Child Support Handbook

30th edition

Michelle Counley and Gwynfor Evans

Child Poverty Action Group

Child Poverty Action Group works on behalf of the more than one in four children in the UK growing up in poverty. It does not have to be like this. We use our understanding of what causes poverty and the impact it has on children's lives to campaign for policies that will prevent and solve poverty – for good. We provide training, advice and information to make sure hard-up families get the financial support they need. We also carry out high-profile legal work to establish and protect families' rights. If you are not already supporting us, please consider making a donation, or ask for details of our membership schemes, training courses and publications.

Published by Child Poverty Action Group
30 Micawber Street, London N1 7TB
Tel: 020 7837 7979
staff@cpag.org.uk
cpag.org.uk

A CIP record for this book is available from the British Library

ISBN: 978 1910715 90 1

Child Poverty Action Group is a charity registered in England and Wales (registration number 294841) and in Scotland (registration number SC039339), and is a company limited by guarantee, registered in England (registration number 1993854). VAT number: 690 808117.

Cover design by Colorido Studios
Internal design by Devious Designs
Content management system by Konnect Soft
Typeset by DLxml, a division of RefineCatch Limited, Bungay, Suffolk
Printed in the UK by CPI Group (UK) Ltd, Croydon CR0 4YY

The authors

Michelle Counley is the Senior Consultant at NACSA, specialising in all aspects of the Child Maintenance Statutory Scheme. Having worked in this area of law since 1995, Michelle has become a leading resource for child maintenance law, providing support and guidance to parents, employers and family lawyers.

Gwynfor Evans is a barrister at 36 Family (36 Group) specialising in matrimonial finance, applications under Schedule 1 to the Children Act 1989, trusts of land, claims under the Inheritance (Provision for Family and Dependants) Act 1975 and other contentious probate matters. Gwynfor is a member of the Family Law Bar Association, the Chancery Law Bar Association and Resolution. He is also an associate member of STEP and a Master of the Bench at Gray's Inn.

Acknowledgements

A huge debt is owed to all the authors and checkers of previous editions and, in particular, to Mark Brough, Will Hadwen and Nick Turnill.

Many thanks to Anne Ketley for compiling the index and Jack Ryan for proofreading the text.

Finally, thanks are also due to officials at the Department for Work and Pensions for patiently answering queries and providing helpful information.

The law described in this book was correct at 1 September 2022.

Contents

Appendices

Abbreviations

ADP	adult disability payment
CDP	child disability payment
CMS	Child Maintenance Service
CSA	Child Support Agency
DfC	Department for Communities (Northern Ireland)
DLA	disability living allowance
DWP	Department for Work and Pensions
ESA	employment and support allowance
EU	European Union
HMCTS	HM Courts and Tribunals Service
HMRC	HM Revenue and Customs
IB	incapacity benefit
ICE	Independent Case Examiner
IS	income support
JSA	jobseeker's allowance
NI	national insurance
NRP	non-resident parent
PAYE	pay as you earn
PC	pension credit
PIP	personal independence payment
PWC	parent/person with care
UC	universal credit

Chapter 1

Introduction

This chapter covers:

1. What is child support

All parents have a legal responsibility to support their children financially until they are 16 and, in some circumstances, until they are 20.[1] Child maintenance paid by parents who do not live with their children is intended to reflect this. Some people make voluntary arrangements to pay maintenance, others have arrangements made by a court order, and some people have maintenance calculated and enforced under the statutory child support scheme run by the Department for Work and Pensions. Some people may pay or receive child maintenance in more than one of these ways.

This *Handbook* explains how the statutory scheme operates. We use the term **'child support'** to refer to maintenance calculated and enforced under the statutory scheme. **'Child maintenance'** is used as a generic term for all types of child maintenance, including child support, voluntary arrangements and payments made under a court order.

2. The statutory child support scheme

The statutory child support scheme calculates the amount of child support people have to pay. It has been in operation since 1993, but has changed significantly since then.

The current system of calculating child support is the third such system and was introduced on 10 December 2012. Since 25 November 2013, all new applications have been dealt with under this system. This third system is sometimes referred to as the '**2012 rules**' or the 'gross income' scheme. All child support cases with ongoing liability are now dealt with under the '2012 rules'.

There are different rates of child support, depending on the parent's gross income (see Chapter 4). The calculation can be varied in certain circumstances (see Chapter 5). Fees may be charged for some aspects of the administration of the system (see p22, p136 and p188).

There are two previous schemes. The first scheme, introduced in 1993, is usually referred to as the '**1993 rules**'. In 2003, this scheme was replaced by a simpler calculation process, the second scheme, usually referred to as the '**2003 rules**'. The first and second schemes are now closed – ie, it is not possible to make new applications under them. Most cases that began under these schemes have now been closed. There may still be arrears due in some cases under the previous schemes, but no ongoing liability to pay child support.

For full details of the '1993 rules' and '2003 rules' and the process of closing these cases, see previous editions of this *Handbook*.

3. Responsibility for the child support scheme

The Department for Work and Pensions (DWP) is responsible for the statutory child support system in Great Britain.

The child support scheme is administered by the **Child Maintenance Service** (CMS), staffed by the DWP.

Note: previous cases were dealt with by the Child Support Agency. Any residual debt from the legacy scheme is now managed by CMS.

The Child Maintenance Service

The CMS is responsible for calculating child support payments and, in some cases, collecting and enforcing them. This includes tracing non-resident parents and investigating parents' financial circumstances.

The CMS has wide powers to gather information. These are covered in Chapter 3. If you think that a child support decision is wrong, you may be able to challenge it (see Chapters 9 and 10). If you are unhappy with the service provided by the CMS, you can make a complaint (see Chapter 11).

4. Arrangements in Northern Ireland

The child support system is largely the same throughout the UK, but Great Britain and Northern Ireland are treated as two separate territories for child support purposes.

There is a separate agency for Northern Ireland, also known as the Child Maintenance Service. It is part of the Department for Communities (DfC), and has the same powers as the Child Maintenance Service in England, Scotland and Wales. There is also an information and support service, known as Child Maintenance Choices, providing information and support to help parents make informed choices about child maintenance arrangements. This service is free.

If this *Handbook* is being used in Northern Ireland, references to the Department for Work and Pensions should be read as references to the DfC. **Note:** some legislative references are different in Northern Ireland.

If an application is made to the statutory child support scheme and the person with care (PWC – see p9), non-resident parent (NRP – see p11) and qualifying child (see p6) do not all reside in the same territory, there are special rules to determine how the application is dealt with.

New applications are generally dealt with by the agency of the territory where the NRP named in the application lives. They are dealt with by the territory in which the applicant lives until the address of the NRP is verified and, if the applicant lives in Great Britain, any application fee (see p22) due is paid.

Outstanding arrears under the '1993 rules' and '2003 rules' are dealt with by the agency of the territory where the PWC lives.[2]

Any calculation made must take into account the rules of the other territory.[3] Because the rules for calculating child support in the two territories are very similar, this should not make any difference in practice.

5. Using this *Handbook*

This *Handbook* explains the rules of the statutory child support scheme and how it is administered by the Child Maintenance Service (CMS). It is intended to help parents who use this scheme and their advisers. It covers the child support scheme in England, Wales and Scotland as at 1 September 2022.

This *Handbook* deals with the current (ie, third) '2012 rules' scheme. In a few places, it highlights important older rules where these are different. For full details of the previous '1993 rules' and '2003 rules' schemes, see the 2014/15 edition of this *Handbook*.

Much of the caselaw relevant to child support was established under the '1993 rules' and '2003 rules'. However, many of the principles still apply to '2012 rules' cases. Where there are likely to be differences in interpretation or difficulties in applying previous caselaw to the '2012 rules', this is explained.

Around 95 per cent of people who apply for child support are women. However, the rules apply in the same way whatever the gender of the person with care of the child or the paying parent, including if both parents are men or both are women. The various parties are therefore referred to in a gender-neutral way in this *Handbook* whenever possible.

Structure of the book

Chapter 1 is an introduction to child support. It explains how to use this *Handbook*.

Chapter 2 explains how applications are made and **Chapter 3** covers how the CMS obtains information. Once all the information is available, the amount of child support can be worked out. **Chapter 4** explains how this is done and **Chapter 5** explains how the amount can be varied in certain circumstances. **Chapter 6** covers decisions. **Chapter 7** explains how child support is collected and paid. **Chapter 8** explains how child support arrears are dealt with and enforced. **Chapters 9 and 10** explain how to change, query or challenge a decision. **Chapter 11** explains how to complain about anything to do with child support.

The **appendices** contain useful addresses and information about reference materials.

The best way to find the information you need is to use the **index** at the back of the book.

Endnotes

Each chapter has endnotes that contain the legal sources, relevant caselaw and other information that support the text. These can be quoted to the CMS if the statement in the text is disputed. Appendix 5 explains the abbreviations used in the endnotes, with information on how to obtain the sources.

The Department for Work and Pensions also now publishes online some of the guidance used in making child support decisions.[4] Anyone concerned about how the CMS has applied a particular aspect of the law in their case may wish to ask the CMS to provide details of any guidance it has taken into account when making the decision.

Notes

1. **What is child support**
   1 s1(1) CSA 1991

4. **Arrangements in Northern Ireland**
   2 Sch 1 para 5(5) CS(NIRA) Regs
   3 Sch 1 para 5(4) and (7) CS(NIRA) Regs

5. **Using this *Handbook***
   4 gov.uk/government/publications/child-maintenance-decision-makers-guide

Chapter 2

Applications

This chapter covers:

1. Who can apply for child support

Both parents (see p7) of a child have a legal duty to contribute to the maintenance of that child.[1] A parent who is not living in the same household as their child (a 'non-resident parent' (NRP)) may be required to pay child support to the person who is the child's main carer (a 'person with care' (PWC)). In most cases, this is the child's other parent, but could be another person – eg, the child's grandparent.

The following people can apply to the Child Maintenance Service (CMS) for child support for a 'qualifying child' (see p6):

- a PWC (see p9);
- a NRP (see p11);
- in Scotland, a child aged 12 or over (provided no application has been made, or is treated as having been made, by the PWC or the NRP).[2]

Child support can only be paid to one PWC of a qualifying child. If there is more than one PWC and they both/all apply for child support, the person whose application is accepted (see p26) receives all the child support. There is an order of priority that the CMS must consider when deciding which application to accept (see p26).

If two or more people in different households care for a qualifying child and at least one, but not all, of them has parental responsibility (see p8) for the child, only those with parental responsibility can apply for child support.[3] For example, if a child is cared for partly by a mother who has parental responsibility and partly by a grandmother who does not have parental responsibility, only the mother can apply. This means that if the person with parental responsibility decides not to apply, another PWC could lose out on child support.

Who is a qualifying child

Child support is only payable for a 'qualifying child'. A child is only a **'qualifying child'** if one or both of their parents are NRPs (see p11).[4]

A **'child'** is defined as a person who is:

- under 16 years of age; *or*
- a young person aged 16–19 inclusive and is a 'qualifying young person' for the purposes of child benefit.

Even if someone is in one of the above groups, they are not a child if they are, or have been, married or in a civil partnership. This applies even if the marriage or civil partnership has been annulled or was never valid – eg, because they were under 16.[5]

The main condition for being a 'qualifying young person' for the purposes of child benefit is to be receiving full-time, non-advanced education (see below) or undertaking certain approved training. See CPAG's *Welfare Benefits and Tax Credits Handbook* for full details of the rules on child benefit.

Full-time, non-advanced education

A course is **non-advanced** if it is up to A level or Higher or Advanced Higher Scottish National Qualifications, or NVQ and SVQ level 3 and below. Courses of degree level and above, Diploma of Higher Education, Higher National Diploma or Higher National Certificate, or NVQ and SVQ level 4 and above count as advanced education.[6]

The young person must attend a recognised educational establishment (such as a school or college). Education elsewhere (eg, at home) must be recognised by the CMS. The CMS can normally only recognise such other education if it was being provided immediately before the young person reached 16, unless there is a statement of special educational needs.[7]

The CMS must treat a young person as receiving **full-time** education if they attend a course with more than 12 hours of weekly contact time. 'Contact time' includes teaching, supervised study, exams and practical or project work which are part of the course. It does not include meal times or unsupervised study, whether on or off school premises. It is the hours of education received that count, not the hours of attendance.[8]

If a young person is not attending such a course (eg, if the contact time is 12 hours or less), the CMS must look at all the facts and decide whether the education is full time.[9]

After leaving school or college, a young person still counts as being in full-time education until child benefit stops being paid. This is:[10]

- at the 'terminal date' (if this is a Sunday, otherwise the first Sunday after the terminal date) after leaving school or college. The terminal date is the last day of February, May, August or November, whichever falls first after leaving school or college; *or*
- if earlier, any week in which the young person is:
  - engaged in remunerative work (ie, work for at least 24 hours a week which is paid, or which is done in expectation of payment); *or*
  - receiving 'other financial support' (ie, receiving, in their own right, income support, income-based jobseeker's allowance, incapacity benefit, working tax credit, employment and support allowance or universal credit).

A young person at school or college can still count as a qualifying child if there is a temporary break in full-time education. It does not matter whether they are under or over 16 when their education is interrupted. A break of up to six months can be allowed. The CMS can allow longer if the break is due to the young person's illness or disability. For someone to continue to count as a qualifying child, any breaks in full-time education must not be followed by a period during which child benefit stops being payable.[11]

Who is a parent

A **'parent'** is a person who is legally the mother or father of the child.[12] This includes:
- a biological parent;
- a parent by adoption;[13]
- a parent under a parental order (used in surrogacy cases).[14]

See also p41 for when the CMS can assume that a person is the parent of a child.

If a child was conceived by artificial insemination or *in vitro* fertilisation (IVF):
- the mother is the woman who gave birth to the child, unless an adoption order or parental order is made;[15]
- the father is the man who provided the sperm (but see below).

If the insemination or IVF took place on or after 1 August 1991 but before 6 April 2009, the father is:
- the mother's husband, unless he did not consent to,[16] or died before, insemination;[17] *or*
- if the insemination was during licensed treatment services provided for the mother and a man, that man.[18] The man and woman must have received treatment services together.[19] This rule does not apply if the woman was inseminated or fertilised outside the UK.[20]

From 6 April 2009, in the case of assisted reproduction:[21]

- a man who is married to, or is a civil partner of, the mother is the father, unless he did not consent;
- if a man and woman are not married or in a civil partnership and the woman has a child as a result of licensed treatment, the man is the father if there is a notice of consent between them.

Two women who are married or civil partners are treated in the same way as a man and woman who are married or civil partners – ie, if one partner gives birth to a child as a result of donor insemination, she is the mother of the child and her partner is automatically the other parent, unless she did not consent to the mother's treatment.[22] If two women are not married or in a civil partnership and one woman has a child as a result of licensed treatment, the other woman can be treated as a parent of the child if no man is treated as the father and there is a notice of consent between the two women.[23]

At the time of creation of an embryo using donor sperm, if the person married to or in a civil partnership with the mother dies before the embryo is placed in the mother, that partner can be treated as the other parent for the purposes of birth registration if that person consented to the treatment, provided no one else is legally treated as the parent of the child.[24]

An **adoption order** means the child is legally the child of the adopter(s).[25] The liability of a biological parent to maintain their child ends on adoption, the adopting parent(s) becoming the only person/people liable to maintain the child.

Note: a person who has legal parental responsibility (see below)[26] is not necessarily a parent for child support purposes.[27] For example, a step-parent who has acquired parental responsibility (except one assumed to be a parent – see p41) cannot be required to pay child support.[28] However, the courts could order them to pay maintenance.

A **foster parent** is not a parent for child support purposes because the child has been placed with them by a local authority (see p9).

Note: the information above is summary and is not intended to be a statement of the law. If you have any queries about how you are affected, seek legal advice.

Parental responsibility

A mother automatically has parental responsibility for her child from birth. If the child's father was married to, or in a civil partnership with, the mother when the child was born, he also automatically has parental responsibility. This continues even if they later divorce or the civil partnership is dissolved.[29]

If the mother is not married to or in a civil partnership with the father, the father has to acquire parental responsibility. A mother can make a formal agreement giving the father parental responsibility.[30] The courts can also grant parental responsibility to a person who applies for it.[31]

If the name of a father who is not married to or in a civil partnership with the mother appears on a birth certificate on or after 1 December 2003, he automatically has parental responsibility.[32] In Scotland, this applies if the father jointly registers a birth on or after 4 May 2006.[33] Unmarried fathers who signed a birth certificate before these dates cannot acquire parental responsibility without going through one of the other routes – ie, arranging a formal agreement with the mother or applying for a court order.

In addition, in England and Wales, if a child's parent is married to or in a civil partnership with someone who is not the child's other parent (ie, a step-parent), they (or if both biological parents have parental responsibility, both parents) can make a parental responsibility agreement with the step-parent, giving them parental responsibility for the child.[34] The courts (in England, Wales and Scotland) can also grant parental responsibility to such a person upon application.[35]

A female partner of the mother of a child conceived on or after 6 April 2009 automatically has parental responsibility if her details are included in the birth registration on or after 1 September 2009.[36]

If a birth certificate was issued before these dates, a female partner can only acquire parental responsibility through one of the other routes.

Who is a person with care

A **'person with care'** (PWC) is a person with whom a child has their home and who usually provides their 'day-to-day care' (see p10).[37]

If the PWC is the child's parent, they are known as the **'parent with care'** (also abbreviated to PWC in this book).[38] **Note:** the CMS uses the term **'receiving parent'**, rather than 'person with care'.

Home

A **'home'** is the physical place where the child lives. It is different from a household (see p11). Although there is no specific definition of 'home' in the child support rules, the child's home is usually clear. A child may have more than one home – in which case, the CMS decides which is their principal home.

The PWC is usually the child's parent or another individual who provides day-to-day care for them, but could also be, for example, an organisation such as a children's home. However, a local authority *cannot* be a PWC, nor can someone who is looking after a child who has been placed with them by the local authority (including, in Scotland, someone who is providing 'continuing care' to a young person after they reach age 16[39]). In England and Wales, a person with whom a local authority has placed a child can be a PWC if they are the child's parent and the local authority has allowed the child to live with them.[40]

Child support can only be paid to one PWC in respect of each qualifying child. If there are two or more people who each provide day-to-day care for the child, it is paid only to one. The person who receives child support could decide on an informal basis to pass some of the money to the other PWC, but that cannot be enforced.

In some situations where the day-to-day care of a child is shared, a parent who provides some care may nonetheless be treated as a non-resident parent (NRP) (see p12).

Day-to-day care

'Day-to-day care' is not specifically defined in the rules. The ordinary meaning of the phrase should be used when deciding who is a PWC and who can therefore receive child support. In most cases, it is clear who has day-to-day care.

Two or more people living in different households may each provide day-to-day care for the same child.

In deciding whether a person has day-to-day care of a qualifying child, the CMS should consider the overall care arrangements. The number of nights a year for which a person provides care may be a guide, but should not be the only consideration.[41] If a mother provides care during the day but her children sleep at their father's home, both may be regarded as providing day-to-day care.[42] The CMS may ask which parent carries out particular care routines and, if necessary, may ask parents to provide supporting evidence from a child's school, GP or other professional body on who has the main care of the child.

A person who is responsible for a child's daily routine may be providing day-to-day care, even if some things are done by another person – eg, a childminder. It may not be necessary for someone to be *with* the child if that person is responsible for the overall care during that time. What matters is the degree to which a person continues to have control over the child and to be responsible for their behaviour and protection.[43]

If a child is placed with their parent by a local authority in England and Wales, even though the local authority is legally responsible, the parent is treated as providing day-to-day care.[44]

If a child is a boarding school boarder or a hospital patient, the person who would otherwise provide day-to-day care is treated as still doing so.[45] The person who is treated as having day-to-day care while a child is at boarding school need not be the person who pays the school fees.[46]

Although it is not explicitly stated in the rules, if a child is temporarily in someone else's care, whoever would otherwise have day-to-day care should be treated as providing care.

If a change in the pattern of care occurs, the CMS should be informed, as this may affect the amount of child support payable and may be grounds for a supersession (see p204). The CMS is likely to take an overall view of the care arrangements rather than make separate decisions for different periods of time.

Who is a non-resident parent

A **'non-resident parent'** (NRP) is a parent (see p7) who is not living in the same household (see below) as their child, the child having their home with a PWC (see p9) – eg, where the parents of a child have separated.[47] Only a NRP can be required to pay child support. **Note:** the CMS uses the term **'paying parent'**, rather than 'non-resident parent'.

Both parents can be NRPs, in which case they can both be required to pay child support to the PWC – eg, to a grandparent who provides day-to-day care for a child.[48]

If a step-parent adopts a child and therefore legally replaces a biological parent, there may be no NRP.[49]

If separated parents reconcile and live together, the NRP is no longer non-resident and the child support calculation ceases to have effect. How soon this happens depends on the circumstances – eg, the nature of the reconciliation and the intentions of the couple. It may mean that the calculation ceases to have effect immediately.

If people share the care of a child, a parent who provides some care for the child may nonetheless be treated as a NRP (see p12).[50]

Household

'Household' is not defined in the child support legislation. A household is something abstract, not something physical like a home (see p9). It is either a single person or a group of people held together by social ties.[51] In many cases, whether or not people are members of the same household is obvious. If it is not obvious, the CMS considers other factors such as the living arrangements of the couple including shared living spaces, payment of household bills, laundry routines and the preparation and eating of meals. No one factor on its own should be conclusive. There does not need to be any settled intention about future arrangements for a household to exist.[52]

The meaning of household has been considered in family law and social security cases as well as child support cases, and this caselaw may be used to help make child support decisions.

Caselaw has established the following.

- There can be two or more separate households in one house.[53]
- One or more members of a household can be temporarily absent from the home without ending their membership of the household.[54]
- There does not need to be a relationship like marriage for people to share a household – eg, two sisters can form a household.[55]

If there is a polygamous marriage, the CMS decides whether the qualifying child lives in a different household from at least one of the parents when establishing whether there is a NRP. There can only ever be two legal parents, regardless of the number of partners either parent may have.

A couple may become members of the same household even if they get back together only briefly, assuming that they are hoping the relationship and their domestic arrangements will be indefinite.[56] In this case, a new household could be formed immediately, whether or not it then ceases to exist a few weeks or months later. A household can be formed as soon as people live together intending to form a household, and before they have arranged joint domestic and financial matters.

Note: a decision by the CMS or First-tier Tribunal that the couple share a household for child support purposes is likely to mean that they share a household for benefit or tax credit purposes. For more information about cohabitation decisions for benefits, see CPAG's *Welfare Benefits and Tax Credits Handbook*.

When a parent with care is treated as a non-resident parent

If both parents share the care of a child for whom a child support application has been made and the CMS accepts that they both have 'day-to-day care', there can only be a liability to pay child support if one of the parents is treated as the NRP.[57]

If one parent is treated as a NRP, they are liable to pay child support, and the entire amount is paid to the other parent (or PWC).

If one or both parents share the child's care with a PWC who is not the child's parent (eg, a grandparent), at least one of the parents must be treated as a NRP in order for there to be a liability to pay child support. Both parents may be treated as non-resident and liable to pay child support to the PWC.

A PWC who applies to the CMS for child support from the NRP but ends up being deemed the NRP and being required to pay child support can request that the application be withdrawn (see p26).

If a PWC is treated as a NRP, the amount of child support they must pay is worked out as usual. However, see p78 for how the amount of care provided affects their liability.

If both parents share the care of a qualifying child equally, no one is liable to pay child support (see p13).

Example

Priya and her partner Tom are separated. Their daughter Mia lives with Priya three nights each week. Priya works some night shifts, so Mia stays with her grandmother two nights each week. Mia stays with Tom for two nights each weekend.

Priya applies for child support. Although Tom also provides day-to-day care, he provides care to a lesser extent than Priya. He is treated as the NRP (see p13) and is liable to pay child support (the amount is adjusted for the care he provides – see p78). All the child support is paid to Priya. She decides to pay two-fifths of it to Mia's grandmother to reflect the regular care she provides.

Who is treated as the non-resident parent

A PWC is treated as the NRP if they provide care to a lesser extent than another PWC.[58] A 'lesser extent' could mean either fewer nights a week on average or fewer hours a week overall, but the starting point must be the care arrangements of the child. The total number of nights spent with each parent cannot be the only deciding factor.[59]

The CMS usually assumes that the parent who does not receive child benefit is providing the lesser amount of care, and is therefore treated as the NRP.[60] This may lead to competing claims for child benefit. If more than one person who is entitled makes a claim for child benefit, an order of priority is used to decide who receives it. For example, the person with whom the child is living has priority over other claimants. If the priority rules do not decide the matter and the claimants cannot come to an agreement, HM Revenue and Customs makes the decision. Priority can be conceded by a higher priority claimant to someone else, in writing.

Note: if someone has elected not to receive child benefit because they would be liable for the 'high-income child benefit charge' via income tax, then child benefit is still treated as payable in respect of the child.[61]

See CPAG's *Welfare Benefits and Tax Credits Handbook* for full details of the child benefit rules.

If you think a decision that you are a NRP is wrong, get advice. You may need to provide the CMS with evidence (eg, a diary), showing the pattern of care.

If the evidence shows that day-to-day care is shared equally between a qualifying child's parents, neither parent is treated as non-resident and there is no liability for child support. This is the case even if the two parents have significantly different levels of income. Receipt of child benefit should not be used as a 'tie-break' to decide who is a NRP if the evidence does not otherwise make it clear.[62] The CMS must consider the *overall* care arrangements when deciding whether day-to-day care is shared equally. It should not focus solely on whether or not the number of nights of care provided by each is equal.[63] So a child being cared for by one parent for a few days more or less than an absolutely equal pattern does not necessarily prevent the CMS from deciding that care is shared equally, although this conclusion is likely to be reached in relatively few cases.[64]

Example

Mel and Dan are divorced. They have two children, Oscar (7) and Sam (5). Every fortnight the children spend five nights with Dan. The rest of the time they live with Mel.

Mel has the children nine out of every 14 nights = approximately 234 nights a year.

Dan has the children five out of every 14 nights = approximately 130 nights a year.

Both parents have day-to-day care.

Because Dan looks after the boys to a lesser extent, he is treated as a NRP and a calculation is carried out to decide how much child support he should pay to Mel.

Mel remains the PWC and has no liability to pay child support.

A year later, Dan has moved onto shift work. One week he has the children four nights, the second week three nights. Mel cares for the children the rest of the time. They now share care equally. As Mel receives child benefit, Dan is still treated as the NRP.
However, the CMS accepts that care is now shared equally and cancels the calculation.

There may be cases where each child of a family spends a different amount of time with the two parents – ie, the mother may be treated as the NRP for one child, and the father for the other. If this is the case, the situation is similar to that of a divided family in which different children live full time with different parents (also known as **'split care'** – see p64). Two separate calculations are carried out.

Example

In the example above, Mel and Dan's work patterns change, and they agree new arrangements for caring for the children. Mel now looks after Oscar for nine nights out of every 14 nights. Dan now looks after Sam for eight nights out of every 14 nights. As Mel looks after Oscar for the greater amount of time, Dan is treated as the NRP for Oscar and is liable to pay child support to Mel. As Dan looks after Sam for the greater amount of time, Mel is treated as the NRP for Sam and is liable to pay child support to Dan.

The child support due is calculated separately for each parent based on their income. The amount due is reduced to take account of the care that parent provides for the child for whom they are the NRP (see p78). The amounts due to be paid by each NRP can be offset so that only the parent with the higher liability actually makes a payment (see p138).

2. When an application can be accepted

The Child Maintenance Service (CMS) will accept an application for child support if it has jurisdiction – ie, if a child is a 'qualifying child' and if all relevant parties (qualifying child, person with care (PWC) and non-resident parent (NRP)) are habitually resident in the UK (see p15).[65]

If the CMS decides that it no longer has jurisdiction because one of the parties is no longer habitually resident in the UK, the decision on child support liability should be superseded and the calculation cancelled (see p131).

The child support scheme has priority over the court-based system. See p17 for the role of the courts if the CMS has jurisdiction for child support.

The CMS cannot accept an application for child support if there are certain maintenance orders made by a court or certain written maintenance agreements for the child(ren) concerned (see p16).

A CMS decision on whether it has jurisdiction can be revised (see Chapter 9) and subsequently appealed to the First-tier Tribunal (see Chapter 10).[66]

Habitual residence

The CMS cannot make a child support calculation unless the qualifying child, PWC and NRP are all 'habitually resident' in the UK.[67] The UK means England, Scotland, Wales and Northern Ireland (including coastal islands like the Isle of Wight). It does not include the Isle of Man or the Channel Islands.[68]

The PWC does not have to be habitually resident if that 'person' is an organisation (see p9).[69]

If a person is not habitually resident in the UK, see p21.

What is habitual residence

A person is habitually resident if they are ordinarily resident in the UK and have been for an appreciable period of time.[70] 'Ordinary residence' means 'residence for a settled purpose'.[71]

There is no set definition of what is an appreciable period of time and no comprehensive list of factors that are relevant when deciding whether a person is habitually resident in the UK. A decision must take into account all circumstances and intentions. Some of the most important factors that are considered include:

- the person's usual centre of interest or connections to a particular place;
- the length, continuity and purpose of residence in the UK;
- the length and purpose of any absence from the UK;
- the person's future intentions;
- the nature of the person's work.

The following principles have been established by caselaw. Cases that do not relate directly to child support are 'persuasive', but do not necessarily have to be followed.[72]

- A person can habitually reside in more than one country, or in none.[73]
- A person may continue to be habitually resident in the UK even though absent from the UK for some time – eg, because they have employment and accommodation elsewhere.[74]
- A person cannot be habitually resident in the UK if they have never been here. There must be actual residence, not just an intention to reside here in the future.
- There is no minimum period of time required to have been living in another country before a new habitual residence can be established, but there must be a 'settled intention' to make the relevant area their home.[75] Evidence of intention must be provided.
- A person leaving the UK intending never to return to reside will stop being habitually resident in the UK on the day they leave.[76] The intention never to return must be a settled intention rather than to see how things will work out in another country.[77]
- A person held in a country against their will may not be habitually resident there, even after long residence (but see p16).[78]
- A person who is in the UK unlawfully may be habitually resident.

If a NRP is not habitually resident in the UK, but is employed by the civil service, the armed forces, a UK based company (ie, a company which employs a person to work outside of the UK but which makes payment arrangements in the UK), a local authority or the NHS, they may be treated as habitually resident and the CMS can still make a calculation.[79]

A person returning to the UK after an absence may have remained habitually resident in the UK during that absence.[80] A temporary absence abroad, such as for a holiday or to visit relatives, does not mean that a person ceases to be habitually resident. When deciding whether someone has ceased to be habitually resident for child support purposes, the emphasis should be on the nature and degree of their connections with the UK, and on any future intentions.[81] Temporary absences should be ignored if there is a reasonable prospect of the person returning to the UK. But the CMS is not likely to regard an absence of more than 12 months as being 'temporary' unless it accepts that there are special circumstances. If the NRP requests a supersession of the calculation because they are no longer habitually resident in the UK, the onus is on them to prove that this is the case.[82]

For details on enforcing payment of child support if the NRP is abroad, see p159.

Children

Whether or not a child is habitually resident is a question of fact that depends on their age and circumstances. The assessment of habitual residence should be centred on the child. The habitual residence of the parent or person with whom a child lives, and the intentions of that person for the child, are relevant but they do not necessarily determine the habitual residence of the child. Their place of habitual residence should reflect a degree of integration in a social and family environment.[83] A new habitual residence may still, however, be established quickly – eg, depending on the degree to which a move is planned and the child disengaged from the social and family environment in the previous country of residence.[84] Historical connections to another country can be important considerations, but the primary focus should be on whether the child's current situation shows that they are habitually resident in the UK.[85]

If there are two people with parental responsibility (see p8) who live in different countries, the habitual residence of the child depends on the circumstances. Any existing residence order, or order for custody or care and control, is an important factor. A young child will usually have the same habitual residence as the person who cares for them. This may not necessarily be the case for a child of school age or an adolescent.[86]

Court orders and written maintenance agreements

If the CMS has jurisdiction to make a calculation (see p14), regardless of whether or not an application is actually made, the child support scheme has priority over the court system in terms of determining regular maintenance payments for qualifying children. This section explains the role of the courts in these circumstances and its relationship with the statutory child support scheme.

Note: it is advisable to obtain legal advice about any court proceedings. The following is not intended to be a comprehensive guide to the law.

The role of the courts if the Child Maintenance Service has jurisdiction

If the CMS has jurisdiction to make a child support calculation, the courts do not normally deal with child maintenance. In general, the courts cannot make, vary or revive an order for periodic payments of child maintenance if the CMS has jurisdiction. The courts can still, however, make orders in certain circumstances – ie, for situations not covered by the child support scheme (see below). The courts can also formalise written maintenance agreements made by the parties (see p18), revoke an existing maintenance order, and enforce payment of any arrears arising from a period before the CMS had jurisdiction.[87]

The child support scheme does not change the courts' powers in relation to other aspects of relationship breakdown (eg, contact and residence orders, maintenance for a spouse or civil partner and the division of property) or the courts' jurisdiction to deal with parentage disputes (see p41).

Orders that can still be made by the courts

If the CMS has jurisdiction, the courts can still make maintenance orders for:[88]

- a young person who is no longer considered by the CMS to be a qualifying child (see p6);
- any stepchildren of the NRP – ie, children who were accepted by that parent as members of their family when they used to live with them, but who are not qualifying children;[89]
- the expenses of a child's education or training;[90]
- additional expenses relating to a child's disability. A child counts as disabled if they receive disability living allowance (DLA), child disability payment (CDP), personal independence payment (PIP) or adult disability payment (ADP), or if they do not receive DLA/CDP/PIP/ADP but are blind, deaf, without speech or are substantially and permanently disabled by illness, injury, mental disorder or congenital deformity.[91] The courts can extend payments beyond the age at which a child may no longer be a qualifying child for child support purposes;[92]
- the PWC;[93]
- a qualifying child in excess of the maximum worked out under child support rules. An assessment based on the maximum gross weekly income first needs to be obtained before a court has jurisdiction to consider whether the NRP's circumstances (eg, if their gross weekly income is substantially over £3,000) justify its making an order for additional child maintenance.[94]

Some of these types of orders are often referred to as 'top-up' orders.

The courts can backdate these maintenance orders to the 'effective date' (see p129) of a child support calculation, if the application is made within six months of that date.[95] Backdating is at the court's discretion and can ensure that other maintenance is in step with child support.

People with court orders for child maintenance can use the CMS's collection and enforcement service for amounts due under these orders, provided child support is also being collected (see p143).

The courts can also make a lump-sum award for a child. This power should not be used to make awards that are intended to provide regular support for the child in place of child support. It should only be used to meet a need for a particular item of capital expenditure – eg, acquiring a home.[96]

If a court makes an order which affects, or is likely to affect, a child support calculation, the relevant court officer must notify the CMS of this if they know a calculation is in force.[97]

Written maintenance agreements

Even if an application could be made to the CMS for child support, parents can still choose to make a maintenance agreement.[98] Maintenance agreements can be informal 'family-based' arrangements, which are flexible but cannot be enforced. They can also be converted into a legally enforceable form – ie, endorsed by a court in a consent order (or made as a registered minute of agreement in Scotland).[99] In this case, the courts can enforce the terms of the agreement through enforcement methods similar to those available to the CMS (see p159).

Maintenance agreements and consent orders

'Maintenance agreement' means an agreement to make (or to secure the making of) periodic payments of maintenance (or aliment in Scotland) to, or for the benefit of, a qualifying child.[100] This does not include any agreement to make a lump-sum payment (a 'capitalised payment'), even if this is intended to be the equivalent of regular child maintenance payments for a future period.[101]

A **'consent order'** is an order made by the court with the written consent of both parties. It is legally binding and can be enforced like any other court order and cannot be changed by one party without the court's permission.

A **'minute of agreement'** is an agreement drawn up between two parties in Scotland in the presence of their solicitors, but without the need for formal court action. If it is registered for preservation and execution in the Books of Council and Session (a public register of formal documents in Scotland), it can be enforced by officers of the courts.

Parents who want a consent order or registered minute of agreement should obtain assistance from a family law solicitor. Consent orders for child maintenance are often made at the same time as other court orders – eg, in financial remedy proceedings. A consent order must be made as part of a formal application to the court and must refer to the family law provisions under which it is made.

When an existing court order prevents a child support application

If there is an informal maintenance agreement for periodic payments for the benefit of a child which was made on or after 5 April 1993, an application can still be made to the CMS for child support for the same child. Any clause included in the agreement that claims to prevent someone from applying to the CMS is void.[102]

An order for periodical payments of maintenance for a child (see below) made by a court before 3 March 2003 prevents an application for any child to whom it relates – ie, the CMS will refuse to make a calculation.[103]

Any such order made on or after 3 March 2003 that has been in force for less than one year also prevents an application. If an agreement is formalised by a consent order or registered minute of agreement made on or after 3 March 2003, it also prevents an application if it has been in force for less than one year.[104]

The wording of the order is important – eg, a consent order containing an order to provide maintenance for the PWC and undertakings to provide maintenance for the children, may not prevent a calculation by the CMS.[105]

Therefore, if a new agreement is made and formalised by a consent order or registered minute of agreement, this will be the basis of the child maintenance payable for at least a year. If a child support application is made within a year of an order made after 3 March 2003, the CMS may hold it until after the one-year period expires and then treat it as an application, rather than reject it and then insist that a new application be made again later.[106]

An application can be made to the CMS, even if there is one of the court orders listed on p17 (orders a court can still make) or if the court order is a 'Segal' ('global maintenance') order. Such an order provides for an automatic pound for pound reduction of global (ie, spousal and child) periodical payments by such sum as is obtained in a later child support calculation.[107]

A court order only prevents an application to the CMS in the following circumstances.

- It requires periodical payments of maintenance (or aliment in Scotland) to be made to, or for the benefit of, a qualifying child.[108] However, because an order only prevents an *application* to the CMS, an order made *after* the application (eg, a 'top-up order' – see p17) does not stop the CMS making a calculation, or prevent the CMS from revising or enforcing an existing calculation. A court order directing capital payments (ie, not periodical payments) does not count as an order for these purposes.[109]
- It must be in force. The meaning of 'in force' is not defined in the legislation, and so you may wish to obtain advice, as this can be a complex issue. The fact that parties may have waived their rights under an order, or agreed to make different arrangements, does not affect the status of the order itself.[110] It may be arguable that an order is in force only if it is still relevant – eg, the NRP against whom the order was made is still a NRP.[111] An order is in force if some undertakings or arrangements, such as those that determine with whom the

child lives, are still in effect, even though there is no further liability for maintenance payments[112] or if the liability for child maintenance under the order has not yet begun.[113] If a court decides that it has no power to vary or to enforce an order, an application can be made to the CMS.[114]

- It must be made under one of certain legal provisions (see Appendix 2).[115] The order usually states the legal provision under which it was made.

If you cannot apply to the CMS because of an order, you can ask the court to:
- vary or enforce the amount of maintenance under the order; *or*
- revoke the order.

Although the courts can revoke child maintenance orders, this is not usually done simply to allow an application to be made to the CMS.[116] If you are considering asking for an order to be revoked, get advice on the likely child support calculation.

How a child support calculation affects a court order or maintenance agreement

If the CMS is aware that an order is in force, it must notify all the parties and the relevant court when it makes a calculation.[117]

When a child support calculation is made, any existing court order or maintenance agreement either ceases to have effect or has effect in a modified form in relation to periodic payments from the effective date of the calculation (see p129).[118]

These rules apply even to 'clean break' orders or agreements. There are conflicting court decisions on whether the child support scheme allows the court to reopen the capital or property part of such an order.[119] The arrangement may be self-adjusting to address the effect of a child support calculation. This could mean, for example, a legal charge on the transferred home so that the NRP could recover any child support paid from the transferred property.[120] It could also mean an order that the NRP top up any future child support to a certain total amount of maintenance.[121]

If the order includes provisions for additional maintenance (eg, for a child's education or training expenses or for a disabled child's special needs), only the elements for periodic maintenance payments for a qualifying child should cease to be in force. If the order is made solely for these additional expenses, it remains in force.[122] Parts of the order for matters other than periodic maintenance for the children named in the calculation (eg, other children or spousal maintenance) remain in force.[123]

Maintenance agreements are unenforceable from the effective date of the child support calculation.[124] This only affects the part of the agreement to pay periodic maintenance for the children named in the calculation. The agreement remains unenforceable until the CMS no longer has the power to make a calculation.[125]

If a court order is cancelled because it was made by mistake when a CMS calculation was in force, any payments made under the order are treated as payments of child support.[126]

If a court order ceases to have effect because of a child support calculation, but the CMS revises its decision and decides no child support is, in fact, payable because the previous decision was made in error, the court order revives and any child support already paid counts as maintenance paid under that order.[127]

The role of the courts if the Child Maintenance Service has no jurisdiction

If the CMS does not have jurisdiction (eg, because one parent or the qualifying child is not habitually resident in the UK), the courts may make, vary or revive a maintenance order.

The High Court has on several occasions provided guidance directing the courts to use the child support scheme as a guide when setting levels of child maintenance.[128] This may avoid child support applications being made as soon as circumstances change and the CMS acquires jurisdiction. If you are seeking an order, ask your solicitor to prepare a calculation. An online calculator is available.[129]

In England and Wales, applications for maintenance are made to the family court or High Court. In Scotland, they are made to the sheriff court or Court of Session. If the application is made within six months, the order can begin from the date that child support ended.[130]

If a child support calculation is cancelled because the NRP moves abroad (see p131), an application for maintenance can be made to the court. The PWC can apply for a 'reciprocal enforcement of maintenance order' to recover maintenance from someone living abroad.[131]

The courts also have the power to enforce orders and agreements, including those made by courts in other countries.[132]

In Scotland, if the CMS ceases to have jurisdiction to make a calculation in respect of a child, an order previously made revives from the date the CMS ceases to have jurisdiction.[133] The same is not explicitly stated for England and Wales, which means that the original order does not revive when CMS involvement ends. However, it could be argued that it should apply, since the court order has not been revoked but simply ceased to have effect for the duration of a child support calculation. If the original order does not revive, a new order or agreement must be obtained.

3. How to apply

Before applying to the Child Maintenance Service (CMS), you must use the online 'Get Help Arranging Child Maintenance' resource.[134] This asks a number of questions to verify eligibility, and the appropriate options for child maintenance arrangements, including family-based arrangements. If you wish to proceed with the application to the CMS, a unique reference number is provided. No application can be made without the reference number.

The 'Get Help Arranging Child Maintenance' service is intended to encourage parents to consider the range of child maintenance options available before applying to the statutory scheme and, in particular, to consider making a private family-based arrangement. It also provides details of other support and information services. If you cannot access the 'Get Help' online service, you must call CMS directly.

Application fees

There is a fee of £20 for making an application to the CMS.[135] The fee is payable whether or not a child support calculation is actually made as a result of the application. An application is not treated as properly made until the fee is paid or is waived by the CMS.

If an application does not proceed because a qualifying child has died before the calculation is made, the fee must be refunded.[136]

The application fee must be waived if:[137]

- the applicant is aged 19 or under on the date of the application; *or*
- the CMS accepts that the applicant has experienced domestic abuse.

The CMS accepts that an applicant has experienced domestic abuse where they:

- have reported the abuse to an 'appropriate person'; *and*
- informed the CMS that they have experienced domestic violence or abuse and that they have reported this to an appropriate person. The CMS must be informed at the time of making the application or in a written declaration that the CMS may ask the applicant to complete (provided the application fee has not already been paid before the declaration has been returned).

Domestic violence/abuse

The CMS has published guidance on how it decides whether a person has experienced domestic violence or abuse.[138]

'Domestic abuse' is defined as 'any incident or pattern of incidents of controlling, coercive or threatening behaviour, violence or abuse towards the applicant which is between persons aged 16 or over who are or have been intimate partners or family members, regardless of gender or sexuality. This can encompass, but is not limited to, the following types of abuse: psychological, physical, sexual, financial, emotional.' Abuse can include a person witnessing the abuse of their child by a current or previous partner.

The CMS has also published guidance on who is accepted as an **'appropriate person'** for these purposes.[139] These are:
- a court;
- the police;
- a medical professional;
- social services;
- a multi-agency risk assessment conference;
- a specialist domestic violence organisation or service, including a refuge;
- an employer;
- educational services;
- a local authority;
- a legal professional;
- specialist support services.

Note: an application fee has not been introduced in Northern Ireland.[140]

Making the application

From 1 April 2022, an application for maintenance is managed online. The 'Get Help Arranging Child Maintenance' site outlines the options available to parents when making decisions about child maintenance payments. If, after answering all of the questions, you wish to proceed with an application to the CMS, a unique reference number is generated which must be provided when making your application. If you lose or forget the unique reference number, you may have to follow the process again before you can apply to the CMS.

If you do not want to make the application online, you must contact the CMS by telephone. Contact details for the CMS can be found on the gov.uk website and in Appendix 1.

The CMS can determine how an application should be made and what information must be provided.[141]

The CMS can require the applicant to provide any evidence or information reasonably needed to process the application (including sufficient information to allow the NRP to be identified).[142] The application is treated as having been properly made only when any information required to process it has also been provided to the CMS.[143] In most cases, the CMS expects to gather information by telephone. An application by a child in Scotland is always dealt with by telephone.

Information required for an application

An applicant is likely to be asked for the following information in the course of making an application:

- personal details – eg, name, address, national insurance (NI) number, date of birth, phone numbers and the best time to ring, and armed forces service number (if applicable);

- child(ren) being applied for – eg, name, date of birth, NI number if 16 or over, who gets child benefit for the child, maintenance arrangements and any shared care arrangements (or local authority care);
- if the PWC is applying, whether the NRP knows that they are named as the parent and whether they know where the PWC lives;
- the child's education (if aged 16–19) – eg, school/college, course, type of course and hours;
- local authority details (if the child is being cared for);
- the NRP's details – eg, name and other names used, address or last known address and when they lived there, NI number, date of birth, employment details, phone numbers and whether the parent is the father or mother of the child;
- payment details – eg, whether child support is to be collected by the CMS, the preferred payment method, frequency of payment, and bank details;
- details of any representative – eg, name, address, phone numbers and the best time to ring. If the representative is a solicitor, an attorney under a power of attorney, Scottish mental health guardian, mental health appointee or receiver, the representative can apply on behalf of the applicant.

The CMS may wish to see original documents to confirm certain details – eg, any relevant court order or power of attorney.

There are penalties for knowingly providing false information (see p37). See Chapter 3 for full details of the information requirements.

Applications with more than one non-resident parent

Applicants can choose from which NRP they wish to apply for child support. If a person has care of qualifying children of more than one NRP, applications may be made for child support from one (or more), but not necessarily all, of them.

When to apply

There are no time limits for applying to the CMS. An application may be made as soon as someone becomes a PWC or a NRP, or at any later date.[144] The NRP must be notified of any liability to pay child support. That notification must include details of the commencement date, known as the 'initial effective date.' Notifications are usually sent to a postal address five days before the initial effective date, although legally only two days are required. However if sent electronically only one day's notice is required.[145]

The CMS cannot make a decision for a liability to pay child maintenance until it receives an effective application (see p25). This means that delaying the application may delay the start of liability. This is the case even if the reason for the delay is that the PWC is considering alternatives, such as setting up voluntary maintenance arrangements. You cannot apply in advance – eg, before the birth of a baby.

If an application is refused

The CMS may refuse to accept an application – eg, because it believes an existing maintenance order prevents an application or because it does not have jurisdiction (see p14). If this happens, you should explain to the CMS why you believe you are entitled to apply and ask for a written decision. If a written decision is issued, you can try to challenge this by requesting a revision (see Chapter 9) and then appealing to the First-tier Tribunal (see Chapter 10). If this is not successful, or if the CMS refuses to respond in writing, a complaint (see Chapter 11) and/or judicial review (see p198) could be considered.

Effective applications

The CMS can only make a child support calculation if the application is 'effective'.[146] This means that applicants must provide information to enable the NRP to be identified and traced and the amount of child support payable to be calculated and recovered (see Chapter 3).[147] If an applicant does not supply this information, the CMS may refuse to process the application (see p26). A PWC applying is not required to provide significant detail such as the NRP's NI number, but will be expected to be able to supply at least the first name and surname of the alleged NRP or the application will be unlikely to proceed.[148]

The CMS cannot refuse to deal with an effective application, even if it considers that processing it would be against the welfare of the children concerned.[149] If the CMS refuses to accept an application, see above.

Once an effective application has been made, the address of the NRP verified and any application fee paid, the CMS must notify the NRP in writing as soon as possible and ask for any information required to determine the child support liability. This applies even if the NRP is the applicant. The NRP is informed of the 'initial effective date' of the application (see p129), the power of the CMS to estimate income in certain circumstances and the rules regarding 'default maintenance decisions' (see p127).[150]

For delays in dealing with applications, including if the NRP is not co-operating, see p125.

Amending the application

An application can be amended at any time before a child support calculation is made, but not so as to take into account a change which occurs after the effective date. For details of this and of changes after the effective date, see p126.

4. Withdrawing or cancelling an application

The applicant no longer wants to proceed

An applicant can at any time, and whether or not a calculation has been made, request that the Child Maintenance Service (CMS) cancels the application. The CMS cannot refuse this request.[151] For more information on when an application is cancelled or a calculation ceases to have effect, see p130. Requests can be made by telephone or in writing to the CMS office processing the application.

The Child Maintenance Service cancels an application

The CMS may cancel an application before a calculation is made if the applicant does not provide information (see below).

The rules are different if the qualifying child dies before the calculation decision is made (see below).

An applicant does not provide information

The CMS can only cancel a case if no effective application has been made (see p25). If a person with care does not provide sufficient information, the CMS can close the case and no child support will be payable.

If there *is* an effective application, a decision must be made and notified to the parties, even if it is a decision not to make a calculation (see p126). If an effective application is cancelled against your wishes, get advice.

The qualifying child dies

If a qualifying child dies before a calculation has been made, a decision on liability is still made for the period up to the date of death. If the child was the only child named in the application, the decision is then cancelled with effect from the date of death; otherwise, it is changed (superseded) with effect from that date.[152]

5. Multiple applications

If more than one person applies for child support in respect of the same qualifying child before the decision on how much child support is payable is made, only one application can go ahead (see below).[153]

If one application is given priority, information provided in the other application may still be taken into account to help make a decision.

Note: once a calculation is in force, any subsequent application for child support made in the same circumstances in respect of the same person with care (PWC), non-resident parent (NRP) and qualifying child(ren) may be treated as a request for a supersession (see p205) or, depending on the circumstances and information contained in the application, as a request for a variation (see Chapter 5).[154]

Which application goes ahead

The Child Maintenance Service (CMS) decides which application goes ahead using the following order of priority.[155]

- In Scotland, an application from a PWC or a NRP has priority over an application from a child.
- In other circumstances, an earlier application has priority over a later one.

In the following circumstances, the CMS treats the applications as a single application in relation to the qualifying child.[156]

- An application is made and both parents of a qualifying child are non-resident – eg, an application made by a PWC who is not the parent of the qualifying child, or by a child in Scotland whose parents are both non-resident.
- Both parents of a qualifying child are non-resident and both apply for child support.

Although the law does not state this explicitly, if more than one application is made by the same person in the same circumstances, they are likely to be treated as one application if the calculation decision has not been made.

Applications for additional children

If there is an existing child support calculation and an application is made for an additional child of the same NRP cared for by the same PWC, this is a relevant change of circumstances. A new calculation is made which supersedes the existing one (see p204).

6. Communicating with the Child Maintenance Service

Once an application is made, parties are encouraged to manage their case online.[157]

The Child Maintenance Service (CMS) preferred method of contact is electronically through the online portal. A webchat facility is available from 8am to 7.30pm, Monday to Friday, and from 9am until 1pm Saturday, although this service is not able to deal with many case specific enquiries, and parents are encouraged to telephone. Although the government intends the majority of communication to be electronic, at the time of writing, the online services are limited. Parents have the option of using other methods of communication if they do not wish to communicate electronically.[158]

The CMS aims to answer telephone calls promptly. The impact of COVID-19 has caused considerable delay in the answering of calls. It should reply to letters, or messages sent through the online portal, resolving the issue or agreeing what will happen next, within three weeks. If you have difficulty in contacting the CMS, or in obtaining a response within a reasonable time, then complain (see Chapter 11).

The CMS does not normally offer face-to-face interviews, but these may be arranged if the CMS considers that the case involves complex issues and an interview may help to resolve them more quickly. An interview may also be considered if someone has communication difficulties which make other methods problematic. A request for a face-to-face interview by anyone involved in a case should be considered seriously if the CMS agrees that it is the most effective way to make contact or if all other ways of progressing the case have been exhausted.

The CMS should also meet any accessibility or language needs of the applicant – eg, English not being the applicant's first language or there being difficulties with using the telephone.

The online portal allows parties to check the progress of an application, set their contact preferences, report certain changes in their circumstances, track the progress of any reported change, report non-payment of child maintenance, upload documents, update personal details, make one-off payments and view calculation and payment details.

It is always advisable to keep copies of letters, take screenshots and make a note of the date, time and content of telephone calls.

Dates of postage

A document sent to the CMS is treated as having been sent on the day the CMS receives it.[159] Although the CMS is taking steps to reduce the number of physical letters being issued, if it posts a document to a person's last known address (or the address the person last notified to the CMS), it is treated as being received two days after the day it was posted.[160] It is understood that this is intended to exclude Sundays and bank holidays. If the CMS issues a document electronically, it is deemed as having been sent at the end of the following day.[161] A document is likely to be treated as having been 'sent' by the CMS if it was properly addressed, pre-paid and posted. Evidence that it was not received does not show that it was not sent.[162]

These rules are important when determining whether something has been done within a time limit.

Note: if no statutory timescale applies for a particular action to be done or for information to be provided, the CMS generally allows 14 days to provide information, and extends this to 16 days to allow for the time taken for information to reach the CMS by post.

Representatives

Anyone dealing with the CMS can appoint a representative to act on their behalf.[163] If the person is not legally qualified, authorisation to act needs to be confirmed in writing, although authorisation for a representative to speak for the duration of a telephone call can take place during that same call if the representative is with you. An authorised or legally qualified representative can complete forms, receive documents and supply information. A person with care may also choose to have payments of child support made to a representative.

A representative who understands the law and/or is experienced in dealing with the CMS may find it easier to get a quick response and clearer information from the CMS, and can advise about rights and options. For information about how to find independent advice, see Appendix 3.

A representative with legal authority to act for a CMS client (eg, someone with power of attorney, a receiver, a mental health appointee or a Scottish mental health guardian) can act for them in every respect, as if they themselves were the client.

The legal advice and assistance scheme in Scotland may help to cover costs in child support cases.

Notes

1. **Who can apply for child support**

1 s1 CSA 1991
2 s7(1) CSA 1991
3 ss5(1) and 54 CSA 1991
4 s3(1) CSA 1991
5 s55(2) and (3) CSA 1991
6 Reg 76 CSMC Regs; s142(2) SSCBA 1992; reg 1(3) CB Regs; CCS/12604/1996
7 Reg 76 CSMC Regs; s142(2) SSCBA 1992; reg 3 CB Regs
8 CCS/1181/2005
9 Reg 76 CSMC Regs; s142(2) SSCBA 1992; reg 1(3) CB Regs; *CF v CMEC (CSM)* [2010] UKUT 39 (AAC); CCS/1181/2005
10 Reg 76 CSMC Regs; regs 1(3), 7 and 8 CB Regs
11 Reg 76 CSMC Regs; s142(2) SSCBA 1992; reg 6 CB Regs
12 s54 CSA 1991
13 s39 AA 1976; s39 A(S)A 1978; s26(2) CSA 1991, Case A
14 ss54 and 54A HF&EA 2008; s26(2) CSA 1991, Case B
15 ss27(2) and (3) and 29(1) HF&EA 1990
16 s28(2) HF&EA 1990; *Re CH (Contact: Parentage)* [1996] 1 FCR 768, [1996] 1 FLR 569, [1996] Fam Law 274
17 s28(6) HF&EA 1990
18 s28(3) HF&EA 1990
19 See *Re D (A Child Appearing by her Guardian Ad Litem)* [2005] UKHL 33
20 Because such a clinic would not have a UK licence: *U v W (A-G intervening)* [1997] 3 WLR 739, [1997] 2 CMLR 431, [1997] 2 FLR 282
21 ss35-37 HF&EA 2008
22 s42 HF&EA 2008
23 ss43 and 44 HF&EA 2008
24 ss40 and 46 HF&EA 2008

25 **EW** s67 A&CA 2002
S s40 A&C(S)A 2007
All s54 CSA 1991, definition of 'parent'
26 **EW** CA 1989
S C(S)A 1995
27 **EW** s3(4) CA 1989
S s3(3) C(S)A 1995
28 R(CS) 6/03
29 s2(1) CA 1989; s3(1) C(S)A 1995
30 ss4(1)(b) and 4ZA(1)(b) CA 1989; s4(1) and 4A(1) C(S)A 1995
31 ss4(1)(c), 4ZA(1)(c), 4A(1)(b) and 5(6) CA 1989; s11 C(S)A 1995
32 s4(1)(a) CA 1989
33 s3(1)(b)(ii) C(S)A 1995
34 s4A CA 1989, as amended by s75 CPA 2004
35 ss4(1)(c), 4ZA(1)(c), 4A(1)(b) and 5(6) CA 1989; s11 C(S)A 1995
36 s4ZA(1)(a) CA 1989; s3(1)(c) and (d) C(S)A 1995
37 s3(3) CSA 1991
38 s54 CSA 1991
39 s3(3)(c) CSA 1991; reg 78(1) CSMC Regs
40 Reg 78(1)(b) and (d) CSMC Regs
41 *MR v SSWP & LM* [2018] UKUT 340 (AAC); *JS v SSWP* [2017] UKUT 296 (AAC); *CF v SSWP & CG (CSM)* [2018] UKUT 276 (AAC)
42 *GR v CMEC (CSM)* [2011] UKUT 101 (AAC)
43 *R(CS)* 11/02; *GR v CMEC (CSM)* [2011] UKUT 101 (AAC)
44 Reg 78(1)(b) and (d) CSMC Regs. This applies if a child is placed under s22C(2) CA 1989 or s81(2) Social Services and Well-being (Wales) Act 2014.
45 Reg 55 CSMC Regs
46 R(CS) 8/98
47 s3(2) CSA 1991
48 s1(3) CSA 1991
49 *RW v SSWP (CSM)* [2013] UKUT 576 (AAC)
50 Reg 50 CSMC Regs
51 *Santos v Santos* [1972] 2 WLR 889, [1972] All ER 246 (CA)
52 CCS/2318/1997
53 CSB/463/1986
54 *R(SB)* 4/83
55 R(SB) 35/85
56 CCS/2332/2006
57 Reg 50 CSMC Regs
58 Reg 50(2) CSMC Regs
59 *JS v SSWP and another (CSM)* [2017] UKUT 296 (AAC)
60 Reg 50(3) CSMC Regs
61 Reg 50(4) CSMC Regs
62 *CF v SSWP and CG (CSM)* [2018] UKUT 276 (AAC)
63 *JS v SSWP and another (CSM)* [2017] UKUT 296 (AAC); *MR v SSWP and LM (CSM)* [2018] UKUT 340 (AAC)
64 *CF v SSWP and CG (CSM)* [2018] UKUT 276 (AAC)

2. **When an application can be accepted**

65 s44(1) CSA 1991; reg 7A CS(MAJ) Regs
66 R(CS) 3/97
67 s44(1) CSA 1991
68 Sch 1 Interpretation Act 1978
69 s44(2) CSA 1991
70 *Nessa v Chief Adjudication Officer* [1998] 2 All ER 728, [1998] 2 FCR 461, [1998] 1 FLR 879, [1998] Fam Law 329 (CA), applying *Re J (A Minor) (Abduction: Custody Rights)* [1990] 2 AC 562, [1990] 3 WLR 492, [1990] 2 All ER 961, [1991] FCR 129, [1990] 2 FLR 442, [1991] Fam Law 57 (HL); *Cruse v Chittum* [1974] 2 All ER 940; *Brokelmann v Barr* [1971] 3 All ER 29; *Langford Property Co v Athanassoglou* [1948] 2 All ER 722
71 *Shah v Barnet LBC* [1983] 2 AC 309, [1983] 2 WLR 16, [1983] 1 All ER 226 (HL)
72 *R (on the application of Nahar) v Social Security Commissioners* [2002] 1 FLR 670
73 CCS/2314/2008; *AF v SSWP (CSM)* [2009] UKUT 3 (AAC); *Armstrong v Armstrong* [2003] EWHC 777 (Fam), [2003] 2 FLR 375
74 *CJ v SSWP and VW (CSM)* [2017] UKUT 498 (AAC); *Arthur v HMRC* [2017] EWCA Civ 1756
75 *AB v CD* [2018] EWHC 1021 (Fam)
76 *Re J (A Minor) (Abduction: Custody Rights)* [1990] 2 AC 562, [1990] 3 WLR 492, [1990] 2 All ER 961, [1991] FCR 129, [1990] 2 FLR 442, [1991] Fam Law 57 (HL)
77 CCS/3574/2008; *H v CMEC* [2009] UKUT 84 (AAC)
78 *Shah v Barnet LBC* [1983] 2 AC 309, [1983] 2 WLR 16, [1983] 1 All ER 226 (HL); *Re Mackenzie* [1940] 4 All ER 310
79 s44(2A) CSA 1991; reg 7A CS(MAJ) Regs
80 R(CS) 5/96
81 R(CS) 5/96
82 CSCS/6/2006
83 *B (A Minor: Habitual Residence)* [2016] EWHC 2174 (Fam); *SR (A Child: Habitual Residence)* [2015] EWHC 742 (Fam)
84 *AB v CD* [2018] EWHC 1021 (Fam)

85 *M (Children) (Habitual Residence: 1980 Hague Child Abduction Convention)* [2020] EWCA Civ 1105
86 *AB v CD* [2018] EWHC 1021 (Fam)
87 s8(1), (3) and (4) CSA 1991. It has been decided that this lack of access to the courts is not inconsistent with Art 6(1) European Convention on Human Rights. See *R v SSWP ex parte Kehoe* [2005] UKHL 48.
88 s8(6)-(10) CSA 1991
89 **EW** MCA 1973
S FL(S)A 1985
90 s8(7) CSA 1991
91 s8(8) and (9) CSA 1991
92 Sch 1 para 3(2)(b) CA 1989. In *C v F* [1997] 3 FCR 405 the court held that where s8(1) CSA 1991 applies, s8(8) CSA 1991 limits this power to children aged under 19. However, this seems to be wrong because the fact that CSA 1991 only applied at the time of the judgment to those aged under 19 cannot prevent an order being made under CA 1989 for a person aged 19 or over.
93 s8(10) CSA 1991
94 s8(6) CSA 1991; *Dickson v Rennie* [2014] EWHC 4306 (Fam)
95 s29(7) MCA 1973; s5(7) DPMCA 1978; Sch 1 para 3(5) and (6) CA 1989, as amended by Sch 3 paras 3, 5 and 10 CSPSSA 2000 respectively
96 Sch 1 para 1(2)(c) CA 1989; *Phillips v Pearce* [1996] 2 FLR 230
97 Reg 6 CS(MAJ) Regs
98 s9(2) CSA 1991
99 **EW** Child Maintenance (Written Agreements) Order 1993 No.620
S Child Support (Written Agreements) (Scotland) Order 1997 No.2943
All s8(5) CSA 1991
100 s9(1) CSA 1991
101 *SJ v SSWP (CSM)* [2014] UKUT 82 (AAC), reported as [2014] AACR 32
102 s9(3) and (4) CSA 1991
103 ss4(10)(a) and 7(10)(a) CSA 1991; reg 2 CS(APD) Regs
104 ss4(10) and 7(10) CSA 1991; reg 2 CS(APD) Regs
105 CCS/316/1998; CCS/8328/1995
106 *YW v CMEC (CSM)* [2011] UKUT 176 (AAC)
107 CCS/4047/2007, citing *Dorney-Kingdom v Dorney-Kingdom* [2000] 2 FLR 855
108 s8(11) CSA 1991
109 CCS/4741/1995, upheld by the Court of Appeal in *AMS v CSO* [1998] 1 FLR 955
110 CCS/4049/2007
111 CCS/4049/2007. This and other cases have disagreed with the conclusions reached in R(CS) 4/96. The Court of Appeal in *Kirkley v Secretary of State for Social Security and the Child Support Officer* (unreported, December 15, 1995) ruling on an application for leave to appeal against R(CS) 4/96 also disagreed with the reasoning. Authorities differ as to whether changes in a child(ren)'s residence (eg, from the PWC to the NRP) mean that an order ceases to have effect (CCS/3127/1995) or not (CCS/2567/1998). In the latter case, the commissioner suggested that it would instead be grounds to seek to vary the court order.
112 CCS/4741/1995
113 CCS/11364/1995
114 Reg 9 CS(MAJ) Regs
115 s8(11) CSA 1991; reg 2 CS(MAJ) Regs. Provisions repealed before 1 April 1980 are not listed.
116 s8(4) CSA 1991; *B v M (Child Support: Revocation of Order)* [1994] 1 FLR 342, [1994] 1 FCR 769, [1994] Fam Law 370
117 Reg 5(1) CS(MAJ) Regs
118 s10(1) and (2) CSA 1991; reg 3(2) CS(MAJ) Regs
119 *Crozier v Crozier* [1994] 1 FLR 126; *Mawson v Mawson* [1994] 2 FLR 985
120 *Smith v McInerney* [1994] 2 FLR 1077. However, an arrangement like this might be void under s9(4) CSA 1991 because it would 'restrict the right to apply for a maintenance assessment', though the commissioner in CCS/2318/1997 thought not.
121 See the arrangement in CCS/2318/1997
122 Reg 3(3) CS(MAJ) Regs
123 Reg 3(2) CS(MAJ) Regs
124 Reg 4 CS(MAJ) Regs
125 Reg 4(3) CS(MAJ) Regs
126 Reg 8(2) CS(MAJ) Regs
127 Reg 8(1) CS(MAJ) Regs
128 *GW v RW* [2003] 2 FLR 108 at 74 (per Mostyn sitting as a DHCJ); *Re TW & TM (Minors)* [2015] EWHC 3054 (Fam) at 7-9; *CB v KB* [2019] EWFC 78 at 48-49 (per Mostyn J)
129 gov.uk/calculate-child-maintenance
130 s29(7) MCA 1973; s5(7) DPMCA 1978; Sch 1 para 3(7) CA 1989

131 **EW** gov.uk/government/publications/countries-where-you-can-enforce-child-maintenance-decisions
S scotcourts.gov.uk/taking-action/frequently-asked-questions/reciprocal-enforcement
132 MO(RE)A 1992
133 Reg 3(4) CS(MAJ) Regs

3. **How to apply**
134 child-maintenance.service.gov.uk/get-help-arranging-child-maintenance
135 s6 CMOPA 2008; reg 3 CSF Regs 2014
136 Reg 5 CSF Regs 2014
137 Reg 4(1)-(3) CSF Regs 2014
138 DWP, *Guidance on Regulation 4(3) of the Child Support Fees Regulations 2014: how the Secretary of State will determine if an applicant is a victim of domestic violence or abuse,* August 2017, available at gov.uk. The CMS uses the cross-governmental definition of domestic abuse under the Domestic Abuse Act 2021. At the time of writing, the guidance has not been amended to reflect this.
139 DWP, *Guidance on Regulation 4(3) of the Child Support Fees Regulations 2014: list of persons to whom an applicant must have reported domestic violence or abuse,* August 2017, available at gov.uk
140 Department for Communities press release, 20 September 2013
141 Reg 9(1) CSMC Regs
142 Reg 9(1) CSMC Regs
143 Reg 9(2) CSMC Regs
144 R(CS) 10/02
145 Reg 12 CSMC Regs; reg 26 CS(ARECI) Regs
146 Reg 9(2) CSMC Regs
147 ss4(4), 6(7) and 7(5) CSA 1991
148 para 37011 DMG
149 R(CS) 4/96; CCS/14/1994; CCS/17/1994; CCS/16535/1996
150 Reg 11 CSMC Regs

4. **Withdrawing or cancelling an application**
151 ss4(6) and 6(5) CSA 1991
152 Reg 18(3) CSMC Regs

5. **Multiple applications**
153 s5(2) CSA 1991; reg 10(1) CSMC Regs
154 *DB v CMEC* [2010] UKUT 356 (AAC). This decision relates to a '2003 rules' case. However, the same principle should apply to the '2012 rules', although this is not explicitly stated in those rules.
155 Reg 10(2) CSMC Regs
156 Reg 10(3) CSMC Regs

6. **Communicating with the Child Maintenance Service**
157 childmaintenanceservice.direct.gov.uk
158 Child Support (Amendments relating to Electronic Communication and Information) (England and Wales and Scotland) Regulations 2022
159 Reg 7(1) CSMC Regs
160 Reg 7(2) CSMC Regs
161 Reg 7(3) CSMC Regs; reg 24 CS(ARECI) Regs
162 R(CS) 1/99
163 Reg 8 CSMC Regs

Chapter 3

Information

This chapter covers:

1. Information-seeking powers

The Child Maintenance Service (CMS) has wide powers to obtain information from (among others) parents, employers, local authorities and HM Revenue and Customs (HMRC).[1] It can require information to be provided in order to make any child support decision.[2]

In addition, the CMS can appoint inspectors who have extensive powers to obtain information. In general, CMS staff seek information by telephone, but may also carry out face-to-face enquiries.

When information can be requested

After a child support application has been made, the non-resident parent (NRP) is notified in writing (see p37). The date this notice is issued sets the 'effective date' for the calculation (see p129). The notice is followed up by a telephone call to the NRP to gather and confirm information.

The CMS can request information in order to:[3]

- determine an application for child support and any issues that arise from it – eg, to establish which parent is the child's main carer if care is shared (see p13);
- make any other decisions – eg, to determine the income of the NRP;
- enable child support to be calculated, collected and enforced.

See p34 for who can be required to give information, and p37 for what happens if someone fails to provide it.

What information can be requested

The CMS can request information on many issues, including:

- the habitual residence of the person with care (PWC), the NRP and any child covered by the application, to determine whether the CMS has jurisdiction;
- the name and address of the PWC and NRP, their marital or civil partnership status, and the relationship of the PWC to any child covered by the application;
- the name, address and date of birth of any child covered by the application, the child's marital or civil partnership status and details of the child's education;
- if there is more than one PWC:
  - who has parental responsibility (or parental rights in Scotland) for any qualifying child; *and*
  - how much time is spent by that child with each PWC;
- who is the parent of a child or, if parentage is disputed, information to determine whether someone can be assumed to be a parent (see p41);
- the name and address of any current or recent employer of a NRP and their gross earnings from that employment;
- if the NRP is self-employed, the address, trading name, gross receipts and expenses, other outgoings and taxable profits of the trade or business;
- any other income of the NRP;
- how much is paid or payable under a court maintenance order or maintenance agreement;
- details of anyone who lives in the same household as the NRP, their relationship, and the date of birth of any children;
- details and statements of any account in the name of the NRP, including bank and building society accounts (and including joint accounts);
- whether someone counts as a qualifying child for child support purposes (see p6);
- information to decide whether a calculation should end (see p130).

Who must provide information

Information can be required from the following, if they have the information or evidence or can reasonably be expected to acquire and provide it:[4]

- a 'relevant person' – ie, the PWC, NRP or child applicant in Scotland (see p35);
- someone who denies parentage of a child (see p35);
- court officials (see p35);
- the Department for Work and Pensions (DWP – see p35);
- HMRC (see p35);
- others, including employers, local authorities and banks (see p36).

Information or evidence can also be given to the CMS when there is no obligation to provide it – eg, from a relative, neighbour or landlord. For information on disclosure by the CMS, see p51.

A relevant person

All child support applicants must provide information required by the CMS to:[5]

- identify and trace a NRP; *or*
- calculate, collect or recover child support.

The PWC and NRP (or a parent treated as non-resident – see p12) must provide the information listed on p34, if requested.[6] A child applicant in Scotland must provide the same information, except information enabling the NRP to be identified.[7]

If information is not provided by a PWC (or child applicant in Scotland), the application may be treated as withdrawn (see p26). If a NRP does not supply the requested information, a 'default maintenance decision' may be made (see p127).

Someone who denies parentage of a child

Someone who denies parentage of a child named in an application is required to give information:[8]

- to identify a NRP; *or*
- to decide whether or not all the relevant people are habitually resident in the UK and therefore whether the CMS has jurisdiction.

This means, for example, that if the CMS only wants to identify someone as the NRP, their employment details would not normally be necessary and so should not be requested until parentage is established.

Court officials

Certain court officials can be required to give information for the purposes listed on p34 – eg, to allow the CMS to:[9]

- identify how much is payable under a court maintenance order;
- collect child support or maintenance under a court order;
- identify any proceedings about a court maintenance order;
- decide whether a maintenance order is in force that may affect whether an application can be made (see p16);
- decide who has parental responsibility for the qualifying child if there is more than one PWC (see p8).

The Department for Work and Pensions

Any DWP agency or anyone providing services to the DWP may give information held for benefit purposes to the CMS.[10]

HM Revenue and Customs

There are specific arrangements for passing information about the NRP's gross income from HMRC to the CMS (see p66).

In addition, HMRC can be required to disclose information or evidence for the purposes listed on p34.[11] Information provided can be used for any function related to child support. If a parent is self-employed, this also includes details of their taxable profits, gross receipts and expenses.

HMRC can provide information about whether a self-employed NRP received a payment under the Self-Employment Income Support Scheme (SEISS) during the coronavirus pandemic. The CMS says that it will only use this information to check a NRP's financial situation if there has been non-compliance with the duty to pay child support. The CMS will not use this information to make or to revise the child support calculation.[12]

It is unlawful for HMRC to give the CMS any other information.[13]

Others

The CMS can also require the following to provide information for the purposes listed on p34:

- current or previous employers of the NRP;[14]
- people or organisations for whom the NRP provides, or has provided, goods or services under a contract.[15] This could include individuals, a company or partnership, or a government department, and means, for example, that a self-employed consultant could be traced and have their income investigated through companies for which they have provided services;
- a person who acts, or has acted, as the NRP's accountant;[16]
- credit reference agencies;[17]
- the local authority in whose area either the NRP or PWC lives or has lived.[18] The CMS may require the local authority to provide information, such as address and bank account details, relating to, for example, rent and council tax or a housing benefit claim;[19]
- the Driver and Vehicle Licensing Agency. In particular, it may be asked for information needed to trace the NRP, and to collect and enforce payments;[20]
- prison authorities;[21]
- banks and building societies. See p169 for details of specific information requirements on banks or building societies in relation to enforcement action to deduct funds from an account, particularly joint or business accounts;[22]
- gas and electricity suppliers;[23]
- persons engaged in investment management or share trading activities;[24]
- the proprietor of an Academy;[25]
- mortgage lenders (qualifying lenders include banks, building societies, insurers and local authorities);[26]
- trustees, managers or administrators of occupational, or personal pension schemes;[27]
- Motor Insurers' Bureau, or a company limited by guarantee, or its officers.[28]

When must the information be provided

A person who has been requested to provide information must do so if that information or evidence is in their possession or if they can reasonably be expected to acquire and provide it.[29] The information must be provided as soon as it is reasonably practicable.[30] The CMS can allow information to be provided by a later date if it is satisfied that the delay is unavoidable.

See p28 for when documents are treated as having been sent and received.

What happens if the correct information is not provided

It is a criminal offence for a person, without reasonable excuse, to fail to provide information, to provide false information or to allow false information to be provided.[31] All requests for information issued by the CMS must state this.[32]

If someone fails to provide information or provides false information, the CMS may decide not to process the application (see p26). If a parent does not give the required information, the CMS may ask another person for the information – eg, an employer or accountant. If a NRP fails to provide information, a default maintenance decision may be made (see p127). A decision based on estimated income could be made in certain circumstances instead (see p71).

The CMS may also go to court, and a fine (currently up to £1,000) can be imposed on anyone who is required to provide information and fails, without reasonable excuse, to do so. Fines are paid to the court, not to the CMS. A NRP who fails to provide information may have both a default maintenance decision and a fine imposed. If the NRP makes an application and the PWC fails to provide information, the PWC can be fined, although this would be rare.

Disputing the information required

A request for information can be challenged (see p198) if:

- it is not relevant to the reason for the request; *or*
- it is of a very different kind from the examples given in the regulations; *or*
- it is made to a person who cannot be required to give it; *or*
- the CMS already has sufficient information to make a full calculation.

If you think this applies to any information the CMS has asked you to provide, explain this, preferably in writing, in order to avoid a penalty. A complaint could also be made (see Chapter 11).

2. Contacting the non-resident parent

When a new child support application is made, the applicant must verify the address of the non-resident parent (NRP) and pay the application fee (see p22). The Child Maintenance Service (CMS) must then notify the NRP in writing as soon as reasonably practical. In most cases, this notification will also include a provisional calculation based on the information gained from the applicant and HM Revenue and Customs (HMRC). The NRP may dispute any of the facts relating to the application at this point (see p37). The date on which liability for child support usually starts (known as the 'initial effective date' – see p129) is specified in the notice. The CMS may telephone the NRP on or before the initial effective date and then confirm this in writing to the parent's last known address. If the CMS does not telephone the parent, it must send written notice to their last known address at least two days before the initial effective date.[33]

If you are the person with care (PWC) and there is a long delay by the CMS in starting this process, you can complain (see Chapter 11).

Tracing the non-resident parent

The CMS can use its information-seeking powers (including contacting the people and agencies on pp34–36) to identify and trace the NRP.

Finding a reliable address

The CMS seeks to confirm the identity and address of the NRP from information given by the PWC, Department for Work and Pensions (DWP) computer records and other methods. The CMS can decide that an address it holds for the NRP can reliably be used as their current address, without having to establish it beyond all reasonable doubt.[34] If the DWP computer gives the NRP's address and it is the same as that of the PWC, this is not considered reliable.

Information from the person with care

When the PWC applies for child support, they are asked for the address of the NRP, or for any information that could help trace them. This could include:

- their middle name(s) and any other names by which they may be known;
- other addresses at which they may have lived;
- their place of work and any previous employers;
- the name and address of their accountant;
- any benefit claims made;
- if they have a car, the registration or make, model, colour and other details.

The CMS may contact the PWC again if additional information is required – eg, if parentage is disputed. A parent may be asked to provide a recent photograph of the NRP if DNA testing may be involved, and to provide any relevant documents, such as a marriage certificate or expired passport. A PWC could also be asked other detailed questions – eg, whether the NRP has ever lived with them. The CMS may contact friends and relatives with whom the NRP may be living. If it does this, it must preserve confidentiality and should not disclose its interest.

The CMS does not normally offer face-to-face interviews (see p27), but these may be arranged if the CMS considers that the case involves complex issues and an interview may help to resolve them more quickly.

Initial contact with the non-resident parent

The initial notification (see p37) to the NRP that an application has been made usually includes a provisional child support calculation, based on the details provided by the applicant and information received by the CMS from HMRC or from other parts of the DWP.[35] This is not a decision, but an illustration of the NRP's child support liability based on the information the CMS currently has. It takes account of any information about shared care provided by the applicant.

The notification advises of the information that the NRP is required to provide for the child support calculation decision to be made. Details of the NRP's income are normally provided to the CMS automatically by HMRC (see p66), unless HMRC has no income data or is unable to supply it, in which case the NRP is asked for this.

A few days after issuing the notification, the CMS telephones the NRP to obtain information for the calculation decision. If the CMS is unable to contact the NRP by telephone, a reminder notice is issued in writing. If there is no response from the parent after 14 days, the CMS may then make the provisional child support calculation final, make a default maintenance decision (see p127) or, in certain circumstances, make a calculation based on estimated income (see p71).

Note: the CMS intends to obtain all (or most) of the information needed to work out child support electronically or by telephone. If the NRP prefers to be contacted in writing, they must request this.

If the parent is unaware of the child or is not named on the birth certificate, the CMS may try to arrange a face-to-face interview, although this is not expected to be done often.

There are special rules for young NRP (see p40).

During the initial phone call, the NRP may be asked questions in order to obtain or to confirm any information needed to make a calculation. This information can also be provided by the parent in writing if they wish.

For example, the NRP may be asked to confirm:

- personal details – eg, name, address, other names used, phone number(s), national insurance (NI) number, date of birth and best contact times;
- details required to confirm whether the CMS has jurisdiction;
- whether they accept parentage for the named qualifying child(ren);
- any means-tested benefits being claimed by, or for, them;
- student details, if appropriate – eg, name of college, course and qualification, and whether it is full or part time (evidence is requested);
- children who live with them – eg, date of birth, NI number (if appropriate) and who gets child benefit for the child (evidence is requested);
- details of any shared care or other special arrangements;
- employment details – eg, job title, employer (name, address and phone number), and start and end dates (if appropriate);
- income details – eg, frequency of pay, gross pay, bonuses and expenses (pay slips may be requested);

- their self-assessment form or tax calculation notice if they are self-employed;
- any other income – eg, pensions;
- payments made to a personal or private pension;
- collection details – eg, when the CMS will collect the child support and bank details, such as account number and sort code;
- representative details – eg, name, address, phone number and best contact times (signed authorisation is needed in certain circumstances).

The NRP is warned that a default maintenance decision (see p127) or, in certain circumstances, a calculation based on an estimate of income (see p71), may be made if there is a failure to provide sufficient information to enable the making of a calculation. At various stages, they are given the opportunity to provide more information, and is usually given at least seven days to do so.

They must also be informed that failure to provide the information requested, or knowingly to provide false information, is a criminal offence (see p37).

Information given can be amended at any time before a calculation is made. See p204 for what happens if there is a change in circumstances after the effective date.

Young non-resident parents

A face-to-face interview is likely to be arranged with a young NRP – ie, one under 16 years of age (or aged 16–19 and treated as a child – see p6). No calculation can be made until the NRP ceases to be treated as a child, but they are asked to confirm parentage for future reference. An adult must be present at the interview.

3. Parentage investigations

Disputes about whether someone is the parent (see p7) of a qualifying child can arise both before and after a child support calculation is made. The dispute can be about one or all of the qualifying children. Parentage is most commonly disputed by alleged non-resident fathers.

If the parentage of a qualifying child is denied or is in doubt, a child support application cannot be decided and a calculation completed in respect of that child unless the Child Maintenance Service (CMS) can assume parentage (see p41) or unless parentage is determined.

An alleged non-resident parent (NRP) may deny parentage during the initial telephone contact with the CMS or in writing before a calculation is made. The CMS can proceed with the calculation for any children for whom parentage is accepted or assumed while investigations are taking place for others.

The CMS carries out investigations to determine whether parentage may be established or assumed. Both the NRP and the person with care (PWC) can submit evidence to resolve the matter, and may be interviewed (see p43). The qualifying child's other parent may also be interviewed if they are not the PWC. The CMS may seek a DNA test or court action to establish parentage. The PWC or alleged NRP may also pursue court action at any time.

If an alleged NRP accepts parentage when responding to CMS enquiries, neither the CMS nor the First-tier Tribunal can then cancel the child support calculation, unless a court decides that they are not, in fact, the parent.[36]

Once a calculation has been made, a NRP who then disputes parentage can request a revision (see Chapter 9). However, they must still pay child support until they provide conclusive evidence that they are not the parent.[37] At this stage, it is not sufficient to deny parentage: evidence must be provided to raise doubt – eg, if the PWC was having another relationship when the child was conceived.

If the alleged NRP provides evidence in the form of a previous negative DNA test or a declaration/declarator of parentage, this is sufficient proof that they are not the parent of a particular child. The child support calculation in respect of that child is then cancelled from the date that child was included in the calculation,[38] and any payments made may be refunded. Whether or not all payments made are refunded may depend on how long after the calculation was made the parent disputed parentage, and a refund may only be made from the date when parentage was denied.[39]

If evidence provided by the alleged NRP is not conclusive but raises a doubt about parentage, the PWC is contacted by the CMS for comments on the NRP's evidence.

- If the PWC accepts that there may be doubt about parentage, a DNA test may be offered.
- If the PWC disputes the NRP's evidence, the decision is not revised. The NRP is advised to obtain a DNA test or declaration/declarator of non-parentage; the CMS does not offer a DNA test in this case. The alleged NRP is informed of their right to appeal to a court.

If a decision is not revised, the alleged NRP may have to apply to the family court (in England and Wales) or the sheriff court (in Scotland) for a declaration/declarator of parentage. A decision to refuse to revise can be challenged (see Chapter 10), but parentage can only ultimately be established by the court.

When someone is assumed to be a parent

If a person denies being the parent of a child, in certain circumstances the CMS must assume that they are the parent. (This does not apply if the child has subsequently been adopted by someone else.) They must then co-operate with the CMS, unless the CMS accepts proof that they are not, in fact, the parent of the child.

The CMS must assume parentage if:[40]

- the person has adopted the child;
- in England, Wales or Northern Ireland, a declaration of parentage or, in Scotland, a declarator of parentage, is in force for that person, including if the PWC or the CMS has applied to court for a declaration on whether the person is a parent of the child;[41]
- in England, Wales or Scotland, the person is a man who;[42]
  - was married to, or in a civil partnership with, the mother at any time between the child's conception and birth; *or*
  - acknowledged his paternity *and* was acknowledged by the mother *and* was named as the father on the birth certificate issued in the UK;
- the person is a man who was found to be the father by a court in England or Wales in proceedings under certain legal provisions (see Appendix 2). The court decision usually states the legal provision under which it was made;[43]
- the person is a man who was found by a court in Northern Ireland to be a father in proceedings under similar legal provisions to those in Appendix 2;[44]
- the person is a man who was found by a court in Scotland to be the father in any action for affiliation or aliment;[45]
- the person is a man who refuses to take a DNA test, or if the result of a test shows that he is the father (even if he refuses to accept it);[46]
- a parental order has been made in favour of that person following an application made within six months of a birth that is the result of a surrogacy arrangement;[47]
- certain types of fertility treatment have been carried out by a licensed clinic and the person is treated as a parent of the child under the Human Fertilisation and Embryology Acts 1990 and 2008.[48]

If none of the above applies, the CMS cannot make a calculation until parentage is admitted by a person or decided by a court.

If no one can be assumed to be a parent, the CMS usually attempts to arrange voluntary DNA testing or applies to court for a declaration/declarator of parentage.

If the alleged NRP disputes that the rules apply (eg, by alleging that the person named in a court order is someone else), they may appeal against the CMS decision. This appeal is dealt with by the family/sheriff court rather than by the First-tier Tribunal.[49]

If the alleged NRP accepts that the rules apply, but disputes that the court order referred to by the CMS is correct (eg, the court declaration/declarator of parentage was wrong), they should consider applying to the court to set aside its order and/or making a late appeal against it. It is not possible to challenge a decision about parentage through the revision and appeals process outlined in this *Handbook*.

Interviews if parentage is disputed

If parentage is denied after the CMS's initial contact, the PWC may be interviewed in order to establish the case to be put to the alleged NRP. In other cases, sufficient information may already be available to contact the NRP. However, both parties are interviewed before offering DNA tests (see p47) and, even if the PWC has already been interviewed or parentage is assumed, they may be reinterviewed to ascertain their response to the alleged NRP's version of events. If the PWC has already completed a parentage statement, they are only reinterviewed if the alleged NRP has new evidence.

Interviews are usually conducted by phone. If someone does not want to be interviewed in this way, an interview may be conducted in the CMS office or at their home. It is not compulsory to take part in any interview, but see p34 for who can be required to provide certain information.

If the PWC or alleged NRP is under 16 (or 16–19 and treated as a child – see p6), their parent or guardian must consent to the application progressing. The young person must have a face-to-face interview in the presence of a parent or guardian. A child support calculation is not made for a young person in these circumstances, but a parentage statement is required for future use. Additional information may be sought about a young alleged NRP to determine whether or not they should be treated as a child – eg, details of their current education or training.

Interviewing the alleged non-resident parent

If the alleged NRP denies parentage, a request is made for evidence of this. Further time to obtain documentary evidence may be permitted: seven days is usually allowed.

If documentary evidence cannot be supplied, the PWC may be interviewed to gather their evidence. If no evidence can be provided to establish or to assume parentage (see p41), the case may progress to DNA testing.

In an interview with an alleged father, the CMS could ask:

- whether he was in the country at any time between the date of conception and the child's birth;
- whether he had sex with the mother and, if so, over what period of time;
- if conception was assisted, whether he agreed to the treatment;
- how long the relationship lasted and whether he lived with the woman as husband and wife;
- whether or not he has had any contact with the child(ren);
- his reasons for thinking that he is not the father;
- whether there is any other information that might support his view.

This is not an exhaustive list. The alleged NRP need only answer such questions if parentage is denied and if the information is needed to decide the issue.

The alleged NRP is sent information about disputing parentage and the reduced-cost DNA test (see p45) before the interview. At the interview, the possibility of DNA testing is explained and agreement is sought.

Interviewing officers should take notes, and details of the interview (including any statement made by the NRP) should be recorded.

If the alleged NRP does not comply with requests to be interviewed, the CMS may consider a home visit or court action.

If the alleged NRP accepts parentage, the CMS makes a child support calculation.

Interviewing the parent with care

If someone has been named as the parent of a qualifying child and denies it, the CMS informs the parent with care of this and explains the procedures that follow.

The PWC is asked for any documentary evidence from which the CMS could assume parentage – eg, a birth or marriage certificate. They are also questioned about their relationship with the alleged NRP.

If no evidence can be provided to establish or assume parentage, the PWC is asked whether they are willing to take a DNA test (see p45).

The CMS asks about the alleged relationship and the circumstances of conception and birth. A mother who is the PWC is likely to be asked personal questions, including:

- the place the child was born and whether the pregnancy was full term;
- the names of the child's parents on the birth certificate;
- the man's reaction to the pregnancy;
- whether the two individuals ever lived together and, if so, when and where;
- whether the PWC considered them to be a couple at the time the child was conceived;
- whether the alleged NRP has ever acknowledged the child;
- whether the alleged NRP has ever paid any maintenance;
- whether there is, or has been, any contact with the alleged NPR's family;
- whether there are any letters or cards acknowledging the child, or witnesses to the association with the alleged NRP;
- whether the child's conception was assisted and, if so, whether the man agreed to the treatment and gave notice of this;
- whether they have any photographs of the alleged NRP;
- whether they are is willing to give evidence in court.

If you are a PWC and consider the question(s) inappropriate, you should question their relevance. If the interviewer insists, you could ask to end the interview to consider whether or not to provide the information. You can ask the interviewer to write down the questions and the reason for them. If, at the interview or later, you refuse to answer any of the questions, you should indicate that you have given all the information that is necessary to trace and identify the father.

A PWC may also be asked to make a parentage statement. You can refuse to sign this and the refusal forms part of the evidence, along with any reasons given. You may ask for a copy of the parentage statement and your reasons for not signing it. The statement is added to the report of the interview and can be used in court proceedings (see p47).

Interviewing a person with care who is not the parent

If both parents are non-resident and an alleged NRP continues to deny parentage after an interview, the PWC may be interviewed. The questions depend on the PWC's relationship with the alleged parents – eg, a grandparent may know the length of the relationship between the parents. They are is asked for the addresses of both parents, and any letters or cards from them. They are also asked why they are looking after the child(ren), whether there is any documentation about the care arrangements and whether they give their consent for the child(ren) in their care to undergo a DNA test (if they have parental responsibility).

DNA testing

DNA testing involves taking a cell sample from the PWC, alleged NRP and qualifying child. The test establishes the genetic fingerprint of the individual and is virtually conclusive. The test is usually done by taking a cheek cell sample from the inside of the mouth using a swab. It is possible for blood to be taken for the DNA test instead, but all parties must use the same method. If young children are involved, a cheek cell sample is usually preferred.

DNA testing is used when parentage cannot be assumed and the parties involved give their consent. If the CMS has applied to a court for a declaration/declarator of parentage, the court may order DNA testing.

The CMS arranges the DNA test through its approved provider, Cellmark Limited. An alleged NRP can also choose to arrange their own test (see p46).

Consent

If there is a dispute about parentage, both the PWC and the alleged NRP are asked to agree to a DNA test. Written consent must be obtained before a test can be carried out. If the qualifying child is under 16, their parent or guardian must give consent.

There are consequences if someone refuses to take the test.

- If the PWC accepts DNA testing, but refuses consent for the child, a court can direct DNA testing if it is in the best interests of the child, but it cannot force the child to take the test.
- If an alleged NRP refuses testing, they may be assumed to be the parent (see p41).[50]
- If a NRP already assumed to be the parent refuses to take a test, the CMS will not revise the calculation.

- If a child support applicant refuses to be tested and/or does not consent for testing of a qualifying child, the case is likely to be closed.
- There is no guidance on what happens when a parent or guardian of a child applicant in Scotland refuses consent, but DWP policy indicates that action may be taken to obtain a declarator of parentage.

The reason for any refusal must be explored. As the DNA test usually involves taking a cheek cell sample, any objections (eg, to blood tests on medical or religious grounds) may not be regarded as reasonable.

If the alleged NRP agrees to the test, but fails to attend the appointment, parentage is assumed unless there are good reasons – eg, they were in hospital, did not receive the test notification or were ill.

If a qualifying child aged 16 or over refuses consent, the NRP must apply to the court for a declaration/declarator of non-parentage.

Paying for a DNA test arranged by the Child Maintenance Service

If an alleged NRP is found to be the father, he is responsible for the costs of tests arranged by the CMS. He is responsible for the costs for himself, the PWC and the child(ren). If he is found not to be the father, a full refund of the cost of the test is made.[51]

At the time of writing, the fee for a test arranged by the CMS is £239.40. The fee is higher if more than one child is tested.[52]

If the alleged NRP says he cannot afford to pay for the test before a calculation is made, the CMS may pay for it, provided he agrees to accept the results and to repay the fee should the test show that he is the father. (If he is liable for child support at the nil rate or flat rate, the CMS may help with the fee in exceptional cases.[53]) If he still refuses to take the DNA test, parentage may be assumed (see p41).

The CMS can recover the costs of the test from the alleged NRP if the test does not exclude him from being the father and:[54]

- he does not now deny that he is the father; *or*
- a court has now made a declaration/declarator of parentage.

Private testing

An alleged NRP may choose to arrange the test himself. The CMS usually allows 40 working days for this. In the meantime, the CMS may still assume parentage if the CMS test has been refused.[55] Prices vary depending on which company is used, but are likely to be higher than for a test arranged by the CMS. If the alleged parent has arranged a test himself, the fee is not refunded if the test is negative.

The test must be carried out by an approved agency[56] and proper security measures must be in place; otherwise, even if the test is negative, the CMS and court will not accept the result.[57]

Tests must involve the PWC; a test with only the alleged NRP and the qualifying child is not accepted. No action can be taken against a PWC who does not consent to a private test. If the alleged NRP cannot arrange a private test because he does not know the PWC's address, the CMS does not provide contact details.

DNA test results

Once the DNA-testing company has received all the samples, the test usually takes 10 days. The results are sent by post to the PWC, the alleged NRP and the CMS. The results are confidential and are not given by telephone.

If the alleged NRP is shown to be the parent, he is also sent notification by the CMS. The CMS also asks for any additional information needed. (The 'effective date' of liability for child support remains the date as recorded in the original notification of the application – see p129.) If the alleged NRP still does not accept parentage, he must take court action to obtain a declaration/declarator of non-parentage. The CMS may make a calculation (or, if already made, refuse to revise one) because a positive DNA test is grounds to assume parentage.

If the DNA tests confirm that the person who took the test as the alleged NRP is not the parent, action is taken to confirm the identity of the person tested. If the alleged NRP sent someone else to take the test, the CMS passes the case to the fraud team. If the wrong person has been traced, the CMS pursues further tracing. If the identity is confirmed, the PWC may be reinterviewed about any other possible NRP.

Court proceedings

When all possible action and investigations have been completed, the CMS may decide to apply to a court for a declaration/declarator of parentage.[58] Court action is rare, as there are other ways of being able to assume parentage (see p41). Examples of situations where court action may be taken include:

- if a DNA test is inconclusive;
- cases involving fertility treatment where an alleged non-resident father denies he consented to the treatment;
- if the PWC disputes the NRP's inconclusive evidence after a child support calculation has been made. In this case, the NRP must apply to court (the CMS may not be involved in this action, but may be informed of the outcome).

If the CMS decides not to take court action, the PWC may initiate proceedings.[59] The PWC or NRP may start court proceedings at any time.

The CMS or the PWC may apply to court for a declaration/declarator of parentage. If the CMS is willing to do so, usually the PWC should not also apply, because this may lead to their paying their own legal costs and, if they lose, those of the alleged NRP (see p48). If the CMS suspends the case, but the PWC wants to go to court then it is suggested that legal advice is sought.

Only the courts have the power to order blood tests (including DNA tests – see p45) in any civil proceedings in which parentage is an issue.[60] If convinced that blood testing would be against the child's interests, the court should not order it.[61] A court can direct that blood tests be used to establish whether or not someone is a parent of the child, but cannot force anyone to give a blood sample. It can, however, overrule a child's lack of consent if it determines it is in the child's interests.[62] However, the court may draw its own adverse conclusions if a person fails to comply, depending on the circumstances of the case.[63] The costs of testing ordered by the court are treated as the costs of the party who applied for the testing.[64] However, if that person wins the case, the court usually orders the losing party to pay costs, which can include the costs of any test. In Scotland, if an alleged NRP applies for a declarator of non-parentage and the CMS does not defend the action, no expenses can be awarded against the CMS.[65]

Outcome of the court proceedings

If no child support calculation has been made, once a declaration/declarator of parentage is issued, the CMS contacts the NRP to gather the information needed to make it.

If the court finds that the person is not the parent, the PWC is approached to establish whether a different alleged NRP can be named. Unless the parent can name an alternative alleged NRP, the case is likely to be closed.

The court can order any party to pay some, or all, of the legal costs of another party – eg, solicitors' fees. Usually, the losing party is ordered to pay the other party's costs.

4. **Further investigations**

The Child Maintenance Service (CMS) may make further enquiries when considering an application. In practice, the CMS usually makes no further investigations if:

- parentage is accepted; *and*
- information is provided to make a calculation; *and*
- any documents requested are provided – eg, a copy of a maintenance agreement, pay slips or a tax calculation notice.

Even if one parent challenges the details provided by the other, the CMS may be reluctant to make any further enquiries unless the parent can provide sufficient evidence to give the CMS reasonable grounds to investigate – ie, to persuade the CMS that there are grounds for a revision or supersession to be considered.

The CMS should not request any corroboration of evidence of a particular fact (ie, other evidence to support what the CMS already has), unless the evidence the CMS has is self-contradictory, improbable or contradicted by other evidence.[66]

Asking the Child Maintenance Service to investigate

If you are not satisfied with the way the CMS has investigated the case, you can ask it to make further enquiries. Contact the CMS, by telephone or through the online portal and explain the situation, asking what enquiries have already been made and suggesting further ones. Refer to the CMS's power to request information (see p33) and to use an inspector to conduct investigations (see below). If the CMS refuses to say what steps have been taken or to make further enquiries, a complaint can be made (see Chapter 11) and judicial review may be possible (see p198).

If an appeal has been made, the First-tier Tribunal can also make enquiries (see Chapter 10). It has more powers than the CMS and it may be easier to persuade it to use them.

If you are dissatisfied with the CMS's enquiries, you can also make your own and pass the information to the CMS.

Inspectors

The CMS can appoint inspectors (which it usually refers to as 'investigating officers') to obtain the information it requires.[67] The CMS may instruct inspectors from its Financial Investigation Unit if concerns are raised about the circumstances of the non-resident parent (NRP), and a face-to-face interview may take place.

Inspectors can enter premises (except those used only as a home) to make enquiries and to inspect documents. Inspectors must have a certificate of appointment, which must be produced when entering premises.[68] They can do so at any reasonable time, either alone or accompanied by anyone they consider appropriate. An inspector must obtain a warrant from the magistrates' court (in England and Wales) or sheriff court (in Scotland) to enter premises if they are occupied and the occupant(s) have refused to allow entry, or are likely to refuse entry without a warrant.[69]

'Premises' can include vehicles, aircraft, moveable structures and offshore installations. Inspectors cannot enter premises by force. The premises that can be entered include ones where the inspector has reasonable grounds to believe that:[70]

- the NRP is, or has been, employed;
- the NRP carries out, or has carried out, a trade;
- there is information held by someone whom the inspector has reasonable grounds for suspecting has information about the NRP acquired in the course of their own trade, profession, vocation or business.

Inspectors usually contact the occupier of the premises by telephone or letter to arrange a mutually suitable time for the entry and inspection. They will also advise the occupier of the duty to provide information and the penalties for failing to do so or for the obstruction of an inspector. Where an inspector intends to apply for a warrant, at least 21 days' notice must be given to the occupier of the intention to do so. A warrant expires one month after being issued.[71]

An inspector can question any person aged 18 or over found on the premises and request information and documents from:[72]

- an occupier of the premises;
- an employer or employee working there;
- anyone else whose work or business is based there;
- an employee or agent of any of the above.

No one is required to give any evidence or to answer any question that might incriminate them or their spouse or civil partner. Deliberately delaying or obstructing an inspector is an offence. Where the premises are occupied, delaying or obstructing an inspector is an offence only if the inspector has a warrant authorising entry. Failing or refusing to answer a question or to provide the evidence requested is also an offence, unless there is a good reason for not doing so.[73] The maximum fine is currently £1,000.

A solicitor is entitled to claim 'privilege' concerning information about a client's confidential affairs and can refuse to give information. The CMS has also given assurances that the powers of inspectors will not be used to investigate other representatives – eg, an adviser. This does not apply to information required from an employer about an employee.

5. Change of circumstances

There is no general duty to give information about any change of circumstances to the Child Maintenance Service (CMS).

However, in some circumstances, there is a duty to disclose information to the CMS if the CMS has the right to request the information.

- The non-resident parent (NRP) must notify the CMS of a change of address within seven days.[74] Any failure to do so, may be construed as a criminal offence and a fine (currently up to £1,000) may be imposed.[75] The NRP must also inform the CMS of certain changes when a deduction from earnings order is in force (see p161). In certain circumstances, the CMS may also require the NRP to notify it of any increase in their gross income (see p76).
- A person with care (PWC) has a duty to tell the CMS if they believe that a calculation has ceased to have effect.[76] This may be because:
  - a relevant person (ie, the PWC, NRP or qualifying child) has died;
  - a relevant person is no longer within CMS jurisdiction – ie, they are not habitually resident in the UK (see p15);
  - the NRP is no longer a NRP of the child(ren) named in the calculation – eg, because the child has been adopted;
  - a child no longer counts as a child, or as a qualifying child (see p6);

- the PWC has stopped being a PWC in relation to the child(ren) named in the calculation.

The PWC must give the reasons for their belief in writing, and may be required to give further information to enable a decision to be made.

The PWC is not required to inform the CMS until the change has taken place.

For the consequences of failing to disclose information when required, see p37.

In practice, any party may want to tell the CMS of changes or of new information that may affect the amount of child support payable. See Chapter 9 for details of when a calculation may be changed.

6. **Disclosure of information**

In the course of its investigations, the Child Maintenance Service (CMS) collects information and evidence about people affected by child support applications. The non-resident parent (NRP) and person with care (PWC) (and a child applicant in Scotland) must be given details of how the amount of child support has been calculated (see p128). The CMS must also give certain other information it has to the courts, to the First-tier Tribunal, to other parts of the Department for Work and Pensions (DWP) and to local authorities.

The CMS cannot give information to third parties without the written permission of the person to whom the information relates. Any unauthorised disclosure of information is a criminal offence.

However, the CMS *can* disclose information given to it by one party (see below) to a child support calculation in order to enable it to explain to another party:[77]

- why an application for child support, or for revision or supersession of a decision, has been rejected;
- why an application cannot proceed or why a calculation will not be made;
- why a calculation has been cancelled or ceases to have effect;
- how the amount of child support has been worked out;
- why a decision has been made not to collect child support, or to stop collection;
- why a particular method of enforcement has been used;
- why enforcement methods have not been used or enforcement has ceased;
- why a decision has been made not to accept part- payment of arrears;
- why a decision has been made not to write off arrears in certain circumstances.

Parties

For the purposes of the CMS's disclosure of information, the **'parties'** are the person who made the application for child support, the PWC, the NRP and a qualifying child.[78] If one of these people has died, and a revision, supersession, appeal or variation request is pending but remains undecided at the date of death, then a representative who was dealing with the request on their behalf is also a party.[79]

Any request for the above information must be made in writing to the CMS, giving reasons.[80] However, the CMS can provide the information without a request.

The CMS must only disclose a person's address (or other information which could reasonably be expected to lead to that person being located) if written permission has been provided[81] (if you are appealing, you should notify the First-tier Tribunal if you do not want your address or other information disclosed – see p217[82]). Also, the CMS must not disclose information which could reasonably be expected to lead to the identification of any person other than a PWC, NRP or a qualifying child.[83]

The CMS can disclose any information to the First-tier Tribunal, to the courts and to anyone with a right of appeal, if it is for proceedings under the child support or benefits legislation.[84]

In practice, in a child support appeal, CMS papers are included in the CMS submission sent to each party (see p211). The CMS can also disclose information to a court which has made, varied or revived a maintenance order or agreement, if that information is required in relation to those proceedings or other matters arising from them.[85] The CMS can also disclose information to local authorities for their use in administering housing benefit.[86]

In certain circumstances, the CMS can disclose information about the NRP to a credit reference agency (see p53). See also p169 for details of information about a NRP that can be disclosed to joint account holders when the CMS is considering enforcement action by deductions from bank accounts.

If you want to see a copy of information about you held by the CMS, you can apply in writing. This information must be supplied without delay, and normally within one month of the request at the latest.[87] It should be provided free of charge (but a reasonable fee based on the administrative costs of providing the information may be charged if a request is unfounded or excessive, particularly if it is repetitive). If you have concerns about the collection, retention, accuracy or use of this information, contact the Information Commissioner's Office.[88]

Disclosure to other government departments

The CMS can disclose information to government departments dealing with benefits, including DWP agencies.[89] This includes information obtained using its powers and information disclosed to the CMS voluntarily.

As the DWP has close links with the Home Office, disclosure may create problems for people from abroad and those prohibited from having recourse to public funds. If you have doubts about whether information should be disclosed to the CMS, get advice first from a law centre or independent advice centre dealing with immigration issues (see Appendix 3). You can only be prosecuted for refusing to give information if it has been requested by the CMS or an inspector (see p49).

CMS staff can exchange information with their counterparts in Northern Ireland and vice versa.

Disclosure to credit reference agencies

The CMS can disclose information about a NRP to credit reference agencies but only that which is relevant to the NRP's financial standing. This means that any arrears of child support are likely to have the same effect on a parent's credit assessment as other debts.

The NRP must consent to the information being passed to the agency, unless a liability order (see p180) is in force against them, in which case such consent is not required.[90] If there is an ongoing appeal by the NRP against the granting of the liability order, the CMS must not disclose information without the NRP's consent until the appeal is concluded.

The following information can be passed to a credit reference agency:[91]

- the parent's name, last known or notified address and date of birth;
- the CMS reference number for the parent's case;
- the date any liability order in force against the parent was made;
- the amount covered by the liability order;
- the address stated in the liability order, if different from the last known or notified address.

The decision to disclose information is a discretionary one. Before passing any information to an agency, the CMS must consider the welfare of any child likely to be affected by the decision (see p124). Before it proceeds, the CMS must then also notify the parent in writing by post, or electronically to their last known or notified address (if they can be traced) that it intends to do so. The notification must be sent at least 21 days before the information is given to an agency.[92]

The CMS can also tell a credit reference agency without first notifying the NRP:[93]

- that the amount covered by the liability order has been paid, and when;
- that a liability order against the parent has been 'set aside' or quashed.

Notes

1. **Information-seeking powers**
1 s14 and Sch 2 CSA 1991
2 s12 CSPSSA 2000
3 Regs 3 and 4(1) CSI Regs
4 Reg 7(1) CSI Regs
5 ss4(4) and 7(5) CSA 1991; reg 3 CSI Regs
6 Regs 3 and 4 CSI Regs
7 Reg 3(2) CSI Regs
8 Reg 5 CSI Regs
9 Reg 6 CSI Regs
10 See s3 SSA 1998
11 Sch 2 para 1 CSA 1991; Sch 6 para 2 CMOPA 2008
12 s127 WRA 2012; paras 38015-7 DMG

13 s6 and Sch 1 Taxes Management Act 1970; s182 Finance Act 1989
14 Reg 4(2)(b) and (3) CSI Regs
15 Reg 4(2)(c) and (3) CSI Regs
16 Reg 4(2)(d) CSI Regs
17 Reg 4(2)(f) CSI Regs – credit reference agencies are as defined by s145(8) Consumer Credit Act 1974 and Art 89B Financial Services and Markets Act 2000 (Regulated Activities) Order 2001 No.544
18 Reg 4(2)(g) CSI Regs
19 s122D SSAA 1992
20 Reg 4(2)(h)(i) CSI Regs
21 Reg 4(2)(h)(ii) CSI Regs
22 Reg 4(2)(i) CSI Regs
23 Reg 4(2)(j) and (k) CSI Regs
24 Reg 4(2) (ka)-(kc) CSI regs
25 Reg 4(2)(kd) CSI regs
26 Reg 4(2)(l) CSI Regs
27 Reg 4(2)(m) CSI Regs
28 Reg 4(2)(n) CSI regs
29 Reg 7(1) CSI Regs
30 Reg 7(2) CSI Regs
31 s14A CSA 1991
32 Reg 8 CSI Regs

2. **Contacting the non-resident parent**
33 Regs 7, 11 and 12 CSMC Regs
34 CCS/2288/2005
35 Child Maintenance and Enforcement Commission, *The Child Support Maintenance Calculation Regulations 2012: a technical consultation on the draft regulations*, December 2011

3. **Parentage investigations**
36 R(CS) 13/98
37 gov.uk/manage-child-maintenance-case/disagreements-about-parentage
38 Reg 14(1)(g) CSMC 2012
39 gov.uk/manage-child-maintenance-case/disagreements-about-parentage; DMG para 59023
40 s26 CSA 1991
41 Under ss55A or 56 Family Law Act 1986, art 32 Matrimonial and Family Proceedings (Northern Ireland) Order 1989 No.677 or s7 LR(PC)(S)A 1986
42 **EW** s26(2) CSA 1991, Cases A1 and A2
S s26(2) CSA 1991, Case E; s5(1) LR(PC)(S)A 1986
43 s26(2) CSA 1991, Case F(a)(i) in 'relevant proceedings' under s12(5) Civil Evidence Act 1968 or affiliation proceedings
44 s26(2) CSA 1991, Case F(a)(i) in 'relevant proceedings' under s8(5) Civil Evidence Act (Northern Ireland) 1971 or affiliation proceedings
45 s26(2) CSA 1991, Case F(a)(ii) in affiliation proceedings
46 s26(2) CSA 1991, Case A3
47 s26(2) CSA 1991, Case B
48 s26(2) CSA 1991, Case B1
49 **EW** Arts 3 and 4 CSA(JC)O
S Arts 2 and 3 CSA(JC)(S)O
50 s26 CSA 1991, Case A3(b)
51 gov.uk/manage-child-maintenance-case/disagreements-about-parentage
52 gov.uk/get-a-dna-test
53 para 45064 DMG
54 s27A CSA 1991
55 s26 CSA 1991, Case A3
56 See the list at gov.uk/get-dna-test
57 For a current list of accredited agencies, see gov.uk/get-dna-test
58 ss27 and 28 CSA 1991
59 **EW** s27(2) CSA 1991
S s7 LR(PC)(S)A 1986
60 s20 FLRA 1969; *Re H (Paternity: Blood Test)* [1996] 2 FLR 65
61 *W v Official Solicitor* [1972] AC 24
62 s21 FLRA 1969
63 s23 FLRA 1969; *Re A (Paternity: Refusal of Blood Test)* [1994] 2 FLR 463
64 s20(6) FLRA 1969
65 s28(2) CSA 1991; s7 LR(PC)(S)A 1986; r152 AS(CSA)(AOCSCR), inserting Act of Sederunt (Sheriff Court Ordinary Cause Rules) 1993 No.1956, Chapter 33.89

4. **Further investigations**
66 *DB v CMEC* [2010] UKUT 356 (AAC)
67 s15(1) CSA 1991
68 s15(8) CSA 1991
69 ss15(4ZA) and 15A CSA 1991
70 s15(4), (4A) and (11) CSA 1991
71 s15A(3)(d) and (8) CSA 1991
72 s15(5) and (6) CSA 1991
73 s15(7), (9) and (9A) CSA 1991

5. **Change of circumstances**
74 s14A(3A) CSA 1991; reg 9 CSI Regs
75 s14A CSA 1991
76 Reg 10 CSI Regs

6. **Disclosure of information**
77 Reg 13 CSI Regs; R(CS) 1/00
78 Reg 13(2)(a) and (b) CSI Regs
79 Reg 13(2)(d) CSI Regs
80 Reg 13(3) CSI Regs
81 Reg 13(4) CSI Regs
82 r19(3) TP(FT) Rules

83 Reg 13(4) CSI Regs
84 Reg 12 CSI Regs
85 Reg 12(3) CSI Regs
86 s122C(2)(a) SSAA 1992
87 EU Reg 2016/679, with effect from 25 May 2018, as it forms part of the law of the UK by virtue of s3 European Union (Withdrawal) Act 2018
88 ico.org.uk
89 s3 SSA 1998
90 s49D(3) CSA 1991
91 Reg 14A(1)(a)-(e) CSI Regs
92 Reg 14A(2) and (3) CSI Regs
93 Reg 14A(1)(f) and (g) and (2) CSI Regs

Chapter 4

Calculating the amount of child support

This chapter covers:

1. The rates of child support

There are four rates of child support:

- nil rate (see p57);
- flat rate (see p58);
- reduced rate (see p59);
- basic rate, including 'basic rate plus' (see p60).

The amount of child support calculated is a weekly amount. In all cases, fractions of a penny are disregarded if they are less than a half, or rounded up to the next penny if a half or over.[1]

If there is more than one non-resident parent (NRP) in relation to a qualifying child, child support is calculated for each parent separately. This means that a person with care (PWC) could receive different rates from each – eg, the flat rate from one NRP and an amount worked out using the basic rate from the other. If there is more than one PWC, see below.

Note: the child support calculation can be varied in certain circumstances – eg, if the NRP has certain special expenses or additional income (see Chapter 5).

If there is more than one person with care

If there is more than one PWC, each caring for a different qualifying child in relation to a NRP, the amount of child support may be apportioned between them in relation to the number of qualifying children each person cares for.[2]

Apportionment occurs after child support has been calculated at the appropriate rate, but before any decrease for shared care (see p78).[3] **Note:** if apportioning the child support due to different PWCs leaves a 'floating' penny leftover, these are retained and paid out when enough have accumulated to split them equally between the PWCs.[4]

In basic and reduced rate cases, if an adjustment is made that reduces the NRP's liability to less than £7 (eg, because of shared care or a variation), the amount payable is £7 apportioned between the PWCs.[5]

Child support liability is calculated for only one PWC in respect of each qualifying child. If, in practice, another person who is not the NRP provides care for a qualifying child, the Child Maintenance Service (CMS) does not apportion the child support between them. The PWC who receives the child support could agree to pass some of it on to any other person who also provides care for the child. However, this would be an informal agreement and would not be monitored or enforced by the CMS.

Nil rate

Some NRPs do not need to pay any child support. This 'nil rate' applies if the NRP:[6]

- is a child (see p6 for the meaning of 'child'); *or*
- is a prisoner (including if serving a prison sentence and detained in hospital); *or*
- is 16 or 17 years old and receiving universal credit (UC) calculated on the basis that there is no earned income (or, if part of a couple, their partner is receiving UC calculated on this basis); *or*
- is 16 or 17 years old and receiving income support (IS), income-based jobseeker's allowance (JSA) or income-related employment and support allowance (ESA) (or, if part of a couple, their partner is receiving one of these benefits for them); *or*
- receives an allowance for work-based training for young people. Young people may receive a training allowance or (in Scotland and Wales) an education maintenance allowance; *or*
- is resident in a care home or independent hospital, or being provided with a care home service or/and independent healthcare service, and receives one of the prescribed benefits for the flat rate (see p58) or has all or part of the cost of their accommodation met by a local authority; *or*
- has a gross income (including income from any of the prescribed benefits for the flat rate) of less than £7 a week.

Example

Kerry is a PWC of two children, Mia and Lewis. Her ex-partner, Craig, is in prison. In this case, the nil rate applies. When he comes out of prison, Kerry could ask for a supersession as their circumstances have changed.

Flat rate

A 'flat rate' of £7 a week applies if the NRP does not qualify for the nil rate and:[7]

- their weekly income is £100 or less; *or*
- they receive one of the following benefits:[8]
  - category A, B, C or D retirement pension;
  - state pension;
  - incapacity benefit;
  - contributory ESA;
  - carer's allowance;
  - maternity allowance;
  - severe disablement allowance;
  - industrial injuries benefit;
  - widowed mother's or widowed parent's allowance;
  - widow's pension;
  - contribution-based JSA;
  - a training allowance (other than for work-based learning for young people);
  - war disablement pension;
  - war widow's, war widower's or surviving civil partner's war pension;
  - payments under the Armed Forces Compensation Scheme;
  - a social security benefit paid by a country other than the UK; *or*
- they, or their partner, get one of the following means-tested benefits:[9]
  - UC calculated on the basis that they do not have any earned income;
  - IS;
  - income-based JSA;
  - income-related ESA;
  - pension credit.

The flat rate can be halved if the NRP has a partner who is also a NRP with a child support calculation in force, and the NRP (or their partner) receives one of the means-tested benefits above. Each pays £3.50.[10] If the NRP is in a polygamous relationship and there is more than one partner who is also a NRP and the NRP or their partner receives one of these means-tested benefits, each is liable to pay £3.50 a week.

If there is more than one PWC caring for different qualifying children, the flat rate is apportioned between them (see p56).

Note: the flat rate is not reduced to take account of any relevant other children (see p62), children abroad or children in family-based arrangement (see p63).

There are special rules about shared care (see p81).

If the flat rate is paid by deductions being made directly from the NRP's benefit (see p139), a collection fee of 20 per cent is added and the deduction is £8.40 a week.

Example

The situation is as in the previous example on p57. Craig has now come out of prison and gets UC. Kerry requests a supersession and Craig pays the flat rate of £7 child support each week (a monthly amount of £36.40 would be deducted from his UC if he pays that way). If Craig moved in with his new partner, Hazel, and claimed UC as a couple, the flat rate of £7 would still apply and Kerry would receive £7 a week. However, if Hazel were also a NRP with a child support application in force, the flat rate would be halved. In this case, Kerry would receive £3.50 a week.

Reduced rate

The reduced rate applies if the NRP does not qualify for the flat rate or the nil rate and their weekly gross income is more than £100 but less than £200. The flat rate of £7 is added to a percentage of the parent's income between £100 and £200[11] – eg, if gross income is £150, the percentage is applied to £50. The percentage depends on the number of qualifying children (see p6), including a child abroad or child in family-based arrangement (see p63) the NRP has, as well as the number of other children who live with them ('relevant other children' – see p62).[12]

Reduced rate percentages

Number of relevant other children	*Number of qualifying children*		
	One	Two	Three or more
None	17%	25%	31%
One	14.1%	21.2%	26.4%
Two	13.2%	19.9%	24.9%
Three or more	12.4%	18.9%	23.8%

Step one

Work out the gross weekly income between £100 and £200.

Step two

Work out the relevant percentage. Apply this percentage to the income worked out in Step one and add this to £7.

Step three

If different qualifying children are cared for by different people with care, apportion the amount worked out in Step two between them, depending on the number of qualifying children each cares for.

Example

Milo is due to pay child support to Emma for two qualifying children, Harry and Lily. Milo lives with his new partner, Cate, and their baby, Max. Max is a relevant other child. Milo's gross income is £180 a week. The reduced rate of child support applies.

Step one:	Gross weekly income = £180 Income between £100 and £200 = £80
Step two:	Relevant percentage for one relevant other child and two qualifying children is 21.2 per cent. £7 + (21.2% x £80) = £7 + £16.96 = £23.96

Milo is due to pay £23.96 child support a week to Emma.

If Lily was being cared for by Emma and Harry stayed with his grandmother, there would still be two qualifying children, each cared for by a different PWC. The child support calculated would need to be apportioned between them.

Step three:	Each person cares for one qualifying child, so the child support is divided by two. £23.96 ÷ 2 = £11.98

Milo now pays Emma £11.98 a week and the grandmother £11.98 a week.

If the NRP shares the care of any qualifying children, the reduced rate may be decreased by applying the shared care rules (see p81).

Basic rate

The basic rate applies if none of the other rates (nil, flat or reduced) apply.[13]

If the NRP has a gross weekly income of £200 or more, child support is calculated using the basic rate. If their gross weekly income is over £800, the 'basic rate plus' applies. The maximum amount of gross weekly income that can be included in the child support calculation is £3,000. Even if a variation for additional income is being applied (see Chapter 5), the amount of gross income taken into account cannot be more than this.[14]

The basic rate is a percentage of the NRP's gross weekly income, depending on the number of qualifying children they have (see p6), including children abroad or children in a family based arrangement (see p63).

If the NRP has other children living with them (relevant other children – see p62), the NRP's gross income is reduced by a certain percentage before the basic rate is calculated. The basic rate is therefore worked out in two steps.

Step one

Work out the gross weekly income of the NRP. Reduce this by the appropriate percentage, depending on the number of relevant other children there are.

Basic rate: reduction in gross income for relevant other children[15]

Number of relevant other children	*Percentage by which gross income is reduced*
One	11%
Two	14%
Three or more	16%

Step two

Work out the amount of child support as a proportion of the gross income calculated in Step one, depending on the number of qualifying children (including any children abroad or children in a family-based arrangement).

- If gross weekly income is £800 a week or less, the basic rate of child support is 12 per cent, 16 per cent or 19 per cent of this gross income.
- If gross income is over £800 a week, the 'basic rate plus' of child support is 12 per cent, 16 per cent or 19 per cent of £800 plus 9 per cent, 12 per cent or 15 per cent of the amount over £800.

Basic rate percentages[16]

Number of qualifying children (including relevant non-resident children)	*Percentage of gross income up to £800*	*Percentage of gross income above £800*
One	12%	9%
Two	16%	12%
Three or more	19%	15%

Example

Alfie and Sasha have separated and their three children, Tia, Zara and Jon, live with Sasha. Alfie lives with his new partner and her daughter, Lola. Alfie's gross weekly income is £450 a week. Tia, Zara and Jon are the qualifying children, and Lola is a relevant other child.

Step one: Alfie's gross weekly income is £450. There is one relevant other child, so this is reduced by 11 per cent.
11% x £450 = £49.50
£450 – £49.50 = £400.50

Step two: There are three qualifying children, so child support is 19 per cent of the remaining gross income.
19% x £400.50 = £76.10
Alfie therefore pays £76.10 a week in child support to Sasha.
Alfie's gross weekly income increases to £979.85, so the 'basic rate plus' applies.

Step one: Alfie's gross weekly income is £979.85. There is one relevant other child, so this is reduced by 11 per cent.
11% x £979.85 = £107.78
£979.85 - £107.78 = £872.07

Step two: This amount is over £800 and there are three qualifying children. So child support is 19 per cent of £800 plus 15 per cent of the 'excess' above £800 – ie, 15 per cent of £72.07.
19% x £800 = £152
15% x £72.07 = £10.81
Alfie therefore now pays £162.81 (£152 + £10.81) a week in child support to Sasha.

Step three

If there is more than one PWC caring for different qualifying children, apportion the amount worked out at Step two between the people with care depending on the number of qualifying children each cares for.

Example

Alfie currently pays £162.81 a week in child support to his ex-wife, Sasha, for his three children, Tia, Zara and Jon. When Jon goes to live with his grandmother, the £162.81 child support is split between Sasha and the grandmother.

Step three: £162.81 is apportioned between two PWC.

Sasha cares for two children and so she receives two-thirds of the child support due. Alfie pays her £108.54 a week.

The grandmother cares for one child and so she receives one-third of the child support due. Alfie pays her £54.27 a week.

If the NRP shares the care of any of the qualifying children, the child support calculated may be decreased by applying the shared care rules (see p81).

Relevant other children

The number of relevant other children affects the calculation of child support. A **'relevant other child'** (or **'relevant child'**) is the term used by the CMS for a child, other than a qualifying child, for whom the NRP or their partner receives child benefit.[17] This can include a child who does not live with the parent all the time – eg, a child at boarding school. It can also include a child for whom the NRP or their partner would get child benefit, but for the fact that:[18]

- the rules about presence in Great Britain are not met; *or*
- the NRP or their partner has elected not to receive child benefit because of a potential liability to the 'high-income child benefit charge'.

If a relevant other child is cared for by a local authority for some or all of the time, then that child continues to count as a relevant other child if the NRP or their partner receives child benefit for them.[19]

See CPAG's *Welfare Benefits and Tax Credits Handbook* for full details of the rules on child benefit.

Child in family-based arrangement

If the NRP is liable to pay maintenance for other children, who are not qualifying children, it affects the calculation of child support. This includes a child of the NRP for whom an application for child support cannot be made because the NRP is liable to pay maintenance under a maintenance order (or registered maintenance agreement in Scotland), an order from an overseas court, or under the legislation of another country.[20] It also includes a child who is not a qualifying child, but is habitually resident in the UK (see p15) and the NRP is paying maintenance under an 'informal' maintenance agreement. The arrangement can be a verbal agreement, but must be between the NRP and PWC of the relevant child, and must be for regular payments for the benefit of the child.[21] Payments made to a third party may also count.

In the 2003 scheme, the term 'relevant non-resident child' was used for a child who would be considered a qualifying child if an application could be made for them if it were not for the restrictions that prevent the application. See p16 for more information about when a court order prevents an application for child support being made. The CMS now use the term 'child in family-based arrangement' for children who do not live with the NRP, but for whom child maintenance is payable.

A child abroad may be treated as a 'child in family-based arrangement' if the NRP has a liability to pay child maintenance under the legislative system of another country and is making such payments. A formal court order to that effect is not required. An informal family-based arrangement to support a child abroad may be sufficient. The CMS will seek evidence of the nature of the arrangement.[22]

When working out the basic and reduced rate of child support (including if payable after a variation), a child abroad or 'child in family-based arrangement', counts as a qualifying child, even though no amount of child support is paid for that child.[23]

The amount of child support calculated is divided by the total number of qualifying children, including any child abroad or 'child in family-based arrangement'. This amount is then multiplied by the number of qualifying children, excluding the child in family-based arrangement, which determines the amount of child support the NRP must pay for the qualifying children. The amount payable for the child abroad or child in family based arrangement (eg, amounts payable under a maintenance order) is not affected by the child support calculation, nor are adjustments made for shared care allowances or because the child is being looked after by the local authority for part of the time.

If there is more than one PWC, each caring for a different qualifying child, the child support is apportioned between them in relation to the number of qualifying children they care for, including any adjustment for shared care.[24] If the total amount payable by the NRP is less than £7, they pay £7 instead, apportioned between the PWCs as appropriate.[25]

Example

Sean lives with his new partner, Amber, and her son, Ben. Sean has three other children. Two (Ella and Kai) are cared for by Natasha; one (Immy) is cared for by Ruth. Sean has a court order for child maintenance for Immy and pays £45 a week maintenance to Ruth. Ruth cannot apply for child support as the court order is in force. In this case:

Ella and Kai are qualifying children.

Ben is a relevant other child (even though he is not Sean's child, Sean's new partner, Amber, gets child benefit for him).

Immy is a 'child in family-based arrangement'.

Sean's gross income is £675 a week. His child support is worked out using the basic rate as follows.

Step one: Sean's gross income is £675. There is one relevant other child, so this is reduced by 11 per cent.
11% x £675 = £74.25
£675 – £74.25 = £600.75

Step two: There are two qualifying children and one child in family-based arrangement. So child support is 19 per cent of £600.75.
19% x £600.75 = £114.14

Step three: Divide the child support by the number of qualifying children, including the child in family-based arrangement – ie, divide £114.14 by 3 = £38.05.
Multiply £38.05 by the number of qualifying children, excluding the child in family-based arrangement – ie, £38.05 x 2 = £76.10.
Sean is due to pay £76.10 a week child support to Natasha.
Ruth receives her usual court order maintenance of £45 a week.
Note: if Ruth could apply for child support, she would receive £38.04 (£114.14 – £76.10).

If the situation changes and Ella is now cared for by her grandmother and Kai is still cared for by Natasha, apportionment applies between Natasha and the grandmother. As each cares for one qualifying child, each would receive £38.05 a week child support.

Divided families

If a couple has more than one child together and at least one child is living with each parent, child support liability is still calculated for both parents. However, the amounts may be offset so that only the parent with the higher liability makes a balancing payment, while the other parent does not pay anything.[26] The CMS may use the term 'split care' when referring to this situation.

2. The non-resident parent's income

The amount of child support payable is based on the non-resident parent (NRP)'s gross weekly income.

'Gross weekly income' is calculated by using either the NRP's 'historic income' (see p66) or 'current income' (see p69) at the 'effective date' of the application (see p129) and converting this into a weekly amount.[27] The rules on the type of income taken into account are complex and are based on how income is treated for income tax purposes. It is not the total income on which tax is due which counts, but the total income on which the parent is 'charged to tax'.[28]

Both historic income and current income are composite figures of all income from relevant sources. The NRP's income is assessed on either one or the other. There is no scope for income from employment to be based on current income and income from self-employment to be based on historic income or vice versa.[29]

Income from sources other than those described in this section is not counted. Taxable social security benefits are not included, except that incapacity benefit (IB), contributory employment and support allowance (ESA), jobseeker's allowance (JSA) and income support (IS) are included in the historic income figure provided by HM Revenue and Customs (HMRC). Working tax credit is *not* counted as part of the NRP's income.

In some cases, income that is not counted in gross income for the calculation can be taken into account by a variation (see Chapter 5). For example, if the NRP has unearned income from property or investments, or has valuable assets that do not generate a declared income, the person with care (PWC) could ask for a variation on the grounds that the NRP has additional income. However, in many cases, an application for a variation is only likely to be made if the PWC is aware that the NRP has other sources of income or assets. A decision to refuse a variation can be disputed further (see Chapter 10)

Note: the government has announced plans to allow unearned income to be included in the initial calculation, without an application for a variation being necessary (see p98).[30] No date has yet been set for these changes to take effect.

Pension contributions are deducted when calculating gross weekly income. No other deductions are taken into account. See p69 for further details.

All the parties (ie, the PWC, the NRP and, in Scotland, any child applicant) are notified of the income figure used in the child support calculation. This applies whether the calculation is based on historic income or current income (including if current income is estimated). This does not include a breakdown of the types of income included.[31] See p128 for further details on the notification of decisions.

Note: if the Child Maintenance Service (CMS) does not have sufficient information to make a calculation, it may make a default maintenance decision (see p127).

There are special rules for annual reviews of income (see p73), periodic checks if current income is being used (see p75) and for reporting changes to current income (see p76).

Historic income

In most cases, the child support calculation uses a NRP's 'historic' income. The CMS obtains income information directly from HMRC using an automated system. This approach aims to reduce delays, avoid the supply of inaccurate information and limit demands on employers.

The historic income figure takes into account the NRP's taxable income from:[32]

- employment – ie, their income from earnings (see p68); *and*
- pensions (see p68); *and*
- the taxable amount of the following social security benefits: IB, contributory ESA, JSA and IS (**note:** a parent currently receiving one of these benefits usually pays the flat rate – see p58); *and*
- any profits from self-employment (see p68).

The CMS requests a historic income figure for the latest available tax year from HMRC no more than 30 days before the initial 'effective date' (see p129). The 'latest available tax year' is the most recent tax year for which HMRC has received information about the NRP under either:[33]

- the pay as you earn (PAYE) scheme, for which employers complete end-of-year returns on the taxable earnings of their employees; *or*
- the annual self-assessment returns completed by individual taxpayers on various sources of income.

The latest available tax year must be one of the six tax years before the date the information is sought.[34]

The CMS does not have any discretion to use different income figures[35] – eg, if there is evidence that the NRP has under-reported their income in the self-assessment (but see p69 for when 'current' income is used for the calculation instead of 'historic' income).

The CMS does not automatically receive a breakdown of the historic income figure, but may request a breakdown from HMRC if one party queries the figure. The CMS does not normally provide the breakdown to the parties, but may give the breakdown to the NRP. The CMS will not provide the breakdown to the PWC.

If HMRC supplies a figure that is not from the most recent tax year for which it has received information, this is not a valid historic income figure. The CMS can make a further request to HMRC for an up-to-date historic income figure. It should consider doing so particularly where it is not suitable to use current income, as the automated system can normally only request a historic income figure once each year. However, if there is good reason to doubt the validity of the figure provided by HMRC (including reason to doubt whether it is, in fact, for the latest available tax year), the CMS should make a further request.[36] The First-tier Tribunal considering an appeal may direct the CMS to do so.[37]

Self-assessment information is usually available to the CMS by February or March in the year following the end of the tax year on 5 April. Information from PAYE returns is available earlier. If HMRC has information from both the PAYE scheme and a self-assessment for the latest available tax year, information from the self-assessment is used, as it is expected to be more comprehensive.[38]

Information about all forms of a person's taxable income must relate to the same tax year. If an application is made in June 2022, PAYE information may be available for 2021/22 , but the most recent self-assessment information is likely to be for 2020/21. What matters is not the availability of one form of information for a tax year, but HMRC's identification of the total amount that was charged to tax for the year. For a person who has to complete a self-assessment, HMRC cannot determine total income until the self-assessment is received, even if it appears that the PAYE information is complete. So, in this example, the latest available tax year for which HMRC can supply information in June 2022 is 2020/21.[39]

For pension contributions in the relevant year, see p69.

The rules on the type of income included are intended to ensure that parents are treated consistently, whether the information held on them by HMRC comes from the PAYE scheme or from self-assessment.

The use of historic income information from HMRC means that taxable payments to those in the following occupations or offices are *not* disregarded:
- auxiliary coastguards;
- part-time firefighters and lifeboat crew members;
- reserve or territorial force members;
- local authority councillors.

Maintaining consistency, however, means that some types of income captured by self-assessment are not counted as gross weekly income for the calculation, even though HMRC may hold reliable information about them. This includes some taxable social security benefits and some allowances claimed by employees against taxable earnings.[40]

If a parent is both employed and self-employed, it is possible that at the time the calculation is made PAYE details are available for the most recently completed tax year, but self-assessment only for the year before this. Information on employment income is therefore likely to reflect the parent's current circumstances more accurately.

Income from employment

When HMRC provides information on historic income from employment, gross pay is used. **'Gross pay'** is all payments, such as salary, wages, fees, bonuses, commission, tips and overtime, before any income tax or national insurance contributions are deducted. HMRC deducts contributions to an approved personal or occupational pension scheme. Deductions should also be made for any other allowable deductions (eg, expenses) that will not be taxed.[41] Payments from an employer to reimburse an employee for legitimate work-related expenses should not be counted in gross pay.[42]

Statutory sick pay, statutory maternity pay, statutory adoption pay, statutory parental bereavement pay, statutory paternity pay and statutory shared parental pay are treated as employment income.

Anything of direct monetary value to the employee that derives from the employment or office is also treated as earnings.[43] There are certain exemptions.[44]

A lump-sum redundancy payment is not earnings but a compensation for lost employment. It is not taxed as earnings. To the extent that it exceeds the £30,000 tax-free threshold, it is taxed as other employment income and so may be included in the historic income figure.[45]

Income from self-employment

Historic income from self-employment is based on the taxable profits from any 'trade, profession or vocation' in the latest available tax year for which a self-assessment has been completed – ie, the profits in the accounting period that ended in the tax year.[46] For example, if a self-employed parent's accounting year ends in June 2021, which is in tax year 2021/22, the self-assessment for that period is not due until 19 months later in January 2023.[47]

If a business is run on a commercial basis and has made a loss, gross income is nil for that tax year. In certain circumstances, a loss in a previous year can be carried forward and deducted from profits in the next and later tax years. HMRC deducts such losses when determining the historic income figure for self-employment.[48]

Pension income

Income (before tax) from a personal or occupational pension, or an annuity or other kind of taxable pension income, counts towards gross weekly income.[49]

The full details of pension income that is taxable are complex.[50] Tax-free lump sums paid under an approved personal pension scheme, retirement annuity contract or tax-exempt pension scheme are ignored completely. A lump sum counts if it is for cashing in a small pension, if the fund is too small to pay a pension (within the 'trivial commutation' limit) or if an occupational pension scheme winds up.[51] If a pension is paid because of a work-related illness or disability caused by an injury on duty, only the amount that would have been paid had the parent retired on non-work-related ill-health grounds counts. Any extra amount paid is ignored.[52] Various war disablement pensions are also not counted.[53]

Pension income for these purposes does not include UK social security pensions, even though they are taxable and appear on a self-assessment return.[54] This means that the following are not counted:[55]

- retirement pension;
- graduated retirement benefit;
- industrial death benefit;
- widowed mother's allowance;
- widowed parent's allowance;
- widow's pension.

Pension contributions

Contributions to an approved personal or occupational pension scheme (ie, a scheme registered with HMRC) by the NRP in the relevant tax year are deducted from the gross income figure. In many cases, these will already have been deducted by the employer when any payment was made. In this case, the deductions are not included in gross income.[56]

If the NRP has income from employment or self-employment and has made pension contributions during the relevant tax year that have not been deducted by the employer (eg, they were made directly to a personal pension scheme), the weekly average amount of these can be deducted from the gross income figure.[57] There is no limit on the amount of pension contributions that can be deducted. However, if a PWC is aware of the amount of contributions and considers them to be excessive, or considers that arrangements have been set up deliberately to reduce liability for child support (eg, if the NRP has made a salary sacrifice arrangement in return for increased employer contributions), then an application may be made for a variation on the grounds of diversion of income (see p102).

Note that, because tax relief is given on personal pension contributions, actual contributions are less than the gross amount included in the pension plan. It is the higher gross amount that should be deducted from current income. The CMS does not deduct a higher gross amount to reflect higher rate tax relief, as granting this relief requires a decision by HMRC that it will not yet have been able to make at the time that current income is being assessed. If a gross amount including higher rate tax relief is being claimed, the CMS is likely to require evidence in the form of an HMRC calculation notice.

Current income

In certain cases, historic income information may not be available or may differ significantly from the NRP's current circumstances. In this case, the calculation can be based on the NRP's current income. In contrast to the situation with historic income, the source of the current income figure is not limited to HMRC.[58]

The CMS approaches the parent to verify their employment or self-employment details and, in some cases, may contact their employer or accountant for information. The CMS also has access to the 'real-time information' records held by HMRC.

The CMS may seek information on current income if:[59]

- no historic income figure is available – ie, HMRC does not have information for any one of the six tax years before the date of the CMS's request;[60] *or*
- the CMS is unable, for whatever reason, to request or to obtain the required information from HMRC – eg, because of problems with the automatic data-sharing system; *or*
- there is at least a 25 per cent difference between the amount of current income and historic income.

If HMRC supplies a historic income figure of 'nil', the CMS accepts this and does not use current income in this case. If the CMS then becomes aware that the NRP has *any* current income, it is automatically treated as at least 25 per cent different from the nil historic income figure and a new calculation decision can be made.[61]

The 25 per cent threshold for change applies to the total income figures. Both historic income and current income are composite figures of all income from relevant sources. The 25 per cent threshold cannot be applied to income from employment and income from self-employment separately, but to the total. Once the threshold is reached, the parent's gross weekly income is calculated on current income as a whole.[62] Current income must only take into account the income from any employment held as at the effective date.[63]

If a PWC believes a NRP with nil historic income has current earnings, a revision or supersession (see Chapter 9) may be requested. If you are a PWC, you are most likely to want to dispute the accuracy of a nil historic income figure used and may ask for current income to be considered once you have applied for child support and the CMS has started to gather information. The CMS is only likely to investigate further if the PWC provides information that gives the CMS reasonable grounds to suspect that the NRP has current earnings.

'Current income' is the total (calculated or estimated) income from:[64]

- employment; *and*
- self-employment; *and*
- pensions.

Income from the taxable benefits included in historic income (see p66) is not counted in current income. **Note:** a parent currently receiving one of those benefits usually pays the flat rate (see p58).

The appropriate method for the treatment for pension contributions is discussed on p69.

If any payment is made in a currency other than sterling, charges for converting it to sterling are deducted from the current income figure.[65]

Estimating current income

The CMS can estimate a parent's current income if the information about it is insufficient or unreliable and:[66]

- the historic income is nil and there is any amount of current income – ie, current income is automatically treated as being 25 per cent different from historic income; *or*
- no historic income information is available, or the CMS is unable, for whatever reason, to request or obtain the required information from HMRC.

The CMS is likely to use this power to encourage NRPs to co-operate with providing details of their current income. It can base an estimate on any assumptions about any facts. Assumptions may be based on any information already held about the NRP's circumstances. If the CMS is satisfied that the NRP works in a particular occupation, it can assume that they have the average weekly income of a person engaged in that occupation in a particular area of the UK.[67] It may use information such as the Office for National Statistics' *Annual Survey of Hours and Earnings*, which gives average earnings for occupations and regions. This can apply to income from employment or from self-employment. A parent who works part- time or has lower than average wages for any reason should make sure the CMS is aware of this.

If there is no historic income information available, the CMS has not been able to gather information about current income and it does not have enough information to estimate current income, it may make a 'default maintenance decision' (see p127).

Income from employment

Income from employment is defined for current income purposes in broadly the same way as for historic income (see p68). Gross earnings are taken into account, not including approved pension contributions.

Current income is intended to be assessed in a way that, wherever possible, results in a stable amount of child support liability being set. If the NRP receives any income from a salary, wages or other periodic payments and the CMS considers that this is a settled regular amount likely to continue for the foreseeable future, it converts this into a weekly amount.[68]

If earnings are less frequent or are not a regular settled amount for some other reason, the CMS averages the amounts over an appropriate period before the effective date of the decision and converts this to a weekly amount. Averaging is likely to be used if, for example, the parent is a seasonal worker or has an irregular pattern of hours, shifts or overtime.[69]

Some taxable amounts may be paid at different intervals from regular pay. The total of any bonus or commission payments in the last 12 months that have been made separately, or for a different period than other income, is also converted to a weekly amount.[70]

The detailed rules on what income from employment is taxable are complex. Anything of direct monetary value to an employee that derives from the employment or office is also treated as earnings, and the amount received in the past 12 months converted into a weekly amount.[71] There are certain exemptions that are not treated as earnings.[72]

A lump-sum redundancy payment is not 'earnings' but compensation for lost employment. It is not taxed as earnings and so it is not included in current income.[73] However, to the extent that it exceeds the £30,000 tax-free threshold, it is taxed as other employment income and so should be included.

Income from self-employment

Income from self-employment is defined for current income purposes in the same way as for historic income – ie, as the taxable profits from any 'trade, profession or vocation' (see p68).

Profits are determined for the most recently completed tax year or accounting period that a parent would normally report in a self-assessment. The CMS may ask for a self-assessment summary for the most recently completed relevant period, even if the self-assessment has not yet been submitted to HMRC.[74] If no full tax year or accounting period has been completed (eg, if the NRP is newly self-employed), the profits are estimated for the current period. The total profit for the period is converted into a weekly amount.[75] The current income of an established business is normally expected to relate to an annual period equal to that covered by most self-assessments. A shorter period is only expected to be used for a new business. In this case, the CMS tries to identify estimated or projected annual profits – eg, using any completed profit and loss accounts to date and also business plans.

It is the profits from the self-employment in which the NRP is engaged on the effective date that are determined. If the CMS accepts that the parent had ceased trading on the effective date, then the assessment will be that there are no profits, that current income is nil and that the parent no other source of income. The CMS will then consider whether the parent receives a benefit that would lead to liability to pay the flat rate.

If the parent is a partner in a business, the profits are apportioned according to their share.[76]

Note: where there is evidence that a self-employed NRP received a payment from the Self-Employment Income Support Scheme established by HMRC to support businesses during the coronavirus pandemic, this information alone is not be used to make a calculation, or to revise or supercede an existing calculation.[77] It may, however, be used as evidence of a parent's ability to pay child support when considering enforcement action (see Chapter 8).[78]

Pension income

Pension income is defined for current income purposes in the same way as for historic income (see p68). If current income is being used, the CMS averages pension income over an appropriate period to give a weekly amount.[79]

Income from outside the UK

Income from outside the UK is included in gross income if it falls into one of the categories of taxable income from employment, self-employment or pensions. The detailed rules on what income is taxable are complex. Overseas income is also included even if no UK tax is paid but tax has been paid in a country with which the UK has a 'double taxation' treaty.[80] The CMS seeks information about the tax status of parents who are abroad but cannot compel them to provide information. It cannot ask its Financial Investigations Unit to investigate foreign tax returns.[81]

The following are some types of income that are disregarded:

- social security payments from outside the UK, equivalent to non-taxable UK benefits;[82]
- one-tenth of the amount of any overseas pension or of a pension payable in the UK by the governments of certain other countries;[83]
- tax-free lump-sum payments under an overseas pension scheme;[84]
- income the parent is prevented from transferring to the UK by law or by the government of the country where the income arises or because foreign currency cannot be obtained in that country.[85]

Annual reviews

The CMS must conduct an annual review of gross weekly income. This is done whether gross income is based on historic income or on current income.[86]

The review date is normally on the anniversary of the initial effective date (see p129), but the CMS can use a different date for a particular case or type of case.[87]

If a child support calculation is already in force and a new application is made in relation to the same NRP for a different qualifying child, the review dates for the two cases are aligned. This allows the NRP's income to be assessed at the same time for all cases in which they are involved. The first review date for the new case is on the next review date for the calculation already in force.[88] If both parents are non-resident and applications for child support from both have been treated as one application (see p26), the CMS can use different review dates for each NRP.[89]

In order to conduct the review, the CMS requests an updated historic income figure for the latest available tax year from HMRC.[90] It can request this no earlier than 30 days before the review date.[91] If no new income information is available from HMRC and the current calculation is based on estimated income or is a default maintenance decision, the CMS will request the NRP to provide information. If insufficient reliable information is available, the CMS estimates current income (see p71) or make a default maintenance decision (see p127).

If the gross weekly income shown by the updated figure is different from the historic income figure previously used, the CMS supersedes the calculation decision. The supersession decision takes effect from the review date.[92]

If gross weekly income is based on current income, the current income is compared with the updated historic income figure. If current income is still at least 25 per cent different from the updated historic income, the current income figure is still used. If it is within 25 per cent, the updated historic income figure is used and the calculation is superseded, with effect from the review date.

If a variation to the calculation on the grounds of additional income (see p97) is in force, the CMS may also request updated information on unearned income in the latest available tax year when it asks HMRC for the updated historic income figure. If unearned income has changed, a supersession decision can be made. This takes effect from the review date.[93] Variations on other grounds are not affected by the review process.

When the CMS gets the updated historic income figure, it writes to the PWC and NRP (and child applicant in Scotland) giving details of the income figure to be used for the coming year. This includes a breakdown of the calculation, including details such as qualifying children, relevant other children, other maintenance arrangements taken into account and shared care. This notification is not a formal decision that can be challenged, but a notification that the calculation is expected to be based on this information. The parties have 30 days to notify the CMS of any changes and provide any additional information or evidence.[94]

The formal decision on the child support calculation for the coming year is then issued to the parties on the effective date of the annual review. This formal decision can be challenged by the parties.

Any changes reported by any of the parties during this 30-day period may also result in a supersession of the current child support calculation from the date the change is reported.

Example

Alfie is paying £76.10 a week child support to Sasha for their three children. This is based on historic income information, showing his gross weekly income to be £450. The annual review date is 8 March.

On 6 February (30 days before the annual review), the CMS receives updated historic income information, showing a gross weekly income of £500, and notifies Alfie and Sasha. The CMS receives evidence from Alfie on 12 February, showing that he has changed his working pattern and that his current gross weekly income is now £320.

This current income figure varies by more than 25 per cent from the updated historic income figure of £500, so Alfie's new child support liability from 8 March is based on the current income figure of £320 gross weekly income.

Step one: Alfie's gross weekly income is £320. There is one relevant other child, which means this is reduced by 11 per cent.
11% x £320 = £35.20
£320 – £35.20 = £284.80

Step two: There are three qualifying children, so child support is 19 per cent of the remaining gross income.
19% x £284.80 = £54.11

Alfie will therefore pay £54.11 a week in child support to Sasha from the review date.

The CMS also compares the new current income figure of £320 with the historic income figure used in Alfie's existing child support liability (£450). This is also more than 25 per cent different, so there are grounds for a supersession of the existing liability (see p206). Alfie's liability from the date he reported the change (12 February) until the review date (8 March) is also changed to £54.11 a week.

Periodic checks of current income

The CMS can undertake a 'periodic check' of a parent's current income if:[95]

- gross weekly income has been based on current income; *and*
- no supersession decision changing the amount has been made for at least 11 months.

A periodic check is likely to happen if the current income figure has not been updated at the annual review and is still at least 25 per cent different from the updated historic income figure obtained at the review.

This periodic check is separate from the annual review process and is not normally done at the same time. If current income is used to determine gross weekly income, in some cases this may only have been in place for a short time at the annual review date. Once it has been in place for 11 months, a periodic current income check takes place.

If current income has previously been used, but the annual review results in historic income now being used, a periodic check of current income is not undertaken. Therefore, if a periodic check is due to take place around the same time as the annual review, the annual review is done first.

The NRP must provide updated evidence of current income for the periodic check.[96] Any updated evidence on current income is compared against the updated historic income figure for the latest available tax year that was provided at the most recent annual review. Any information provided by a PWC can also be considered.

If the PWC requests a supersession while the periodic check is being conducted and provides any relevant information, this is considered as part of the periodic check.[97]

If the evidence provided by the NRP is sufficient to make a new decision on current income, a supersession of the calculation decision is made.[98] If the evidence shows that the up-to-date current income figure varies by at least 25 per cent from the most recently updated historic income figure, the calculation continues to be based on the current income. If the current income is no longer at least 25 per cent different, a supersession decision is made with gross weekly income based on the updated historic income figure. If the NRP fails to provide evidence for the periodic check, the CMS may decide to supersede the calculation decision and use the updated historic income figure for gross weekly income.[99]

The effective date of a supersession decision arising from a periodic check of current income is the day the decision is made.[100] This is usually expected to be 30 days after the CMS writes to the NRP to request the updated income details.[101]

If there has been a change in current income that should have been reported by the NRP (ie, a change of 25 per cent or more that the NRP should reasonably have expected to have led to an increased liability for child support – see below), a supersession will be conducted before the periodic check of current income. The effective date for the supersession decision is the date the income changed.[102]

Example

Dami's child support for his two children was calculated based on his current income of £400 a week because there was no historic income information available from HMRC. The effective date of the calculation is 12 March 2021.

Dami does not report any changes in his current income. No updated historic income information is available from HMRC when the annual review is conducted on 12 March 2022. Since the current income has been used for more than 11 months, the CMS decides to carry out a periodic check. When gathering evidence for the periodic check of current income, the CMS discovers that Dami's gross income increased to £550 a week on 1 April 2021. A supersession decision based on this new income is made with the effective date of 1 April 2021.

If Dami had reported the change of income at the time and a supersession decision was made, his gross weekly income of £550 would still have been in place at the annual review date of 12 March 2022. By then, that current income figure would have been in place for more than 11 months, so a periodic check of current income is still made. During the periodic check, the CMS receives information that Dami's gross weekly income will increase to £700 on 1 April 2022. A supersession decision is made with an effective date of 1 April 2022, with the calculation being based on this new current income figure.

Change of circumstances

The CMS intends calculations to remain in place for a reasonable period. In many cases, a calculation based on historic income is likely to remain in force for the year ahead.

If gross weekly income is based on current income, a supersession for any income based change of circumstances will proceed only if the current income has changed by at least 25 per cent.[103] Calculations are not adjusted for smaller or short-term changes in income – eg, due to temporary sickness, temporary promotion and seasonal work.

If current income has changed by at least 25 per cent, a supersession decision is made, even if the change means that current income is now less than 25 per cent different from the historic income figure for the latest available tax year.[104]

Example

Alfie is paying £76.10 a week child support to Sasha for their three children. This is based on current income information, showing his gross weekly income to be £450. Alfie's current income was used at the time the calculation was made as it was more than 25 per cent different from the historic income data provided by HMRC, which showed his gross weekly income to be £300.

After the calculation has been in force for a few months, Alfie provides the CMS with new evidence, showing that he has changed his working pattern and his current gross weekly income is now £320.

This new current income figure is more than 25 per cent different from the current income figure used to make the calculation decision. The CMS makes a supersession decision and calculates his child support liability based on a gross weekly income of £320. This takes effect from the date it received the new evidence. This can be done even though £320 is less than 25 per cent different from the most recent historic income figure.

Even if current income has not changed by 25 per cent, a supersession decision can still be made if:[105]

- the supersession results from changes that are considered by the CMS at an annual review or periodic check; *or*
- the supersession is made on the grounds that the original decision was based on an error of law (see p205); *or*
- the CMS supersedes a calculation that was based on an estimate of current income.

Certain changes to historic income (eg, if the historic income information is changed by HMRC, or if the NRP amends a self-assessment) are grounds for the calculation to be revised.[106] However, HMRC does not routinely inform the CMS of minor changes, and so a revision is only likely to be done if the NRP or PWC queries the accuracy of the historic income figure.

For full details of revisions and supersessions of decisions, see Chapter 9.

Reporting changes in income

With a few exceptions, parents are not required to report changes in their circumstances on a routine basis. However, there are specific duties on NRPs to report certain changes in their income. See p76 for details of other changes that must be reported.

If a parent's gross weekly income is based on their current income, they may be informed by the CMS that they must report relevant changes of circumstances. They are informed of this in the written notification of the child support calculation decision. Any such change must be reported in writing, or by using the options available online, within 14 days of its occurring. The CMS may specify a longer period.[107] Failure to provide the required information may be an offence (see p37).[108]

If the NRP is paying child support at the basic rate (including 'basic rate plus'), reduced rate or flat rate and gross weekly income is based on their current income from employment, they must tell the CMS if they:[109]

- start a new job; *or*
- receive a new rate of pay for their existing job; *or*
- change their working pattern in their existing job.

These changes must be reported if the parent could reasonably be expected to know that they may lead to an increased amount of child support being due. This duty does not apply to those who are self-employed.

Fluctuations in wages from week to week or month to month may not necessarily need to be reported. However, the parent must tell the CMS if their wages increase so that over a longer period (ie, five payments if paid weekly, three if paid fortnightly, and two if paid four-weekly or monthly) the average weekly amount is at least 25 per cent more than the gross weekly income that was taken into account in the calculation.[110]

If the NRP is liable for the nil rate and gross weekly income is based on current income, they must tell the CMS if their gross weekly income increases to £7 or more. This duty applies to income from employment, self-employment and pensions (including income from any of the benefits that qualify for the flat rate).[111]

If gross weekly income is based on historic income, there is no duty on the NRP to notify the CMS if current income becomes (at some point during the year after the calculation decision is made) more than 25 per cent different from the most recent historic income figure. However, if this does happen, the PWC or the NRP could apply for the calculation to be superseded. If the PWC alleges that the current income is at least 25 per cent more than the historic income figure used in the calculation, the CMS is only likely to investigate this if provided with information that shows reasonable grounds.

Note: temporary measures were introduced to consider any significant changes to a NRP's income due to the coronavirus pandemic. Those measures are no longer in place, but if NRPs are still affected by the pandemic, they should report this to the CMS.

3. **Shared care**

A number of people may be involved in caring for a qualifying child. The term **'shared care'** is used in this *Handbook* to describe a situation where there is more than one person looking after a particular child and those people live in different households. If the people providing care live in the same household (see p11), this is not shared care.[112]

If parents share the care of a qualifying child equally, there is no liability for child support (see p13). However, if one parent provides day-to-day care for a child *to a lesser extent* than the other parent (or person with care (PWC)), they may be treated as a non-resident parent (NRP) and be liable to pay child support (see p13).[113]

If a parent who is (or who is treated as) non-resident provides sufficient care (see below) for a qualifying child, then the liability for child support may be reduced to reflect the care provided.

If a qualifying child is looked after by a local authority for part of the time, see p86.[114]

Note: 'shared care' is different from the situation where different children of the same family have different homes. If the children of a family are divided between two households (eg, if one child lives with one parent and another child with the other parent), two separate child support calculations are carried out. In one, the first parent is the PWC and the second parent is the NRP. In the second, the roles are reversed. This situation is referred to as 'divided families' in this *Handbook*. The Child Maintenance Service (CMS) may refer to this as **'split care'** (see p64).

If a non-resident parent shares care

In order for the shared care to affect the child support calculation, a NRP must look after, or be expected to look after, a qualifying child for at least 52 nights a year (ie, one night a week) on average. The care must be provided overnight, and the NRP and the child must stay at the same address.[115] The care could be provided away from the NRP's normal home – eg, while on holiday or at a relative's home. The NRP could also look after the child overnight in the PWC's home while the PWC is away from home during the relevant nights.[116]

The CMS determines the number of nights that count for shared care, based on the number of nights the NRP is expected to provide overnight care for the qualifying child(ren) during the 12 months starting with the effective date of the calculation.[117]

The CMS can use a shorter period than this if it considers it is appropriate to do so – eg, if both parents have agreed a pattern of shared care for a shorter period.[118] If a shorter period is used, the number of nights of care in that period must be in the same ratio as 52 nights is to 12 months in order to amount to shared care.

In determining the number of nights of shared care, the CMS looks at all the evidence. Usually, this information is obtained at the time of the child support application – ie, from telephone contact with the PWC and NRP or from written material provided by them. The CMS must consider:[119]

- the terms of any agreement between the PWC and the NRP, or the terms of any court order providing for child arrangements concerning the NRP and the qualifying child; *or*

- if there is no such agreement or order, any pattern of care that has been established over the previous 12 months (or such shorter period as the CMS deems appropriate).

Child arrangements ordered by a court or agreed in writing, or a past pattern of care, are only evidence that must be considered, and are not decisive proof of the care situation. The CMS can decide the weight to be given to the child arrangements in a court order. It is required to consider such arrangements, not to give effect to them, and so it will consider the reality of what is happening. If the CMS has good reason (eg, evidence that the arrangements had not been followed in practice), the CMS may decide that the arrangements or pattern should not be the basis for determining the nights of care.[120]

If the evidence of the PWC and of the NRP conflicts, further evidence may be required to resolve the issue. Parents should keep a note of the nights the child spends with them and, in case of a dispute, be willing to supply further evidence – eg, a diary. The CMS (and, in any subsequent appeal, the First-tier Tribunal) must then determine the number of nights spent in each person's care over the period.[121]

The CMS does not routinely review whether agreed shared care arrangements are being kept to. If it is reported that an agreement about shared care is not being complied with, the CMS may seek further evidence from the parties to allow the calculation to be revised or superseded.

If the CMS accepts that the PWC and NRP have agreed to share care, but there is not enough evidence to determine the number of nights of shared care, it can assume that the NRP provides care for one night a week. This assumption can be made if the parties provide conflicting evidence and the number of nights of shared care cannot be determined, even if both parties agree that shared care is provided on more than one night a week. The assumption is applied until a supersession is requested and there is sufficient evidence to determine the actual number of nights of shared care.[122]

If the qualifying child is a boarder at a boarding school or a hospital patient, any night spent there counts as a night with the person who would normally have been looking after the child on that night (see p85).[123]

Note: if a NRP is providing some care, but not as much as 52 nights a year on average, the child support calculation is not adjusted to take account of the level of care provided, and they are expected to pay the same amount of child support as if they were not looking after the child at all. This means, for example, that a parent who provides *some* regular care for their children may pay the same amount of child support as one who does not. However, a NRP in this situation can apply for the calculation to be varied on the grounds that the contact costs are 'special expenses'. A variation for contact costs may also be considered, even if the contact *is* enough to count as shared care and so affect the calculation. See Chapter 5 for details on variations.

The effect of shared care on the flat rate

If a NRP has been assessed as liable for the flat rate of child support because their gross weekly income is less than £100, this is not adjusted to take into account any care they provide. However, the amount of child support due is reduced to nil if they:[124]

- are liable to pay the flat rate because they are in receipt of a relevant benefit or they or their partner receives one of the relevant means-tested benefits (see p58), including if a reduced flat rate of £3.50 applies; *and*
- care for the qualifying child for at least 52 nights a year.

The flat rate of £7 is apportioned in relation to the number of qualifying children before any adjustment for shared care is made (see p56). This may mean that a NRP's liability reduces to nil for one PWC because of shared care. However, the NRP is still liable for the remaining amounts to the other PWC(s), in which case they pay an amount which is less than £7.

Example

Alistair is the NRP of Oliver, who lives with his older brother Neil, and Katie, who lives with her mother, Rachel. Alistair looks after Katie one or two nights a week. Both Neil and Rachel apply for child support. Alistair receives income-related employment and support allowance (ESA).

Step one: Alistair is due to pay child support at the flat rate of £7, as he gets income related ESA.

Step two: Apportion the flat rate of £7 between the PWCs in relation to the qualifying children each cares for – ie, the amount is halved.
To Neil for Oliver = £3.50
To Rachel for Katie = £3.50

Step three: Alistair cares for Katie over 52 nights a year, so the amount due to Rachel reduces to nil.
Alistair remains liable to pay £3.50 in child support to Neil for Oliver.

The effect of shared care on the basic and reduced rate

If a NRP shares the care of a qualifying child for 52 or more nights a year, the liability for child support at the basic rate (including 'basic rate plus') or reduced rate is reduced by an appropriate fraction, depending on the number of nights of shared care.[125] If there is more than one qualifying child, see p83.

Number of nights	*Fraction to subtract*
52 to 103	One-seventh
104 to 155	Two-sevenths
156 to 174	Three-sevenths
175 or more	One-half

If a NRP shares the care of a qualifying child for a sufficient number of nights for the one-half fraction to apply, an additional £7 decrease in the child support liability is applied in respect of that child.[126] This is known as **'abatement'** and is applied for each child for whom at least 175 nights of shared care applies.

If the decrease results in a NRR being liable to pay a PWC less than £7, the flat rate of £7 is paid instead.[127] This includes the situation where the total amount of child support due to all the people with care is decreased to less than £7. In this case, the £7 is apportioned between them in relation to the number of qualifying children.

Example

Remi shares the care of Theo with Libby, the PWC. He looks after Theo on average two nights at the weekend and for a couple of weeks in the school holidays. Although Remi provides day-to-day care of Theo, he is treated as a NRP as he does so to a lesser extent than Libby. Remi's gross weekly income is £480.

Step one: Basic rate of child support = 12% x £480 = £57.60

Step two: **Apply decrease for shared care**
Remi shares care in the 104–155 band (two-sevenths).
£57.60 child support must be decreased by two-sevenths – ie,
£57.60 – £16.46 = £41.14

Remi pays Libby £41.14 a week.

Note: if Remi has costs for keeping in contact with Theo, he may also be able to apply for a variation (see p92).

Remi increases the amount of time he cares for Theo to three nights one week and four nights the next. In this case, Remi shares care for over 175 nights and the one-half fraction is applied. Remi's child support calculated under the basic rate remains at £57.60.

Step two: £57.60 decreased by one-half and a further £7 subtracted – ie,
£28.80 – £7 = £21.80

Because of the increase in shared care, Remi pays £21.80 to Libby.

Remi's circumstances change again and his gross weekly income is now £160.

Step one: Reduced rate of child support = £7 + (17% x £60) = £7 + £10.20 = £17.20

Step two: **Apply decrease for shared care**
The fraction to apply remains at one-half, with a further £7 subtracted.
(50% x £17.20) – £7 = £8.60 – £7 = £1.60

Step three: Child support due is below £7, so Remi pays £7 a week to Libby.

Note: if the increased amount of time Remi spends caring for Theo is accepted as meaning that care is shared equally with Libby, the child support calculation may be cancelled (see p13).

If there is more than one qualifying child

If a PWC and NRP have more than one qualifying child, the fractions that apply for shared care for each qualifying child are added together, then divided by the number of qualifying children.[128] This applies where care is shared for some, but not all, of the qualifying children or if there are shared care arrangements for each qualifying child.

Example

Luke is the NRP of Lea and Dylan. Both are cared for by their grandmother, Jean. Lea does not like staying with Luke and only does so occasionally. However, Dylan stays with him on Friday and Saturday nights. Both children stay with him for a few days at Christmas and during the school holidays. Luke's gross weekly income is £420.

Step one: Basic rate of child support for two children = 16% x £420 = £67.20

Step two: **Apply decrease for shared care**
Lea does not stay with Luke for sufficient days for it to count as shared care.
Dylan is in the 104–155 band (two-sevenths).
The fractions which apply are added together and divided by two, as there are two qualifying children cared for by Jean.
(0 + 2/7) ÷ 2 = 2/14
Luke's child support is decreased by 2/14 of £67.20 = £9.60

Because of the shared care, Luke must pay £57.60 (£67.20 – £9.60) to Jean.

Note: if Luke has expenses for keeping in contact with Lea and Dylan, he may also be able to apply for a variation (see p92).

Lea increases the amount of time she spends with her father and now this counts as shared care.

Step two: Lea is in the 52–103 band (one-seventh).
Dylan is in the 104–155 band (two-sevenths).
The fractions are added together and divided by two – ie, 3/7 ÷ 2 = 3/14
The child support due is therefore decreased by 3/14 because of shared care.
Luke's child support is decreased by 3/14 of £67.20 = £14.40

Because of shared care, Luke must now pay £52.80 (£67.20 – £14.40) to Jean.

Dylan stays in the care of his father more often and so:

Step two: Lea is in the 52–103 band (one-seventh).
Dylan is in the 175 or more band (one-half).
The decrease is (1/7 + 1/2) ÷ 2 = 9/28
9/28 x £67.20 = £21.60
£67.20 – £21.60 = £45.60. However, because care for Dylan is in the one-half band, the further £7 reduction applies and the amount of child support due is decreased by a further £7.

Luke now pays Jean £38.60 (£45.60 – £7).

Note: if the increased amount of time Luke spends caring for Dylan is accepted as meaning that care is shared equally with Jean, then no child support may be payable for Dylan (see p13).

If care is shared for more than one child with different persons with care

A NRP may be liable to pay child support to more than one PWC (eg, if a father has two children who live with two different mothers) and may share the care of the children with them.

Child support liability is calculated for only one PWC in respect of each qualifying child. The child support due is first apportioned between the PWCs in proportion to the number of qualifying children each cares for. The amount payable to each is then adjusted to take account of any shared care the NRP provides for the child(ren).

If a second person who is not the NRP provides care for a qualifying child, the CMS does not apportion the child support liability between them. The PWC could agree to pass on some of the child support – eg, an amount reflecting the number of days a week the other person has care of the child. However, this would be an informal arrangement and is not monitored or enforced by the CMS.

Example

Ewan is the NRP of two children – Holly, whose PWC is Ellen, and Jamie, whose PWC is Laura. Ewan looks after Holly when Ellen is on night shifts, which is every other week apart from holidays, and takes her camping with him on the odd weekend. Jamie and Laura live further away, so Ewan only sees Jamie for a long weekend once a month and two weeks in the summer holidays. Ewan's gross weekly income is £387.50.

Step one:	The basic rate of child support applies for two qualifying children. 16% x £387.50 = £62 The child support due is apportioned between each PWC. Ellen and Laura each care for one qualifying child, so the child support is halved between them. To Ellen for Holly = £31 To Laura for Jamie = £31
Step two:	**Apply decrease for shared care** *Child support paid to Ellen for Holly* Holly is in the 156–174 band (three-sevenths). 3/7 x £31 = £13.29 £31 – £13.29 = £17.71 *Child support paid to Laura for Jamie* Jamie is in the 52–103 band (one-seventh). 1/7 x £31 = £4.43 £31 – £4.43 = £26.57
Step three:	The total child support due is £17.71 (to Ellen) + £26.57 (to Laura) = £44.28

A qualifying child is in hospital or at boarding school

If a qualifying child is in hospital or at boarding school, any night spent there counts as a night with the person who would normally provide care at that time.[129] This includes nights normally spent with a NRP,[130] PWC or local authority.[131]

These nights count in determining whether care of the child is shared and when establishing who is a PWC (see p9) or which parent is to be treated as non-resident (see p13).

Example

Mohammed, who has been living with his mother during the week and spending Friday nights with his father, goes to boarding school. The time as a boarder continues to be treated as if he were living with his mother. Even if the care arrangement changes, so that Mohammed spends alternate weekends with his father, the nights at school still count as having been spent with his mother.

If the parents agree, or the periods involved are infrequent, the case may be straightforward. However, if the arrangements break down, a normal pattern cannot be established or the parents disagree, the CMS must make a decision on shared care.

Example

Neve is a qualifying child cared for most of the time by her mother, Sarah, although her father, Stuart, looks after her on Wednesday and Saturday nights. Over the past year Neve has undergone treatment for cancer, which has resulted in her spending periods in hospital. Because of this, Stuart has only looked after Neve for 42 nights in the year. On 16 of the remaining nights that Neve should have stayed with him, she was in hospital. On the other nights that Neve should have stayed with Stuart, she was unwell and wanted to stay with Sarah. The CMS must decide whether to consider Neve as staying with Stuart for 58 nights or accept that the intention was for her to stay with Stuart on 104 nights in the year. Both parents have the right to challenge the CMS's decision.

If a night spent in hospital or at boarding school would not otherwise have been a night spent with a PWC, a NRP who shares care or with a local authority who has part-time care, the child is treated as being in the principal provider's care for that night. For example, if a babysitter looks after a child one night a week, then the child goes into hospital, the babysitter is not a PWC, NRP or local authority. Therefore, that night is treated as one normally spent with the principal provider of day-to-day care.

A local authority provides part-time care

If a local authority has part-time care of a qualifying child for 52 nights or more in the 12-month period ending with the effective date of the calculation decision (see p129), the child support to be paid by the NRP may be decreased.[132] This applies if:

- a NRP is liable to pay the basic rate (including 'basic rate plus') or reduced rate, (including if a variation has been made which results in a liability for child support at either of these rates);[133] *and*
- the local authority provides care for at least one night a week on average, but not more than five (see below).

Part-time local authority care has no effect on the flat rate of child support.

A local authority cannot be a PWC.[134] If a child is being looked after by a local authority for more than five nights a week, no child support is payable by the NRP.[135] If a child is at a boarding school, even if this is publicly funded education provision, the child is not treated as being looked after by the local authority.[136]

The CMS may use a period other than the 12 months ending with the effective date if it considers it to be more representative of the current arrangements. A future period may also be considered if the qualifying child is to go into local authority care on or after the effective date.[137] If an alternative period is used, the number of nights of care must be at least in the same ratio as 52 nights to 12 months[138] (nights spent in hospital or at boarding school that normally would have been spent in care are included – see p85).

The child support calculation is only affected if a qualifying child is being looked after by a local authority. If a relevant other child (see p62) is being looked after by a local authority (either full or part time), the calculation is not affected, provided the NRP or their partner continues to receive child benefit for the child (or has elected not to receive child benefit because it would render them liable for the 'high-income child benefit charge' in income tax).[139]

The decrease for part-time local authority care

The basic or reduced rate of child support is decreased in relation to the number of nights the qualifying child spends in local authority care.[140] This calculation may be carried out either on its own if a NRP does not share care, or alongside one carried out because a NRP does share care (see p79).

The effect of part-time local authority care

Number of nights	*Fraction to subtract*
52 to 103	One-seventh
104 to 155	Two-sevenths
156 to 207	Three-sevenths
208 to 259	Four-sevenths
260 to 262	Five-sevenths

If a PWC and NRP have more than one qualifying child, the fractions that apply for each qualifying child in local authority care are added together and divided by the number of qualifying children for whom child support is calculated.[141] This applies if one child or all the children are being looked after by the local authority.

If the decrease because of part-time local authority care would reduce the amount of child support to less than £7, the amount due is £7.[142]

Example

Jake is the NRP of Michael and Leanne. Michael has just been placed under local authority supervision, which means that over the next six months he will spend four nights a week in a residential unit and the rest of the time with his mother, Naomi. Jake has a gross weekly income of £350 and currently pays child support of £56 (basic rate). This must now be superseded because of the local authority care. The CMS supersedes the decision, considering the ratio in the six-month period.

Step one: The basic rate of child support for two qualifying children applies.
16% x £350 = £56

Step two: **Apply the decrease because of part-time local authority care**
Local authority care for Michael is in the 208–259 band (four-sevenths).
The fractions which apply are added together and divided by the number of qualifying children – ie, (0 + 4/7) ÷ 2 = 4/14
Jake's child support is decreased by 4/14 of £56 = £16

Jake now pays Naomi £40 (£56 – £16).

If Leanne were also in care for two nights a week:

Step one: Same as above.

Step two: Local authority care for Leanne is in the 104–155 band (two-sevenths).
Local authority care for Michael is in the 208–259 band (four-sevenths).
The fractions are added together and divided by two:
(2/7 + 4/7) = 6/7 ÷ 2 = 6/14
Jake's child support decreases by 6/14 of £56 = £24

Jake now pays Naomi £32 (£56 – £24).

A non-resident parent shares care and the local authority has part-time care

If a NRP shares the care of a qualifying child and a local authority also has part-time care of a qualifying child in relation to the same PWC, the appropriate fractions are worked out under each provision and are added together.[143] The NRP's child support liability is then decreased by this fraction.

If this decrease would result in a NRP being due to pay less than £7, then the liability is £7.[144]

This calculation is carried out at Step two.

Example

Jake is the NRP of Michael and Leanne. Michael is still under local authority supervision and spends four nights a week in a residential unit and the rest of the time with his mother, Naomi. Jake's child support is £56 a week. Leanne spends one night a week with Jake, but Michael does not.

Step two: Jake cares for Leanne in the 52–103 band (one-seventh).
The fractions which apply are added together and divided by the number of qualifying children – ie,
(0 + 1/7) ÷ 2 = 1/14
Jake's child support liability because of shared care is reduced by 1/14.
Because Michael is in local authority care, the child support due is reduced by 4/14.
1/14 + 4/14 = 5/14
Jake's child support liability is reduced by £20 (ie, 5/14 x £56).

Jake now pays Naomi £36 (£56 – £20).

If Leanne were also in care two nights a week, but still spends one night a week with Jake:

Step two: Jake's child support liability because of shared care is reduced by 1/14 (as above).
Local authority care for Leanne is in the 104–155 band (two-sevenths).
Local authority care for Michael is in the 208–259 band (four-sevenths).
The fractions are added together and divided by two:
(2/7 + 4/7) = 6/7 ÷ 2 = 6/14
1/14 + 6/14 = 7/14 = 1/2
Jake's child support liability is reduced by £28 (1/2 x £56).

Jake now pays Naomi £28 (£56 – £28).

Notes

1. **The rates of child support**

1 Reg 6 CSMC Regs
2 Sch 1 para 6 CSA 1991
3 Sch 1 para 1(2) CSA 1991
4 para 51010 DMG
5 Sch 1 para 7(7) CSA 1991
6 Sch 1 para 5(b) CSA 1991; reg 45 CSMC Regs
7 Sch 1 para 4 CSA 1991
8 Sch 1 para 4(1)(b) CSA 1991; reg 44(1) CSMC Regs
9 Sch 1 para 4(1)(c) CSA 1991; reg 44(2) CSMC Regs
10 Sch 1 para 4(2) CSA 1991; reg 44(3) CSMC Regs
11 Sch 1 para 3 CSA 1991
12 Reg 43 CSMC Regs
13 Sch 1 para 1(1) CSA 1991
14 Sch 1 para 10(3) CSA 1991
15 Sch 1 para 2 CSA 1991; reg 2 CSM(CBR) Regs
16 Sch 1 para 2 CSA 1991; reg 2 CSM(CBR) Regs
17 Sch 1 para 10C CSA 1991
18 Sch 1 para 10C(2)(b) CSA 1991; reg 77 CSMC Regs
19 Reg 54 CSMC Regs
20 Reg 52 CSMC Regs
21 Reg 48 CSMC regs
22 *GC v SSWP & AE (CSM)* [2019] UKUT 199 (AAC)
23 Sch 1 para 5A CSA 1991; regs 48 and 52 CSMC Regs
24 Sch 1 para 6 CSA 1991
25 Sch 1 paras 5A and 7(7) CSA 1991
26 Reg 5 CS(MPA) Regs

2. **The non-resident parent's income**

27 Reg 34(1) CSMC Regs
28 *FQ v SWWP and MM (CSM)* [2016] UKUT 446 (AAC), reported as [2017] AACR 24
29 *EB v SSWP and CW (CSM)* [2019] UKUT 321 (AAC)
30 DWP, *The Child Maintenance Compliance and Arrears Strategy: government response to the consultation*, July 2018
31 Reg 25(1)(b) CSMC Regs
32 Reg 36(1) CSMC Regs
33 Reg 4(1) CSMC Regs
34 Reg 4(1) CSMC Regs
35 *IW v SSWP and DW (CSM)* [2016] UKUT 312 (AAC)
36 *SB v SSWP and TB (CSM)* [2016] UKUT 84 (AAC); *IW v SSWP and DW (CSM)* [2016] UKUT 312 (AAC); *IH v SSWP and EH (CSM)* [2018] UKUT 142 (AAC)
37 *AR v SSWP and LR (CSM)* [2017] UKUT 69 (AAC), reported as [2017] AACR 23
38 Reg 36(5) CSMC Regs
39 *AR v SSWP, HMRC & LR (No.2) (CSM)* [2019] UKUT 151 (AAC)
40 Reg 36(1)(c) CSMC Regs
41 Reg 36(2) CSMC Regs; in *SH v SSWP, CH and HMRC (CSM)* [2018] UKUT 157 (AAC), reported as [2019] AACR 1, it was decided that reg 36 as originally enacted was internally contradictory and the then para (2)(b) should be disregarded. Para (2) was subsequently substituted - see reg 14 CS(MA) Regs 2019 and Explanatory Memorandum.
42 *AR v SSWP and LR (CSM)* [2017] UKUT 69 (AAC), reported as [2017] AACR 23
43 Part 3 IT(EP)A 2003
44 Part 4 IT(EP)A 2003
45 *BB v SSWP and CB (CSM)* [2019] UKUT 314 (AAC)
46 Reg 36(1)(d) CSMC Regs; s5 IT(TOI)A 2005
47 s198 IT(TOI)A 2005
48 Reg 36(4) CSMC Regs
49 Reg 36(1)(b) CSMC Regs
50 Part 9 IT(EP)A 2003
51 s637 IT(EP)A 2003
52 s644 IT(EP)A 2003
53 ss638-41 IT(EP)A 2003
54 Reg 36(3) CSMC Regs
55 s577(1) IT(EP)A 2003
56 Reg 38(5) CSMC Regs
57 Reg 40 CSMC Regs
58 *IW v SSWP and DW (CSM)* [2016] UKUT 312 (AAC)
59 Reg 34(2) CSMC Regs
60 Reg 4(2) CSMC Regs
61 Reg 34(2A) CSMC Regs
62 *EB v SSWP and CW (CSM)* [2019] UKUT 321 (AAC)
63 *HH v SSWP and ASP (CSM)* [2021] UKUT 280 (AAC)
64 Reg 37(1) CSMC Regs

65 Reg 37(2) CSMC Regs
66 Reg 42(1) CSMC Regs
67 Reg 42(2) CSMC Regs
68 Reg 38(2)(a) CSMC Regs
69 Reg 38(2)(b) CSMC Regs
70 Reg 38(3) CSMC Regs
71 Part 3 IT(EP)A 2003; reg 38(4) CSMC Regs
72 Part 4 IT(EP)A 2003
73 *BB v SSWP and CB (CSM)* [2019] UKUT 314 (AAC)
74 para 97035 DMG
75 Reg 39(2), (3) and (4) CSMC Regs
76 Reg 39(1), (5) and (6) CSMC Regs
77 para 97031 DMG
78 para 38017/38018DMG
79 Reg 41 CSMC Regs
80 See gov.uk/government/collections/tax-treaties for details
81 Parliamentary question 240473, 3 April 2019, available at questions-statements.parliament.uk/written-questions/detail/2019-04-03/240473
82 s681 IT(EP)A 2003
83 ss567 and 615 IT(EP)A 2003
84 s637 IT(EP)A 2003
85 s575(2)(b) IT(EP)A 2003
86 Reg 19(1) CSMC Regs
87 Reg 19(2) CSMC Regs
88 Reg 19(3) CSMC Regs
89 Reg 19(4) CSMC Regs
90 Reg 20(1) CSMC Regs
91 Reg 35(2)(b) CSMC Regs
92 Reg 20(2) CSMC Regs
93 Reg 21(2) CSMC Regs
94 Child Maintenance and Enforcement Commission, *The Child Support Maintenance Calculation Regulations 2012: a technical consultation on the draft regulations*, December 2011
95 Reg 22(1) CSMC Regs
96 Reg 22(1) CSMC Regs
97 Child Maintenance and Enforcement Commission, *The Child Support Maintenance Calculation Regulations 2012: a technical consultation on the draft regulations*, December 2011
98 Reg 22(3) CSMC Regs
99 Reg 22(2) CSMC Regs
100 Reg 22(4) CSMC Regs
101 Child Maintenance and Enforcement Commission, *The Child Support Maintenance Calculation Regulations 2012: a technical consultation on the draft regulations*, December 2011
102 Reg 22(5) CSMC Regs
103 Reg 23(1) and (2) CSMC Regs
104 Reg 23(4) CSMC Regs
105 Reg 23(3) CSMC Regs
106 Reg 14(1)(f) CSMC Regs; *FQ v SSWP and MM (CSM)* [2016] UKUT 446 (AAC), reported as [2017] AACR 24
107 Reg 9A(1), (4) and (5) CSI Regs
108 s14A(3A) CSA 1991
109 Reg 9A(2) and (6)(a) CSI Regs
110 Reg 9A(2) and (6)(b) CSI Regs
111 Reg 9A(3), (9) and (10) CSI Regs

3. **Shared care**

112 Reg 50(1)(b) CSMC Regs
113 Reg 50(2) CSMC Regs
114 Regs 46, 47 and 50-55 CSMC Regs
115 Sch 1 para 7(4) CSA 1991; reg 46(5)(a) CSMC Regs
116 R(CS) 7/08
117 Reg 46(2) CSMC Regs
118 Reg 46(3) CSMC Regs
119 Reg 46(4) CSMC Regs
120 CCS/2885/2005; *JH v SSWP and LH (CSM)* [2016] UKUT 440 (AAC); *JS v SSWP and ZS (CSM)* [2018] UKUT 181 (AAC); *EA v SSWP and SA (CS)* [2019] UKUT 149 (AAC)
121 CCS/11728/1996
122 Sch 1 para 9(2) CSA 1991; reg 47 CSMC Regs
123 Reg 55 CSMC Regs
124 Sch 1 para 8 CSA 1991
125 Sch 1 para 7 CSA 1991
126 Sch 1 para 7(6) CSA 1991
127 Sch 1 para 7(7) CSA 1991
128 Sch 1 para 7(5) CSA 1991
129 Reg 55 CSMC Regs
130 Reg 46(5)(c) CSMC Regs
131 Reg 53(11) CSMC Regs
132 Reg 53(2) and (4) CSMC Regs
133 Reg 53(1) CSMC Regs
134 Reg 78(1)(a) CSMC Regs
135 Reg 53(10) CSMC Regs
136 R(CS) 1/04; R(CS) 2/04
137 Reg 53(2)(c) CSMC Regs
138 Reg 53(5) CSMC Regs
139 Reg 54 CSMC Regs
140 Reg 53(6) CSMC Regs
141 Reg 53(7) CSMC Regs
142 Reg 53(9) CSMC Regs
143 Reg 53(8) CSMC Regs
144 Reg 53(9) CSMC Regs

Chapter 5

Variations

This chapter covers:

1. What is a variation

A child support calculation can be varied in certain circumstances. A variation allows situations that are not taken into account by the usual calculation to be considered by the Child Maintenance Service (CMS).

A variation can only be made on one of the specified grounds and only if it would be 'just and equitable' to do so (see p92).

You can apply for a variation either before or after a calculation is made.[1]

If an application for a variation is successful, it may result in a child support calculation being made or, if a calculation already exists, its being revised or superseded with the variation incorporated.

If a default maintenance decision (see p127) is in force, an application for it to be varied may contain sufficient information for it to be revised and replaced with a calculation.

Variations are one of the areas of child support law in which disputes frequently arise. There is much caselaw on variations, and it is best to get advice if you are unsure. Many of the principles established in caselaw were decided on the rules for '2003 rules' (the second scheme) cases, but they also apply to variations in '2012 rules' (the current, third scheme) cases.

2. **Grounds for a variation**

A variation can be made for:

- special expenses (see below);
- additional income (see p97).

Special expenses

A non-resident parent (NRP) can apply for a variation to have their child support liability reduced on the grounds that they are liable for one or more of the following special expenses:[2]

- costs of maintaining contact with the qualifying child(ren) (see below);
- costs of a long-term illness or disability of a 'relevant other child' (ie, a child who lives with them) – see p94;
- previous debts, incurred before the couple separated (see p95);
- boarding school fees paid for qualifying children (see p96);
- costs of repaying a mortgage on the home of the person with care (PWC) and qualifying child(ren) (see p97).

Except for costs associated with an illness or disability of a relevant other child, special expenses can only be considered if they are over £10, regardless of the NRP's income. If expenses are being considered in more than one category, the £10 threshold applies separately to each. If the expenses in any category are less than £10 a week, a variation is not allowed on that ground. If the expenses in any category are £10 or more a week, the whole amount is counted in full (not just the excess over £10).[3]

The Child Maintenance Service (CMS) can also substitute a lower amount for any special expenses it considers are unreasonably high or have been unreasonably incurred. This may be below the threshold amount or nil. In the case of contact costs, any reduced amount must not be so low that it makes it impossible for the NRP to maintain contact with the child at the level of frequency stated in any court order, provided that contact is actually taking place.[4]

A variation for special expenses reduces the gross weekly income of the NRP that is taken into account in the child support calculation.[5]

Contact costs

A variation can be considered if the NRP incurs costs, or is reasonably expected to incur costs, in relation to contact with the qualifying child(ren).[6] The costs can be for the NRP or the child. The cost of a travelling companion can also be included – eg, because of disability or long-term illness (of the NRP or the child) or the child's young age. Costs of contact with another child (eg, a child who might have been a qualifying child but for the fact that the child does not live in the UK) do not count.[7]

Expenses for contact costs may be considered even if they arise for contact that is also being counted as part of a shared care arrangement.

The following count as contact costs:[8]

- public transport fares;
- fuel for a private car. To determine whether the cost for fuel is reasonable, the CMS may compare the amount claimed with an appropriate figure for a car of the same engine size and fuel type as that used;
- taxi fares, if the illness or disability of the NRP or qualifying child makes it impractical to use another form of transport;
- car hire, if the cost of the journey would be less than by public transport or taxis, or a combination of both;
- accommodation costs for the parent or the child for overnight stays, if a return journey on the same day is impractical, or the pattern of care includes contact over two or more days. The cost of meals does not count (apart from the cost of breakfast, if that is included in the accommodation costs);
- minor incidental costs associated with travelling, such as road or bridge tolls or fees. This may include parking fees and ticket reservation fees if it was necessary to incur these to maintain contact with the child. Other costs necessary to maintain contact with the child, such as fees for a contact centre if a court requires contact to be supervised, do not count.[9]

The costs are based on an established pattern of visits, if one exists.[10] If there is no current established pattern, a previous one may be referred to if contact is to begin again. Alternatively, an intended pattern, agreed between the NRP and PWC, may also be used. The pattern set out in a court order may also be used. When contact is set out in a court order, it may only specify an upper limit on visits.

The costs are calculated as an average weekly amount. This is based on a 12-month, or shorter, period that ends immediately before the day the variation would take effect.[11] If it is based on a pattern of contact that has ended before the date of the variation application, the CMS considers the costs incurred between the effective date of the variation and the date on which it would cease – ie, the date on which the circumstances giving rise to the variation end.[12] In other cases, it can be based on anticipated costs.

If a NRP returns from abroad and contact is only one reason for the trip, the CMS may limit costs to those of travel from their home in the UK.

Changes in contact may mean the variation is also changed. If contact stops, even through no fault of the NRP, the calculation may be superseded to reflect this.

Example

Bethan has a gross weekly income of £788 and pays the basic rate of child support of £126.08 a week to Ivan for Ava and Freya. She claims a special expenses cost for contact with her children, amounting to £4,100 over a six-month period since the girls attend boarding school. This includes travel from Northern Ireland by ferry, petrol and overnight stays in hotels, amounting to 12 nights over the six-month period.

The amounts included are considered reasonable in the circumstances and the weekly amount is calculated:

£4,100 ÷ 26 = £157.69 a week on average.

This is above the threshold of £10. Therefore, a variation of £157.69 for contact costs may be considered, and Bethan's gross income reduced by this amount.

Bethan's gross weekly income is now treated as being £630.31 (£788 – £157.69). The amount of child support due is now £100.85 a week (£630.31 x 16%, as the basic rate applies and there are two qualifying children).

Costs of a relevant other child's long-term illness or disability

A variation can be considered if the NRP incurs costs for a long-term illness or disability of a relevant other child (see p62).[13]

A long-term illness is one that exists at the date of the variation application or from the date the variation would take effect. It must be likely to last for at least a further 52 weeks or be terminal.[14] A child is considered disabled if:[15]

- they get the care component of disability living allowance (DLA) or child disability payment (CDP), the daily living component of personal independence payment (PIP) or adult disability payment (ADP) or armed forces independence payment; *or*
- they would get the DLA/CDP care component or the PIP/ADP daily living component but for the fact that they are in hospital; *or*
- they are registered blind. If they have ceased to be registered because of improved eyesight, they are still treated as if registered blind for 28 days. (**Note:** in Scotland, the system of registering a person as blind or severely sight impaired no longer applies to children under 16. If that affects your ability to apply for a variation under this rule, seek advice.)

Note: receipt of the mobility component of DLA or PIP does *not* count for this purpose. It is presumed that this is also intended to apply to the mobility component of CDP and ADP, although the rules do not specifically provide for that.[16]

The reasonable additional costs of any of the following count:[17]

- personal care, attendance or communication needs;
- mobility;
- domestic help;
- medical aids that cannot be provided on the NHS;

- heating, clothing and laundry;
- food essential for a diet recommended by a medical practitioner;
- adaptations to the NRP's home;
- day care, respite care or rehabilitation.

If an aid or appliance can be provided on the NHS, a variation is not normally agreed, even if the item is not available because of a lack of funds at a particular time. However, a variation may be considered if there is likely to be a serious delay in supplying an item which would prevent the child's condition from seriously deteriorating. The CMS may also consider the cost of the aid and whether it can be obtained at a cheaper price.

Any financial help towards these costs from any source, paid to the NRP or a member of their household, is deducted if it relates to the expense claimed.[18] Any DLA/CDP care component, PIP/ADP daily living component or armed forces independence payment being paid for the relevant other child is also deducted from the costs. If DLA/CDP, PIP/ADP or armed forces independence payment has been applied for, but is not yet in payment, it can be taken into account if it covers the date the variation starts.

Debts of the relationship

A variation can be considered if the NRP is repaying debts incurred before becoming a NRP of the qualifying child. These costs can count as special expenses, provided the debt arose when the NRP and the PWC were a couple.[19] The loan must have been taken out for the benefit of at least one of the following:[20]

- the NRP and PWC jointly;
- the PWC alone, if the NRP is liable for the repayments;
- a person who is not a child, but at the time the loan was taken:
  - was a child; *and*
  - lived with the NRP and PWC; *and*
  - was the child of the NRP, PWC or both of them;
- the qualifying child;
- any child other than the qualifying child who at the time the debt was incurred:
  - lived with the NRP and PWC; *and*
  - is a child of the PWC.

Loans only count if they are from a qualifying lender, or from a NRP's current or former employer.[21] Qualifying lenders include banks, building societies or other registered lenders – eg, hire purchase.[22]

The following do *not* count as debts for this purpose:[23]

- debts incurred to buy something which the NRP kept for their own use after the relationship ended;[24]

- a debt for which the NRP took responsibility under a court order or a financial settlement with their ex-partner;
- a debt for which a variation has previously been agreed, but which has not been repaid in the period for which the variation has been applied to the child support calculation;
- debts of a business or trade;
- secured mortgage repayments, except for amounts to buy, repair or improve the home of the PWC and qualifying child;
- endowment or insurance premiums, except those to buy, repair or improve the home of the PWC and qualifying child;
- gambling debts;
- legal costs of the separation, divorce or dissolution of the civil partnership;
- credit card repayments;
- overdrafts, unless taken out for a specified amount repayable over a specified period;
- fines imposed on the NRP;
- any debt incurred to repay one of the above;
- any other debt the CMS considers reasonable to exclude.

Payments on a loan taken out to pay off any negative equity on the former joint home once it has been sold do not count as debts, as the PWC no longer lives there.

In some circumstances, a loan taken out to repay a previous debt which would have counted may be considered a prior debt. This means that a debt incurred *after* a person has become a NRP may be grounds for a variation, although conditions may apply which may exclude them.[25] This can apply whether paying off the previous debt is the sole purpose, or only part of the purpose, of incurring the new debt.[26]

A variation is normally based on the original debt repayment period; any rescheduling of the debt is usually ignored. However, if the person who applied for the variation has been unemployed or ill and the creditors have agreed to extend the repayment period, the CMS can take the extended period into account.

Boarding school fees

A variation can be considered if the NRP incurs, or reasonably expects to incur, costs for the maintenance element of boarding school fees for the qualifying child.[27] Only term-time costs for non-advanced education at a recognised educational establishment can be included.[28]

If the maintenance element cannot be distinguished from other school fees, the CMS can decide what to include, but this amount should not be more than 35 per cent of the total fees.[29]

If the NRP receives financial help to pay the fees, or pays part of the fees with someone else, a proportion of the costs is included. This is calculated in the same ratio as the maintenance element to overall fees.[30]

In all cases, a variation for boarding school fees must not reduce the amount of income used to calculate child support by more than 50 per cent.[31]

Example

Bethan has a gross weekly income of £788 and pays the basic rate of child support of £126.08 a week to Ivan for Ava and Freya. Bethan claims special expenses for her contribution to the costs of Ava and Freya's boarding school. She pays the school £1,500 a term – ie, £4,500 a year. Ivan pays the rest of the fees – ie, £4,500 a year.

The fees for each child each term are £1,500 and the maintenance element is £500 a term. Bethan's contribution to the maintenance element of the fees is £250 a child each term – ie, £500. Over the three terms this amounts to £1,500, which is converted into a weekly figure (£1,500 ÷ 365 x 7 = £28.77). This is above the threshold of £10, so a variation for a contribution to boarding school fees of £28.77 may be considered. **Note:** if this is accepted, it does not reduce her gross income by more than 50 per cent.

Payments for mortgages, loans and insurance policies

A variation can be considered if the NRP makes payments to a mortgage lender, insurance company or PWC for a mortgage or loan if:[32]

- it was taken out to buy, or carry out repairs or improvements to, the property by someone other than the NRP; *and*
- the payments are not made because of a debt or other legal liability of the NRP for the period in which the variation is applied; *and*
- the property was the PWC and NRP's home when they were a couple, and it is still the home of the PWC and qualifying child(ren); *and*
- the NRP has no legal or financial rights in the property – eg, a charge or equitable interest.

Payments may also be considered for an insurance or endowment policy taken out to discharge a mortgage or loan as above, except if the NRP is entitled to any part of the proceeds when the policy matures.[33]

See also p142 for information on when payments made by a NRP to a third party may be offset against child support owed.

Additional income

A PWC can apply for a variation on the grounds that the NRP has certain additional income that has not been taken into account when calculating their child support liability. A variation results in the income being added to their gross weekly income used for the calculation, increasing the amount of child support due. **Note:** a variation can only be considered to the extent that it will result in the NRP's gross weekly income not exceeding £3,000. So, if a NRP's gross weekly income is £2,900 and a variation would result in £350 a week additional income, only £100 of that additional income is taken into account.[34]

A variation can be considered if the NRP:

- has unearned income – ie, income that has not been counted in gross weekly income (see below);
- is on the nil or flat rate in certain circumstances, but has gross weekly income of more than £100 (see p101);
- has 'diverted' income (p102);
- has 'notional income' from assets worth over £31,250 (see p104).

Unearned income

A variation can be considered if the NRP has taxable unearned income of £2,500 or more a year.[35] Not all taxable income counts. **'Unearned income'** for this purpose is income that is subject to UK income tax from:[36]

- land or property (see p99);
- savings and investments (see p100);
- other miscellaneous sources (see p101).

Note: the definitions of the different types of income that are classed as unearned for this purpose are complex and rely on how the sources of the income are treated for income tax purposes. This chapter includes only a summary of some of the main types.

Information on unearned income is collected by HM Revenue and Customs (HMRC) through self-assessment tax returns, and it provides details of the amount in the latest available tax year to the CMS. The CMS only requests this following an application for a variation. **Note:** the government has announced plans to allow unearned income to be included in the initial calculation, rather than only being taken into account after an application for a variation.[37] At the time of writing, no date has been set for this change to take effect.

The CMS can decide the amount of unearned income based on the most recent tax year if:[38]

- the latest available tax year is not the most recent tax year; *or*
- the information for the latest available tax year does not include a self-assessment; *or*
- the CMS is unable, for whatever reason, to request or obtain the information from HMRC – eg, because there has been a failure in the automatic data-sharing system.

The CMS bases the variation decision on actual unearned income figures for a complete tax year. The use of HMRC figures also means that the CMS does not rely on the PWC to provide evidence of the NRP's financial circumstances.

If the CMS agrees to make a variation on this ground, the unearned income is converted into a weekly amount and added to the existing gross weekly income.[39] If the NRP has paid approved pension contributions that have not otherwise been taken into account in the child support calculation, the average weekly amount of these contributions is deducted from the unearned income amount. The pension contributions must have been made in the same tax year to which the unearned income relates.[40]

If the NRP has sold an asset for a capital gain that would be taxable, this is not, in itself, a ground for a variation. However, the proceeds of the sale could be an asset that is assumed to produce notional income (see p104).

Income from land or property

Any taxable income from the use of property or land in the UK or elsewhere counts as additional income. **Note:** if there is no declared income from it, the capital value of property or land may be treated as an asset and a variation considered on the grounds of 'notional income' (see p104).

In most cases, property income is the rent from tenants or licensees. Certain other payments also count, including:[41]

- ground rent and feu duties;
- if property is let furnished, any payment by the tenant for the use of the furniture;
- premiums and other similar lump sums received for granting certain leases;
- income from caravans or houseboats where these are not moved around various locations;
- service charges from tenants for certain services normally provided by a landlord – eg, cleaning of communal areas, fuel and heating, and repairs;
- deposits/bonds from tenants.

Any expenses incurred wholly and exclusively for the purpose of the property business and that are not of a capital nature (such as the cost of furniture, appliances and improvements to the property) are first deducted from the taxable income.[42] Some of the main categories of allowable expenses include:[43]

- council tax, business rates and water charges, if the agreement specifies that these are the responsibility of the landlord;
- the cost of maintenance and repairs (but not improvements);
- in some cases, the cost of certain energy efficiency measures installed before 6 April 2015;
- for fully furnished properties, certain costs for the wear and tear or renewal of furnishings;
- insurance premiums for contents, building and loss of rent;
- interest on a mortgage or loan taken out to purchase the property (although the amount of mortgage interest which can be deducted has been gradually reducing since 2016/17 such that it was nil by 2020/21);[44]

- the cost of providing services, including the wages of gardeners and cleaners;
- letting agent fees, and certain legal and accountancy fees;
- rent, ground rent and service charges;
- other direct costs – eg, phone calls, stationery and advertising for new tenants.

If only part of a property is let and part is occupied by the NRP, a suitable proportion of the charges can be deducted. Any loss on a property business can usually be set against the property business profits of the following year.[45]

Rent and other income from property outside the UK is treated in the same way. Losses on overseas property cannot be offset against profits on UK property, and vice versa.

If a NRP rents out a room in their home under the 'rent-a-room' scheme, the first £7,500 (for the tax year 2022/23) of income a year is not taxable. When calculating the income in this case, expenses cannot be deducted.[46]

Income from property rented as a business (eg, running a hotel, B&B or guest house), or from services not normally offered by a landlord (such as meals, laundry or room cleaning), usually counts as income from self-employment (see p65). Rental income from tied houses and caravan sites, and income from other land-related activity, such as farming and market gardening, are also treated as income from self-employment.[47]

Income from savings and investments

Any taxable income from savings and investments counts as additional income. **Note:** if there is no declared income from them, the capital value of any savings or investments may be treated as an asset and a variation considered on the grounds of 'notional income' (see p104).

HMRC is unlikely to have details of this sort of unearned income for a NRP who is an employee unless it is at least £10,000 a year (and so would require a self-assessment tax return to be completed). If a NRP appears to have income from savings and investments of more than the unearned income threshold of £2,500 a year, but less than £10,000 a year, the CMS will ask the NRP for evidence.

The main types of income that count are:[48]

- interest on invested money, including outside the UK – eg, interest on savings in a bank (including income from selling a right to receive interest);
- dividends and other distributions from UK companies (including the tax credit payable with the dividend), and foreign dividends;
- discounts from securities – ie, the profit from trading in securities such as government stocks and bonds;
- income from government stocks and bonds;
- taxable payments from a life assurance policy, life annuity contract or capital redemption policy;
- payments from a trust;
- payments from the estate of someone who has died;

- interest arising from a debt;
- artificial transactions in futures and options.

Certain types of savings and investment income are exempt from tax and therefore disregarded. These include:[49]

- interest, dividends or bonuses from an individual investment plan, such as an ISA;
- income from certified save as you earn schemes;
- interest under an employee share scheme;
- income from national savings certificates and tax reserve certificates;
- venture capital trust dividends;
- tax-exempt annual payments made by an individual in the UK not for commercial reasons – eg, from a covenant;
- periodic or annuity payments of personal injury damages;
- annuity payments from a Criminal Injuries Compensation Scheme award;
- gains from dealing in certain commodities, financial futures and options;
- the capital element of purchased life annuities;
- tax-free health and employment insurance or immediate-needs annuity payments.

Miscellaneous income

Any taxable income from other miscellaneous sources may count as additional income. This can include, for example, casual income from one-off jobs, royalties and other income from intellectual property such as sales of patent rights.[50]

Certain types of income that are exempt from tax are not counted, including:[51]

- income from an educational bursary or scholarship;
- payments to adopters;
- certain foreign maintenance payments;
- certain compensation payments to World War Two victims;
- income from domestic electricity microgeneration;
- winnings from premium bonds, lotteries and gambling.

Income of a non-resident parent liable for the nil or flat rate

In certain circumstances, if a NRP has been assessed as liable for the nil rate (see p57) or flat rate (see p58) of child support and has income which would otherwise be taken into account in a child support calculation, a variation can be considered.

A variation on this ground is possible if the NRP has gross weekly income of more than £100 that would normally be taken into account were it not for the fact that the parent is liable for:[52]

- the nil rate because they are:
  - a child; *or*
  - a prisoner; *or*
  - receiving an allowance for work-based training for young people; *or*

  - resident in a care home or independent hospital, or is being provided with a care home service and/or independent healthcare service and receiving one of the qualifying benefits for the flat rate (see p58), or has the whole or part of the cost of their accommodation met by a local authority; *or*
- the flat rate as a result of being in receipt of a qualifying benefit (see p58). This does not apply if the qualifying benefit is one of the means-tested benefits.

If the CMS agrees to make a variation on this ground, the NRP is treated as having the whole amount of the income for the purpose of calculating a new child support liability. Child support is calculated on this income at the reduced rate (see p59), basic rate or basic rate plus (see p60) as appropriate. The liability calculated in this way is then added to the nil or flat rate.[53]

If a variation has been agreed on this ground, information about the additional income is sought and treated in the same way as for gross weekly income used in the child support calculation. Historic income information from HMRC for the latest available tax year is normally used. If current income is at least 25 per cent different from the historic income, current income can be used for the variation. If current income is used, the NRP must notify the CMS if it changes by 25 per cent or more (see p77).

Diverted income

A variation can be considered if:[54]
- the NRP can control, whether directly or indirectly, the amount of income they receive or the amount that is taken into account as their gross income; *and*
- the CMS is satisfied that the NRP has unreasonably reduced the amount of income that would have been received (and which would have been taken into account in the child support calculation or under a variation) by 'diverting' it to someone else or for some other purpose. The diversion does not have to have been arranged specifically to avoid child support responsibilities. The CMS (or First-tier Tribunal) has a broad discretion to judge what is unreasonable in the circumstances.[55]

This applies to income that would count as gross weekly income and to income that would count as unearned income.

The NRP may have diverted income:
- to a third party – eg, a new partner or close family member;
- to a business (eg, by taking a lower income[56]) or by making excessive contributions to a pension scheme from which the NRP will benefit later. In this situation, it must be also considered to be reasonable to make a variation;
- towards other purposes – eg, if company assets are used for private use or business funds for day-to-day expenditure.

Converting earnings from a form that counts as income to one that results in their being excluded in the calculation can be classed as diverting income.[57] The fact that a NRP has failed to take advantage of an opportunity to generate income (eg, by choosing to work only part time, or by having a second property and choosing not to let it out) does not mean that income has been diverted; in order to count as diverted income, the money that might have been generated must be paid to someone else or for another purpose.[58]

The fact that a NRP has disposed of or diverted *capital* does not mean that they have diverted *income*, even if the capital may have been a source of income.

The CMS is likely to consider that pension contributions in excess of 12 per cent of gross income are excessive. However, each case should be considered individually, taking account of all the circumstances (such as the parent's age, the age at which they started making contributions, any contributions paid by an employer, any advice received about the appropriate level of contributions, etc).[59]

Example

Marcus runs his own import/export business, employing his new partner, Shamira, and his brother. His brother is paid £800 a week and he and Shamira each receive £400. His ex-wife, Helene, gets basic rate child support of £64 for their two children. Helene applies for a variation because she thinks Marcus is diverting income via the company, especially as Shamira does not seem to do any work.

Shamira's salary could be a token payment, and Marcus takes less from the business than he pays his brother. The CMS considers that, on balance, there could be diversion of income via the company and Shamira's wages. Given its contentious nature, the case is referred to the First-tier Tribunal.

Deciding whether a parent has the ability to control their income or whether a reduction in income received is unreasonable can be difficult – eg, if a parent is a director, employee or shareholder of a small business. Many cases may require detailed investigation of the circumstances and the CMS is likely to refer such cases to its Financial Investigations Unit. The way that money is held and distributed in the business is important, particularly whether this follows recognised business and accounting practices and/or is done for justified business reasons.[60] What counts is whether the parent has the ability to control the income in practice (eg, if it is clear that other shareholders involved in a business will agree to their proposed distribution of funds) and whether or not this could be legally enforced.[61] The fact that income is moved legitimately within a business (eg, a transfer of all or part of a shareholding in a small business) may still, nonetheless, mean that it is found to have been done to divert income.[62]

The full weekly equivalent amount of any diverted income is added to gross weekly income to calculate the new amount of child support (subject to gross weekly income being capped at £3,000).[63]

Notional income from assets

A variation can be considered if a NRP has certain high-value assets.[64] A variation on this ground may be appropriate if they appear to have an affluent lifestyle, and sources of income that would be taken into account in the calculation cannot be identified. If they have significant assets, the CMS can assume a weekly notional income from them.

It is understood that the CMS will not apply a variation on both unearned income grounds and on notional income grounds in respect of the same asset. For example, a NRP owns a second property which is let out. The income from the rent is declared to HMRC and may be grounds for a variation on the basis of having taxable unearned income. The CMS would not also consider a variation on the grounds of having notional income from the property in this case, as it would be unlikely to be considered just and equitable (see p113). Where there is a declared income from the asset, the 'unearned income' ground (see p98) is likely to be the focus. The main aim of the 'notional income from assets' ground is to target parents who appear to be able to support themselves in a way that does not correspond to their declared income.

The CMS must be satisfied that the NRP has a legal or beneficial interest in the asset. This includes any asset which is subject to a trust where the NRP is a beneficiary of the trust.[65]

'Asset' means:[66]

- money – eg, cash, deposits in a bank, building society, post office or credit union account, premium bonds or savings certificates. This also includes any money due to the NRP if the CMS is satisfied that it would be reasonable to require it to be paid to them immediately;
- gold, silver or platinum bullion bars or coins;
- a virtual currency which is capable of being exchanged for money – eg, bitcoin;
- land or rights in or over land. A legal or beneficial interest in land is not counted if the land is the primary residence of the NRP or their child(ren);
- shares, stocks and unit trusts and gilt-edged securities;
- a claim or right to property which has not been enforced on the date of the application for a variation if the CMS is satisfied that enforcement would be reasonable.

An asset only counts for this purpose if its total value is more than £31,250. A variation on this ground is therefore not possible if a NRP has a large number of low-value assets, even if their combined total value is well over £31,250. The CMS says that if a NRP has a number of items of one class of assets, these will be treated as one asset.[67] For example, a number of gold coins are counted as one asset, and shares in more than one company are counted as one asset. However, in some cases there may be a dispute about whether a set of rights is to be treated as one asset.[68]

If an asset is subject to a mortgage or charge, its value is established after the amount due on the mortgage or charge is deducted. If an asset is worth less than an outstanding mortgage or charge on it, the 'negative equity' cannot be offset against the value of another asset the NRP has. However, the CMS may consider this when deciding whether it is just and equitable to agree a variation (see p113).[69]

The CMS does not count assets if:[70]

- they have been received by the NRP as compensation for personal injury;
- they are being used in the course of the NRP's trade or business. Shares are not used in the course of a trade or business if the trade or business is not that of the NRP – eg, if they have invested in a company or even own one, but it is not their trade or business;
- it is satisfied that the assets could have been purchased from the NRP's gross weekly income that has already been taken into account in the child support calculation;
- they will need to be sold to meet any extra child support required to be paid as a result of an 'additional income' variation and the CMS is satisfied that the sale would cause hardship to a child of the NRP, or would be unreasonable, taking account of all relevant circumstances. **Note:** it is understood that this is intended to apply only where the asset will need to be sold to meet the extra child support due as a result of a variation on *this* ground, although the wording of the law suggests it applies if an asset would have to be sold to meet the extra due as a result of *any* additional income ground. If you think this applies to your case, get advice.

The income assumed from the assets is determined by using the statutory rate of interest which applies on the date the variation takes effect.[71] This is currently 8 per cent.[72] Eight per cent of the value of the assets is then divided by 52 to give a weekly notional income that is added to the NRP's gross weekly income. This means that a variation on this ground will be considered if the notional income from assets is over £2,500 a year – ie, £31,250 x 8 per cent.

Example

Adam pays child support to Rea for their two children. Rea discovers that Adam has recently inherited a property worth £253,500, £40,300 cash and shares worth £17,000. He has also recently bought a second sports car, worth £55,000. Rea applies for a variation on the grounds that Adam should be considered to have notional income from assets.

The shares are an asset, but as their value is not over £31,250, they are not taken into account. The sports car does not fall within the meaning of an 'asset' for this purpose. The property and the cash each count as assets. A weekly notional income of £390 is calculated for the property (ie, £253,500 x 8 per cent ÷ 52). A weekly notional income of £62 is calculated for the cash (ie, £40,300 x 8 per cent ÷ 52). A variation may therefore be considered on the basis that Adam has £452 (£390 + £62) a week additional income.

If Adam's gross weekly income for the standard child support calculation is £2,700, only £300 a week additional income is taken into account as this brings his gross weekly income up to the capped amount of £3,000.

Changes in additional income

Variations on unearned income grounds are based on information provided by HMRC. They are considered by the CMS at the annual review (see p73).

As part of the annual review process, the CMS may request updated information and may make a supersession decision on the basis of that information. The supersession decision takes effect from the review date.[73]

If the CMS accepts that the NRP had unearned income in a past tax year but no longer has unearned income in the current tax year (eg, if an income-generating property has been sold), it can treat the parent as having no unearned income.[74]

A calculation decision that includes a variation on the ground that the NRP has gross weekly income of more than £100 based on current income can be superseded before the annual review date if their current income changes by at least 25 per cent.

There is no obligation on parents who have unearned income included in their gross weekly income to report changes in this.

A variation based on diverted income, or notional income from assets, is not reviewed routinely, as it is not based on information provided by HMRC. There is no obligation to report any changes to diverted or notional income from assets, but a PWC or NRP (or child applicant in Scotland) can apply for a supersession at any time if the circumstances relating to the notional or diverted income change.

3. Applying for a variation

A person with care, non-resident parent or a child applicant in Scotland can all apply for a variation.[75] An authorised representative can also apply. In certain circumstances, the Child Maintenance Service (CMS) has discretion to reinstate a previous variation without an application being made (see p118).

An application for a variation can be made by phone, through the online portal or in writing.[76] In exceptional cases, the CMS may insist on a written application – eg, because complicated special expenses are being considered.

The application must state the grounds on which it is made.[77] If it does not, or at least give a reason, it is not accepted as having been properly made.

Example

1. Liam applies for a variation because he believes his child support is too high. The CMS does not accept it as a properly made application.
2. Liam applies for a variation because he believes his child support is too high and he cannot afford it because of the high cost of pet food. The CMS accepts the application as properly made, but then rejects it as it is not on one of the specified grounds.
3. Liam applies for a variation because he believes his child support is too high because he cannot now afford the kennel costs he incurs when he travels to see his children. The CMS

accepts the application as properly made and it is given a preliminary consideration (see p108). It rejects the application as kennel costs are not one of the specified grounds. Had Liam referred to other contact costs (eg, travel), his application may have proceeded.

An application for a variation can be made before a child support calculation decision has been made.[78] If a calculation is already in force and a new application is made by the same person, the CMS may (but does not have to) treat it as a request for a variation, depending on the circumstances and the information contained in it,[79] even if the application did not expressly ask for a variation.[80] An appeal can also be treated as an application for a variation if it would be more advantageous to the person appealing. The CMS must bear in mind, however, that what is advantageous to the appellant may not be to another party to the calculation.[81]

If an application for a variation is made, but there is insufficient information to decide whether to proceed, the CMS may request further information. This should be provided within 14 days, or a longer period if it is reasonable in the circumstances – eg, if the applicant is in hospital.[82] If the time limit is exceeded without good cause, the effective date of the variation may be affected. If the information is not provided, the CMS has the discretion either to reject the application or to proceed.[83]

There is no specific provision to allow an application for a variation to be amended or withdrawn. In practice, an application could be withdrawn verbally or in writing at any time before a decision is made on it. If a change relates to a period after the effective date of an application, a separate new application for a variation could be made and a separate decision would be made for the period covered by each circumstance.

Two or more applications for a variation may be considered at the same time. In addition, if appropriate, an application made on one ground may be treated as an application on a different ground.[84]

4. What happens after an application is made

Once an application has been made, the procedure is as follows.

- The Child Maintenance Service (CMS) considers the application (see p108).
- Unless the application is rejected, the other parties are notified and asked to make representations. This is known as 'contesting' (see p109).
- The CMS may make an interim maintenance decision (see p110) or impose a regular payment condition on the non-resident parent (NRP) (see p110).
- The CMS decides whether or not to vary the amount of child support payable (see p112).

The CMS may also pass a case to the First-tier Tribunal for a determination if the case involves complex or contentious issues (see p111).

The application may not proceed in the above way if the CMS refuses to consider it further – eg, because:[85]

- one of the grounds for rejection is established (see below); *or*
- it is withdrawn; *or*
- the regular payment condition (see p110) has not been met.

Considering the application

Once an application is properly made, the CMS considers whether it should go ahead (this is a 'preliminary consideration').[86] At this point, the CMS may reject the application for a variation and decide to:

- revise or supersede the child support calculation, or refuse to revise or supersede it; *or*
- make the calculation, or make a default maintenance decision (see p127).

Grounds for rejecting an application

The CMS may reject an application for a variation after a preliminary consideration if:[87]

- there are no grounds for a variation; *or*
- it has insufficient information to decide the child support application and so a default maintenance decision is likely to be made; *or*
- the applicant does not state a ground or provide sufficient information to allow a ground to be identified; *or*
- the requirements of the stated ground are not met, or the applicant has not given any information that supports the ground or which is sufficient to allow further enquiries to be made; *or*
- a default maintenance decision is in force; *or*
- the NRP is liable to pay the nil rate, or to pay the flat rate because they or their partner gets universal credit calculated on the basis of no earned income, income support, income-based jobseeker's allowance, income-related employment and support allowance or pension credit (see p58); *or*
- a variation was sought on the grounds that the NRP has additional income, but gross weekly income is already at least £3,000; *or*
- the NRP has applied for a variation on special expenses grounds and:
  - the amount of the expenses is below the £10 threshold (see p92); *or*
  - they are already paying £7 or less child support a week; *or*
  - after deducting special expenses, their gross weekly income is still above the capped amount of £3,000; *or*
  - gross weekly income has been estimated because insufficient information was available.

Contesting the application

If it has not rejected an application, the CMS usually then notifies the other relevant parties. This may include notification being available through the self-service portal, but may be done by telephone or in writing. It must include the grounds on which the application has been made and provide any information or evidence the applicant has given to support it or which has been obtained by the CMS, except information that must not be disclosed (see below).[88]

The CMS may invite the other parties to the child support calculation to make representations within 14 days about anything to do with the application. The 14-day time limit may be extended if the CMS is satisfied that it is reasonable.[89]

The CMS does not need to notify the other parties if:[90]

- it is satisfied that, on the available information, it will not apply the variation; *or*
- the application is on the grounds of unearned income, the latest available tax year information from HM Revenue and Customs (HMRC) does not show unearned income above the £2,500 threshold and the CMS does not have further information that justifies making further enquiries; *or*
- a previously agreed variation can be reinstated without an application (see p118).

The CMS tends to notify the other parties of any such contest online or in writing depending on the contact preferences set.

The other parties may respond online, or in writing. If no contesting information is provided, the CMS may make a decision on the application as it stands.[91]

Any information provided by another party, other than that which must not be disclosed, may be forwarded to the applicant if the CMS considers this reasonable. The applicant is given 14 days to comment on the evidence or information supplied by the other party. This 14-day time limit may also be extended if the CMS is satisfied that it is reasonable. The application must not be decided until this period is over.[92]

It is possible that the applicant may supply further information outside the 14-day time limit and the CMS may already have decided in the meantime to proceed with the application and to notify the other parties. In this case, the further information is likely to be passed to the other parties and a further 14 days from the date of this notification (or longer if the CMS is satisfied that it is reasonable) is allowed for representations.

Information that must not be disclosed

In addition to the general rules on disclosing information (see p51), there are additional rules for variations. Supporting evidence or information from one party is not given to another party if it contains:[93]

- details of an illness or disability of a relevant other child if the NRP has requested that this not be disclosed and the CMS agrees;
- medical evidence that has not been disclosed to the applicant or a relevant person (ie, person with care (PWC), NRP or child applicant in Scotland) and which would be harmful to them;
- the address of a relevant person or qualifying child, or information that could lead to their location, and there is a risk of harm or undue distress to them or to any other child(ren) living with them.

If you request that information is not to be disclosed, this is discussed with you. It may be possible to make an amended application which does not include the relevant details. If you refuse to allow disclosure of information that is relevant for the other party to contest the application, your application could be rejected. However, there may be a good reason for non-disclosure, and each case should be considered on its own merits.

Interim maintenance decision

If an application for a variation is made before the child support calculation decision has been made, the CMS may make an interim maintenance decision.[94] The amount of the interim maintenance is the child support calculated in the normal way, ignoring the variation. An interim maintenance decision is not often used as the maintenance calculation is issued which may later be revised if the variation is successful.

An interim maintenance decision can be challenged in the usual way. However, when a calculation is made which replaces this, any appeal against the interim decision may lapse.[95] If the interim maintenance decision is superseded, the usual rule tolerating a change of up to and including 25 per cent in current income (see p76) does not apply.

Regular payment condition

If a NRP has applied for a variation, the CMS may impose a regular payment condition on them if they have:[96]
- a poor payment record or arrears; *or*
- failed to make payments while the variation application was being contested and considered; *or*
- special expenses that make it difficult for them to meet their child support liability.

The amount due under a regular payment condition is either:[97]
- the child support calculated, including that set under an interim maintenance decision; *or*
- the amount that would be due if the variation were agreed.

This means that if the CMS believes that the variation application will be successful, it may set a regular payment condition that adjusts the child support calculated to reflect the variation, reducing the financial burden on the parent. However, if it believes that the application will be unsuccessful and a regular payment condition is imposed, it is set at the calculation rate.

A regular payment condition does not affect the amount of child support the NRP is liable to pay. Therefore, if the amount set is lower than the amount due, there will be arrears if the variation application fails.

The regular payment condition is set independently of any other arrears arrangement the parent may have. It ends when either the CMS makes a final decision on the calculation (whether or not the variation is agreed) or when the variation application is withdrawn.[98]

When a regular payment condition is imposed, the NRP and PWC (and a qualifying child applicant in Scotland) are sent written notification.[99] This makes it clear that if the condition is not met, the application for a variation may lapse.[100]

If a NRP does not meet the regular payment condition within one month of this notification, written notification of this is sent to all the relevant parties.[101] If the regular payment condition has not been met, the CMS may refuse to consider the application for a variation.[102] A refusal to consider the application cannot be appealed.

Referral to the First-tier Tribunal

Once the application has passed the preliminary consideration and contest stage, it may be passed to the First-tier Tribunal for a determination on whether the variation should take place.[103] This normally only occurs if a particularly contentious or unusual issue is being considered.

If a referral is made, it can only be withdrawn by the CMS. The tribunal can proceed even if the parties come to an agreement.[104] It is also possible for an applicant to add a further ground of variation to an application before it is decided by the tribunal.[105] The tribunal applies the same rules as the CMS and decides whether the variation should happen.[106] It then passes it back to the CMS to make the child support calculation.[107] This decision by the CMS (ie, to revise or supersede, or to refuse to revise or supersede, the child support calculation) may then be challenged in the normal way (see Chapters 9 and 10).

5. Decisions on variations

The Child Maintenance Service (CMS) has some discretion when determining variation applications. It must bear in mind the general principles of child support law – ie, that:[108]

- a parent is responsible for maintaining their children when they can afford to do so; *and*
- a parent is responsible for maintaining all of their children equally; *and*
- the welfare of any child affected by an application for a variation must be taken into account (see p124).

In addition, the CMS must be satisfied that:[109]

- the grounds are met; *and*
- it is just and equitable to agree to the variation (see p113).

The CMS must take into account any representations made by any of the relevant parties to the application.[110]

If the person with care (PWC) applies for a variation and the CMS needs further information before making a decision, the onus is on the CMS to investigate. There is no onus on the PWC to prove that a variation is justified. The CMS must consider any information that is available to it (eg, information that it can obtain from HM Revenue and Customs), and must take appropriate steps to obtain any such further information.[111]

The CMS must not agree to make a variation if:[112]

- it has insufficient information to make a child support calculation and so would make a default maintenance decision (see p127); *or*
- any of the circumstances apply that would lead to a variation application being rejected after a preliminary consideration (see p108).

A variation is applied by revising or superseding the child support calculation decision. Whether the decision is revised or superseded depends on when the variation application is made. If the grounds for the variation existed at the time the original calculation decision was made, the decision may be revised. If the grounds result from a change of circumstances, the decision may be superseded.

If the CMS agrees to a variation, it can:[113]

- revise or supersede the calculation/replace the interim maintenance decision (see p110); *or*
- make a calculation (this may replace an interim maintenance decision or default maintenance decision – see p127).

In some cases, a variation may be agreed which makes no difference to the amount of child support calculated. A revision or supersession is still carried out, as each decision gives further appeal rights.

Once a variation is made, it is considered each time there is a revision or supersession of the calculation under the usual revision/supersession rules. Some changes in circumstances may mean that the variation ceases to have effect, in which case the calculation may be suspended or cancelled in order to remove the variation element. In certain cases, if there is a further change in circumstances, the variation may be reinstated by the CMS without an application (see p118). In other cases, a new request for a variation may need to be made.

Just and equitable

Even though the grounds are met, a variation is only agreed if it is 'just and equitable' to do so.[114]

There are no specific factors that the CMS must take into account in deciding whether it is just and equitable to make a variation. However, examples of factors that are likely to be considered include:

- the welfare of any child likely to be affected by the proposed variation (see p124);
- whether a variation would lead the non-resident parent (NRP) or PWC to give up employment;
- if the applicant is the NRP, whether there is any liability to pay child maintenance under a court order or agreement made before the effective date of the child support calculation;
- if the NRP has applied for a special expenses variation, whether they could make financial arrangements to cover those expenses or could pay for them from money currently spent on non-essentials.

This decision is discretionary and the CMS must make it based on the individual circumstances of the case.

The following must *not* be taken into account:[115]

- whether or not the child's conception was planned;
- who was responsible for the breakdown of the relationship between the NRP and the PWC;
- whether the NRP or PWC is in a new relationship with someone who is not the qualifying child's parent;
- any contact arrangements and whether or not they are being kept to;
- the income or assets of anyone other than the NRP;
- any failure of the NRP to pay child support or maintenance under a court order or written agreement;
- the fact that a NRP pays school fees (because the child support legislation leaves the courts to make orders on tuition fees – see p17);[116]
- representations from individuals other than the PWC, NRP or a qualifying child applicant in Scotland.

The CMS must reach a positive conclusion that it is just and equitable to agree to a variation, and not simply that there is no reason not to do so.[117] All factors should be considered, but the CMS (or the First-tier Tribunal on a referral – see p111) decides what weight to give to them.[118] This may mean taking into account circumstances for which either party could have sought a variation, even if they did not. For example, since contact costs affect the financial circumstances of a NRP, it may be just and equitable to take these into account when deciding on the variation, even if the application was about something else (and may have been made at the request of the PWC).[119] It may also be just and equitable to consider additional payments by the NRP for expenses that could not have been grounds for a variation.[120] If such wider financial circumstances are taken into account, it must be made clear to all parties on what basis the variation has been decided.

The just and equitable rule cannot be used to increase the amount by which the variation would change the calculation beyond the amount that the ground for variation would suggest.[121] However, the amount may be reduced.[122] For example, the CMS decides that a NRP has notional income from assets of £62 a week. The CMS may decide that it is just and equitable in all the circumstances that only £50 a week additional income is taken into account instead of £62. The CMS cannot decide that it would be just and equitable to take £70 a week into account.

The effect of the variation

The effect of the variation should not reduce the total amount of child support paid to less than £7, and should not increase the maximum amount of gross income to be taken into account to above the capped amount of £3,000.[123] The following sections examine the effect of a variation on different grounds, including where there is more than one ground. The CMS calls these 'concurrent variations'.

If the NRP shares the care of the qualifying child(ren), the shared care reduction is applied to the child support liability after the variation has been applied.[124]

Special expenses

All special expenses amounts are aggregated (taking account of the threshold rules). The total amount of the NRP's relevant expenses is converted into a weekly amount and deducted from their gross weekly income. The calculation is then carried out as normal, using this new total.[125]

If the effect of the variation would be to reduce the child support liability to below the flat rate of £7, the NRP is still liable to pay £7.[126]

If the gross weekly income is above the £3,000 capped amount, the special expenses are subtracted from the actual gross weekly income. If this results in a figure that is still above £3,000, the special expenses variation is refused.[127]

Example

Bethan has a gross weekly income of £788 and pays basic rate child support of £126.08 to Ivan for Ava and Freya. She applies for a variation because she has special expenses for the cost of contact with her children, amounting to £4,100 over a six-month period, and she contributes to the maintenance element of their boarding school fees of £500 a term.

Her weekly special expenses are worked out as £157.69 for contact and £28.77 for boarding school costs, totalling £186.46. Both types of special expenses are over the £10 threshold, and so the total amount of £186.46 a week is allowed.

This is deducted from her gross weekly income: £788 – £186.46 = £601.54

Her child support is now worked out in the usual way: 16% x £601.54 = £96.25

The variation for special expenses has reduced her child support liability from £126.08 a week to £96.25.

Additional income

The amount of any additional income is converted to a weekly amount and is added to the NRP's gross weekly income. If this results in a gross income figure above the £3,000 capped amount, the gross income taken into account is restricted to £3,000.[128]

If a variation on additional income grounds is agreed and the child support without the variation would be the flat rate of £7, the amount of child support is £7 plus the amount calculated on the additional income.[129]

Example

Helene believes that Marcus is diverting income via his company and applies for a variation. The CMS refers the case to the First-tier Tribunal. The tribunal determines that there should be a variation for additional income on the grounds that Marcus has diverted income, with a weekly value of £360. This amount is added to Marcus's gross weekly income of £400 used in the child support calculation. His gross weekly income is now £760. The amount he is now due to pay Helene is £121.60 a week (£760 x 16%).

If Marcus had been paying the flat rate of child support and the variation for additional income of £360 occurred, the child support due would then be:

Child support at the basic rate for two qualifying children: 16% x £360 = £57.60

The amount of child support payable: £57.60 + £7 = £64.60

If Marcus's gross weekly income used in the child support calculation had been £2,800, taking account of the diverted income would increase his gross weekly income to the capped amount of £3,000. The remaining £160 of additional income would make no difference to the child support calculation.

If there is more than one variation

If there is more than one variation element (ie, on both special expenses and additional income grounds, known as a 'concurrent variation'), the results of each variation are added together.[130]

- This aggregate figure is then added to the actual gross weekly income, capping the income at £3,000.
- If the total amount of child support is £7 or less, £7 is still payable. The amount payable is apportioned between the people with care, if appropriate.[131]

Example

Marcus has a gross income of £400 a week and pays his ex-wife Helene basic rate child support of £64 a week for their two children. The CMS decides that there should be a variation for additional income on the grounds that he has diverted income via his company, with a weekly value of £360. The CMS also decides that there should be a variation on special expenses grounds as Marcus has contact costs of £32 a week for visiting his children and pays £24 a week for debts of the relationship.

The special expenses Marcus pays are deducted from his additional income:

£360 – (£32 + £24) = £304

This amount is added to the gross weekly income: £304 + £400 = £704

Child support at the basic rate for two qualifying children: 16% x £704 = £112.64

The combined effect of the variations is that Marcus now pays Helene an additional £48.64 child support a week.

When a variation takes effect

If the ground for the variation existed at the initial effective date (see p129) of the child support calculation, the variation takes effect on that date if either:

- the application for a variation is made before the calculation is made;[132] *or*
- the application for a variation is made within 30 days of the notification date for the calculation, or within a longer period if the CMS allows a late application for a revision (see p201).[133]

The exception to this is if the NRP applied for a variation on the grounds of previous debts or payments in respect of certain mortgages, loans or insurance policies before the child support calculation was made, and payments towards these are treated as voluntary payments in the initial payment period (see p147). In this case, the variation takes effect from the date on which the NRP was notified of the amount of their child support liability.[134]

If the ground did not apply at the initial effective date of the child support calculation, the variation takes effect from:

- the date the ground arose, if this is after the initial effective date but before the calculation is made;[135] *or*

- the date of the variation application;[136] *or*
- the date on which the ground is expected to arise, if the application for variation is made in advance.[137]

If an application for a variation is made before the child support calculation is made and the ground has ceased to exist by the date the calculation is made, the variation is applied for the period the ground existed.[138]

There may be a number of different grounds, agreed over time, and each may have a different date from when it takes effect.

Example

Tara applies for child support. The effective date is 27 August 2021. She is notified of her calculation on 19 September 2021. She takes advice and applies for a variation on the basis that an additional income ground applied on 27 August 2021. She makes this application on 8 October 2021 – ie, within 30 days of being notified of the decision on her child support. The variation is agreed and the calculation is revised on 15 November 2021 with effect from 27 August 2021.

Juan, her ex-partner, takes advice and on 3 December 2021 applies for a variation on the grounds that he has been paying off a loan for a car which they bought before splitting up and which Tara needs, as she lives in a secluded cottage. He is also just about to start paying boarding school fees for their eldest child in late December. The variation is agreed and a revision is made on 3 January 2022 in which the element for previous debts takes effect from 3 December 2021 and the boarding school fees take effect from 16 December 2021.

Even though the variation for previous debts only applies from December, Juan could ask that the amounts he paid towards the car before the calculation was made be considered as voluntary payments to offset initial arrears. Had Juan taken advice at the same time as Tara and applied for a variation at the same time as she did, on the grounds of previous debts and that his repayments on the car loan were voluntary payments, there could have been a further variation to the calculation, with the decision taking effect from 27 August 2021.

When a variation is not applied

A variation is not applied for any period when:[139]

- the NRP is liable for the nil rate, or for the flat rate because they are getting a means-tested benefit (see p58); *or*
- a variation was sought on additional income grounds, but the NRP's gross weekly income was already above the capped amount of £3,000; *or*
- the NRP applied for the variation on special expenses grounds and:
  - the amount of the expenses is below the threshold (see p92); *or*
  - the NRP is already paying £7 or less child support; *or*

  - after deducting special expenses, the gross weekly income would still be above the capped amount of £3,000; *or*
  - the gross weekly income has been estimated because insufficient information was available.

When a variation ceases to have effect because of a change of circumstances, a supersession is carried out. This takes effect from the day on which the change occurred. If there is a further later change that means that a variation might apply again, a further application for a variation must be made (unless the CMS has discretion to reinstate the variation – see below).

Reinstating a variation

The CMS has the discretion to revise or to supersede a child support calculation in order to reinstate a variation that has previously been agreed, without the need for a new application. This discretion can be applied if:[140]

- a variation ceases to have effect, because a change of circumstances means that:
  - the NRP's liability is reduced to the nil rate or another rate such that the variation cannot be taken into account; *or*
  - the child support calculation has been replaced with a default maintenance decision;

and then:

- a subsequent change of circumstances means the calculation has been revised or superseded so that the NRP is now liable for a rate which can be adjusted to take the variation into account.

Examples of situations where this could apply include where:

- the NRP is sentenced to a prison term and so becomes liable for the nil rate, but subsequently returns to a basic or reduced rate;
- a variation is agreed and on a subsequent application for a revision or supersession the NRP fails to provide information. Therefore, the child support calculation is replaced by a default decision. Later, the information required is provided and this default maintenance decision is replaced with a calculation. The variation may then be reapplied without a fresh application.

The CMS can reinstate a variation straight away without checking whether the circumstances relating to it have changed. If any party is aware of changes to circumstances, they could apply for a revision or supersession. There is no obligation on the CMS to investigate, so decisions are made based on the information available to it. There is no time limit on the period between the variation ceasing to apply and its being reinstated, provided the circumstances that gave rise to the variation remain unchanged.

Example

Liam obtains a variation from his basic rate child support on the grounds of his contact costs with his children. He is later convicted of a criminal offence and sentenced to six months in prison. He becomes liable to pay the nil rate. On his release, he becomes liable at the reduced rate. The CMS is not satisfied that the circumstances relating to his eligibility are still the same as it assumes that the pattern of contact with his children may now be different. The CMS does not reinstate the variation. Liam must make a new application for a variation on the grounds of contact costs.

Had a variation been granted on the grounds of previous debts of the relationship, the CMS may have reinstated the variation without Liam having to make a further application, as there is no reason why this ground and its effect should be changed by his imprisonment.

If the calculation ceases, this discretion does not apply. For example, if a parent moves abroad and the CMS ceases to have jurisdiction, but then they return to the UK, a new application for child support and a new application for a variation must be made. However, in some circumstances, the CMS may be able to reinstate the variation without going through the step of its being contested (see p109).

Challenging a decision

A variation is applied by a decision revising or superseding the child support calculation decision. Once a variation is applied to the calculation, this decision can be challenged by applying for a revision within 30 days (and appealing if necessary). The variation is taken into account in the revision/appeal. Any change of circumstances, whether in relation to the variation or to other factors, can result in a revision or supersession of the calculation under the normal rules, depending on the circumstances (see Chapter 9). This also applies to decisions referred by the CMS to the First-tier Tribunal for a decision.[141]

If an application is made for a revision or a supersession of a decision that includes a variation:[142]

- there is no preliminary consideration; *and*
- the usual rules on seeking further information and allowing the application to be contested apply; *and*
- the factors that must not be taken into account when considering whether it would be just and equitable to agree to a variation still apply (see p113).

However, the CMS does not have to notify the other parties and invite representations if:[143]

- the revised or superseded decision would not be advantageous to the applicant; *or*
- it considers that representations from the other parties would not be relevant.

The CMS may decide to revise or supersede, or not to revise or supersede, the decision and notifies the applicant and any relevant parties, as appropriate.

Notes

1. **What is a variation**
1 ss28A(1) and (3) and 28G(1) and (2) CSA 1991; ss28A-28F and Schs 4A and 4B CSA 1991, as modified by CS(V)(MSP) Regs

2. **Grounds for a variation**
2 Sch 4B CSA 1991; regs 63-67 CSMC Regs
3 Reg 68 CSMC Regs
4 Reg 68(3) and (4) CSMC Regs
5 Reg 72(1) CSMC Regs
6 Reg 63 CSMC Regs
7 *CMEC v NC (CSM)* [2009] UKUT 106 (AAC), reported as [2010] AACR 1
8 Reg 63(1) CSMC Regs
9 R(CS) 5/08; *SM v SSWP and FS (CSM)* [2013] UKUT 445 (AAC)
10 Reg 63(3)(a) CSMC Regs
11 Reg 63(3)(b) CSMC Regs
12 Reg 63(3)(b)(ii) CSMC Regs
13 Reg 64 CSMC Regs
14 Reg 64(2)(d) CSMC Regs
15 Reg 64(2)(a), (b), (f), (g) (ga) and (h) CSMC Regs
16 Reg 64(2) CSMC Regs, as amended by art 18 Social Security (Scotland) Act 2018 (Disability Assistance for Children and Young People) (Consequential Modifications) Order 2021 No.786
17 Reg 64(1) CSMC Regs
18 Reg 64(3) CSMC Regs
19 Reg 65(1) CSMC Regs; R(CS) 3/03
20 Reg 65(2) CSMC Regs
21 Reg 65(3)(k) CSMC Regs
22 Reg 2, definition of 'qualifying lender', CSMC Regs; see also CCS/3674/2007, para 23; s376(4) ICTA 1988
23 Reg 65(3) and (4) CSMC Regs
24 CCS/3674/2007, para 19
25 Reg 65(5) CSMC Regs; R(CS) 3/03; R(CS) 5/03; *T v SSWP and A (CSM)* [2017] UKUT 492 (AAC)
26 R(CS) 3/03
27 Reg 66 CSMC Regs
28 Reg 66(6) CSMC Regs
29 Reg 66(2) CSMC Regs
30 Reg 66(3) and (4) CSMC Regs
31 Reg 66(5) CSMC Regs
32 Reg 67(2)(a) CSMC Regs
33 Reg 67(2)(b) CSMC Regs
34 Reg 73(1) CSMC Regs
35 Sch 4B para 4(1) CSA 1991; reg 69(1) CSMC Regs
36 Reg 69(2) CSMC Regs; Parts 3-5 IT(TOI)A 2005
37 DWP, *Child Maintenance: modernising and improving our service, March 2022*, press release 14 March 2022, available at gov.uk/government/news/children-to-benefit-from-changes-to-child-maintenance-service
38 Reg 69(5) CSMC Regs
39 Reg 69(7) CSMC Regs
40 Reg 69(8) and (9) CSMC Regs
41 Part 3 IT(TOI)A 2005; HMRC, *Property Income Manual*
42 ss33 and 272 and IT(TOI)A 2005
43 Part 3 IT(TOI)A 2005; HMRC, *Property Income Manual*
44 s272A IT(TOI)A 2005
45 Reg 69(4) CSMC Regs; s118 ITA 2007
46 ss309, 784, 786, 788(2) and 789(4) IT(TOI)A 2005; Income Tax (Limit for Rent-a-Room Relief) Order 2015 No.1539
47 ss9, 19, 20, 267 and 273 IT(TOI)A 2005
48 Part 4 IT(TOI)A 2005; HMRC, *Savings and Investment Manual*
49 Part 6 IT(TOI)A 2005; HMRC, *Savings and Investment Manual*
50 ss579, 587, 683 and 687 Part 5 IT(TOI)A 2005
51 Part 6 IT(TOI)A 2005
52 Reg 70 CSMC Regs
53 Reg 70(2) CSMC Regs
54 Reg 71(1) CSMC Regs

55 *G'OB v CMEC (CSM)* [2010] UKUT 6 (AAC)
56 *TB v SSWP and SB (CSM)* [2014] UKUT 301 (AAC); *EH v SSWP (CSM)* [2015] UKUT 621 (AAC); *AB v SSWP and RS* [2021] UKUT 129 (AAC)
57 R(CS) 6/05; CCS/1769/2007
58 *Green v SSWP and Adams (CSM)* [2018] UKUT 240 (AAC), reported as [2019] AACR 3
59 para 36007 DMG; *DW v CMEC (CSM)* [2010] UKUT 196 (AAC)
60 See, for example, *RC v CMEC and WC* [2009] UKUT 62 (AAC), reported as [2011] AACR 38; CCS/1320/2005; CCS/409/2005
61 *PS v SSWP and KH (CSM)* [2015] UKUT 183 (AAC)
62 *AS v SSWP (CSM)* [2018] UKUT 315 (AAC)
63 Reg 71(2) CSMC Regs
64 Sch 4B para 4(1) CSA 1991; reg 69A CSMC Regs
65 Reg 69A(1) and (3) CSMC Regs
66 Reg 69A(2) and (4)(f) CSMC Regs
67 CS(MA) Regs 2018
68 CCS 8/2000; *MG v CMEC (CSM)* [2010] UKUT 83 (AAC), reported as [2010] AACR 37
69 *GL v SSWP and EG (CSM)* [2014] UKUT 209 (AAC)
70 Reg 69A(4) CSMC Regs
71 Reg 69A(7) CSMC Regs
72 Reg 69A(8) CSMC Regs; s17 Judgments Act 1838; Judgment Debts (Rate of Interest) Order 1993 No.564; Sch 2 r7.7 Act of Sederunt (Rules of the Court of Session 1994) 1994 No.1443
73 Reg 21 CSMC Regs
74 Reg 69(6) CSMC Regs

3. **Applying for a variation**
75 s28A(1) CSA 1991
76 s28A(4)(a) CSA 1991
77 s28A(4)(b) CSA 1991
78 s28A(3) CSA 1991
79 *DB v CMEC (CSM)* [2010] UKUT 356 (AAC)
80 *DB v CMEC (CSM)* [2010] UKUT 356 (AAC)
81 R(CS) 2/06
82 Reg 58(1) and (2) CSMC Regs
83 Reg 58(3) CSMC Regs
84 Reg 56(3) and (4) CSMC Regs

4. **What happens after an application is made**
85 s28D(2) CSA 1991
86 s28B CSA 1991
87 s28B CSA 1991; reg 57(1) CSMC Regs
88 Reg 59(1)(a) and (5) CSMC Regs
89 Reg 59(1)(b) CSMC Regs
90 Reg 59(2) CSMC Regs
91 Reg 59(4) CSMC Regs
92 Reg 59(3) CSMC Regs
93 Reg 59(5) CSMC Regs
94 ss12 and 28F(5) CSA 1991
95 s28F(5) CSA 1991
96 s28C CSA 1991; reg 62 CSMC Regs
97 s28C(2) CSA 1991; reg 62(1) CSMC Regs
98 s28C(4) CSA 1991
99 s28C(3) CSA 1991
100 s28C(5) CSA 1991
101 s28C(7) CSA 1991
102 Reg 31(2) and (3) CS(V) Regs
103 s28D(1)(b) CSA 1991
104 *Milton v SSWP* [2006] EWCA Civ 1258
105 R(CS) 3/01
106 s28D(3) CSA 1991
107 R(CS) 5/06

5. **Decisions on variations**
108 ss28E(1) and (2) and 28F(2)(a) CSA 1991; *RC v CMEC and WC* [2009] UKUT 62 (AAC), reported as [2011] AACR 38
109 s28F(1) CSA 1991
110 s28E(3) CSA 1991
111 s28D(2A) and (2B) CSA 1991
112 s28F(3) CSA 1991; reg 57(2) CSMC Regs
113 ss28B(2) and 28F(3) and (4) CSA 1991
114 s28F(1) CSA 1991
115 s28F(2)(b) CSA 1991; reg 60 CSMC Regs
116 *DB v CMEC* [2010] UKUT 356 (AAC)
117 R(CS) 3/01; *RR v SSWP and PR (CSM)* 2022 UKUT 7 (AAC)
118 CSCS/16/2003
119 CCS/1131/2005
120 *SM v SSWP and BM (CSM)* [2016] UKUT 245 (AAC), reported as [2016] AACR 47
121 R(CS) 5/06
122 *DDH v SSWP and DAH (CSM)* [2013] UKUT 299 (AAC)
123 Regs 72(2) and 74(1A) CSMC Regs
124 Reg 74(2)-(4) CSMC Regs
125 Reg 72(1) CSMC Regs
126 Reg 74(1A) CSMC Regs
127 Reg 72(2) CSMC Regs
128 Reg 73(1) CSMC Regs
129 Reg 73(2) CSMC Regs
130 Reg 74(1) CSMC Regs

131 Reg 74(4) CSMC Regs
132 Reg 13(1) CSMC Regs
133 s28G CSA 1991; regs 14(1)(a) and 15 CSMC Regs
134 Reg 13(2) CSMC Regs
135 Reg 13(1)(b) CSMC Regs
136 ss17(4) and 28G CSA 1991
137 Reg 18(2) CSMC Regs
138 Reg 13(3) CSMC Regs
139 Regs 57(1)(d)-(f) and 74(5) CSMC Regs
140 Reg 75 CSMC Regs
141 ss16(1A)(c) and 17(1)(d) CSA 1991; regs 14(1)(a)(ii) and 17(3) CSMC Regs
142 Reg 61(1) CSMC Regs
143 Reg 61(2) CSMC Regs

Chapter 6

Decisions

This chapter covers:

1. Making decisions about child support

Child Maintenance Service (CMS) officials are responsible for making decisions about child support. In doing so, they must apply the law to the facts of each case in an unbiased manner. They have no discretion about how some decisions are made – eg, about the amount of child support due or choosing between alternatives, such as whether a person is habitually resident in the UK or not. CMS officials have to decide what, on the balance of probabilities, the facts indicate.

Some child support decisions, however, are discretionary decisions – eg, whether a variation would be 'just and equitable' (see p113), or how to collect or enforce payments. The CMS only has discretion if, after deciding on the facts of the case and what the law requires, it still has a choice about what decision to make.

Whenever the CMS makes a discretionary decision, it must take into account the principles of child support law and the welfare of any child (see p6 for who counts as a child) likely to be affected by the decision.[1] Only the welfare of a child must be taken into account, not that of any adults involved. However, it is not just qualifying children or those named in the application who must be considered; the situation of *any* child likely to be affected by the decision must be looked at – eg, a child of the non-resident parent (NRP)'s new family, or another child of the NRP who does not live with them.[2]

This duty to consider the welfare of a child also applies to discretionary decisions made by the First-tier Tribunal and Upper Tribunal.

The welfare of a child

The duty to consider the welfare of children is a general principle in child support law.[3] The legislation does not make it the paramount consideration, or impose a duty on the CMS or First-tier Tribunal/Upper Tribunal to promote the welfare of any children,[4] but considerable weight should be given to this principle.[5] In general, it should be considered along with the other principles of child support – eg, that each parent of a qualifying child has a duty to maintain the child.[6]

'Welfare' includes the child's physical, mental and social welfare. For example, if imposing a deduction from earnings order (see p161) would affect a NRP's ability to visit a child and maintain the parental relationship, that child's emotional welfare may be affected. However, an order may mean the parent with care has more money coming in, which may improve the child's physical and social welfare.

Generally, the welfare of a child must be balanced with the benefits of child support being paid for that child or other children. Where the interests of different children are likely to conflict, the decision should not result in one child being unduly disadvantaged in favour of another. It is likely to be rare that the welfare of a child will justify a decision or action that is contrary to the principle that parents should support their children. However, if the NRP has a child in their household who would be adversely affected by the implications of enforcement action, this might mean that certain enforcement action should not be taken. When deciding on enforcement action, the CMS must not use the welfare of the child principle to avoid the full use of its powers, unless it is genuinely appropriate.[7]

The CMS must record its reasons for any decisions it makes on the welfare of all children who could be affected, and it may be useful to ask to see these records. Give the CMS full details as soon as you can about the effect a discretionary decision may have on a child's welfare. If a decision has been made without considering its effect on a child, supply the information and ask the CMS to reconsider. The CMS does not have a specific duty to seek further information on the welfare of children who may be affected but must take into account any issues of which it is aware.

Some decisions that should involve the welfare principle may be challenged (see Chapters 9 and 10). If the decision cannot be appealed (eg, if it is about enforcement), you could consider making a complaint (see Chapter 11) or applying for judicial review (see p198).

In addition to applying welfare principle in child support law, the UK must also comply with its international obligations, including a commitment to the welfare of children under the United Nations Convention on the Rights of the Child. This means that in instances where more than one interpretation of the law is possible, the one chosen should be that which more closely complies with protecting children's welfare.[8]

2. The initial child support decision

Once an effective application has been made (see p25) and the Child Maintenance Service (CMS) has obtained, or tried to obtain, the necessary information, it can:[9]

- make a calculation; *or*
- make a default maintenance decision (see p127); *or*
- refuse to make a calculation (p126).

Details of the case are entered on the CMS computer system and child support is calculated automatically. In most cases, the non-resident parent (NRP) is notified of any 'provisional' calculation at the same time as they are notified of the application. The CMS will attempt to contact the NRP as soon as possible to gather any additional information. The NRP may also contact CMS if the provisional calculation information is wrong.

The CMS aims to issue a 'final' calculation within one month of the application. This may take longer if the CMS has to wait for the NRP to provide details of current income or has difficulty tracing the NRP.

The CMS may also make an interim maintenance decision (see p110) if an application for a variation is made before a decision has been made on a child support calculation. The interim maintenance decision will be replaced by the calculation once the application for a variation has been decided.

Delays in dealing with applications

Initial contact with parents to collect and check information needed to make a calculation and collect payments is done by telephone.

Parents may enquire about the stage of their application, or raise further queries or complaints through the webchat facility, or by telephone. The CMS should provide regular updates to any enquiry raised.

Any delay following the contacting of the NRP does not normally delay the starting date of any calculation (see p129). If the NRP has liability to pay child maintenance under a court order or an agreement, this continues and remains enforceable. Other NRPs should consider putting money aside or making voluntary payments (see p147). Parents who are already contributing voluntarily should check whether these payments might be used to offset initial arrears (see p141).

If the NRP is not co-operating, the CMS may make a default maintenance decision (see p127) and may take legal action against them (see p37). If you have applied for child support and the CMS does not make a default maintenance decision, request that one be made. If this does not happen, you can complain (see p244). In certain circumstances, the CMS can make a calculation based on an estimate of the NRP's income (see p71).

Withdrawing the application

If an application is withdrawn or treated as withdrawn (see p26), the CMS cannot make a calculation. If a calculation is made after the application is withdrawn, it can be challenged (see Chapters 9 and 10).

The application cannot be withdrawn after a decision has been made, but the applicant can ask the CMS to cease acting, in which case the calculation is cancelled (see p130).

Change of circumstances

There is no general requirement to notify the CMS of changes in circumstances. However, both the person with care (PWC) and the NRP are required to notify the CMS of some changes (see p50).

In practice, any party to a child support calculation (ie, PWC, NRP or child applicant in Scotland) may want to tell the CMS of changes or new information that might affect the calculation.

There are also specific rules for when changes of income must be disclosed and which changes result in a calculation being altered (see p76).

When making a decision, the CMS takes into account the information that applied at the date the decision would have effect.[10] Any information about a change after this 'effective date' but before the calculation is made can lead to two or more calculations in respect of different periods. The effective date of each calculation is normally the date the change occurred or is expected to occur.[11]

Changes that occur after a calculation is made may result in a revision or supersession, depending on the nature of the change and when the CMS is notified about the change (see Chapter 9). Changes resulting in a revision or supersession generally take effect from the day on which an event happens or is expected to happen, or on which a decision is made.

Refusal to make a calculation

The CMS *must* refuse to make a calculation if:

- the application was made by a person who is not a NRP or a PWC (or, in Scotland, a qualifying child aged 12 or over) (see p5); *or*
- there is a pre-3 March 2003 court order (registered agreement in Scotland) or written agreement (see p18) in force; *or*
- there is a post-3 March 2003 court order (registered agreement in Scotland) that has been in force for less than one year (see p19); *or*
- not all of the parties are habitually resident in the UK (see p14); *or*
- there is no NRP, either because both parents live in the same household as the child (see p11) or because the CMS does not accept that the person named is a parent of the child (see p7); *or*
- there is no qualifying child (see p6).

The CMS can also delay making a calculation pending the outcome of a 'test case' (see p238). Otherwise, the CMS must make a calculation.[12]

If there is a change of circumstances so that one of these situations applies for a period beginning after the effective date, the CMS makes a calculation that ends on the date of the change.

If a qualifying child dies before the calculation is made, a decision is still made for the period from the effective date to the date of death (see p26).

The CMS cannot refuse to make a calculation just because it has insufficient information or because it may affect the welfare of a child.[13] The CMS may make a default maintenance decision (see below). If the CMS refuses to make a calculation, the applicant (and, if the applicant is a child in Scotland, any PWC or NRP who had been notified of the application) must be notified in writing of the decision, how to apply for a revision or supersession (see Chapter 9) and the right of appeal (see Chapter 10).[14]

A fresh application may be made after the refusal – eg, if there is a change of circumstances, such as the NRP returning to live in the UK.

3. Default maintenance decisions

If the Child Maintenance Service (CMS) does not have enough information to make a calculation, or to revise or supersede a decision, it may make a default maintenance decision.[15]

A default maintenance decision is for a set amount. The amount depends on the number of qualifying children applied for:[16]

- £39 a week if there is one qualifying child;
- £51 a week if there are two qualifying children;
- £64 a week if there are three or more qualifying children.

These amounts may be apportioned (see p56) if there is more than one person with care looking after different qualifying children. Any relevant non-resident children (see p63) are ignored.

Example

Jimmy gets universal credit (UC) and has no earned income. He pays the flat rate of child support for his two children, Jack and Sarah, who live with their mother Julia. In January 2022, the CMS is notified that Jimmy has stopped getting UC. HMRC has no historic income data for Jimmy and he does not respond to requests for current income details. No previous current income details are held by the CMS. Julia is not able to provide any information about Jimmy's circumstances. The CMS has insufficient information to make a calculation based on historic income, current income or estimated income. It makes a default maintenance decision that Jimmy is liable to pay £51 a week child support to Julia.

The 'effective date' of a default maintenance decision is the same as it would have been for a child support calculation decision (see p129).

Notification of a default maintenance decision must state the effective date, the default rate, the number of qualifying children, details of any apportionment and the information needed to make a child support calculation.[17] It should also include details of the right to request a revision, supersession or an appeal.[18]

When a default maintenance decision ends

A default maintenance decision may be revised at any time – eg, when it is replaced by a calculation.[19] In practice, this only happens when the CMS has sufficient information to determine the case properly (ie, to make a calculation) from the effective date. If the information provided relates to a date after the effective date of the default maintenance decision, the default amount remains in place and a supersession is carried out.

4. Notification of decisions

The Child Maintenance Service (CMS) must notify the person with care (PWC) and non-resident parent (NRP) (and child applicant in Scotland) once a child support calculation or interim maintenance decision (see p110) has been made.[20] This also includes default maintenance decisions (but see below). There are similar rules on notifying revision and supersession decisions (see Chapter 9) and decisions to cancel calculations (see p131). A decision does not have full legal effect until the relevant people are notified of it.[21]

There is no requirement for notifications of decisions to be in writing, although in practice most are. The notification of the calculation or interim maintenance decision, or of a decision to revise or supersede a decision, must include information on:[22]

- the effective date (see p129); *and*
- where relevant, the gross weekly income of the NRP, including:
  - whether it is based on historic or current income; *and*
  - if it is based on current income, whether this has been estimated (see p71); *and*
- the number of qualifying children (see p6); *and*
- the number of relevant other children (see p62); *and*
- the weekly rate of child support and any collection fees; *and*
- any variations; *and*
- any adjustments for apportionment (see p56) for shared care by the NRP or part-time local authority care (see p78), or for maintenance being paid for a relevant non-resident child (see p63); *and*
- the rules for requesting a revision, supersession and appeal.[23]

The CMS does not have to include the information above where it has decided not to supersede a decision. However, it should still notify the parties of the decision where practicable, and should include information on the rules for challenging the decision.[24]

The CMS can correct an accidental error in a decision, or in the record of a decision, at any time (see p196). If it does so, it must also notify the PWC and NRP (and child applicant in Scotland) as soon as practicable. This notification must be in writing.[25]

Unless the people concerned have given written permission, a notification should *not* contain:[26]

- the address of anyone else other than the recipient or information that could lead to other people being located; *or*
- information on anyone other than PWC, NRPs or qualifying children.

If there are errors or someone disagrees with the decision, it may be challenged (see Chapter 9).

If there is a court order for maintenance, the court is notified of the calculation.

5. **When liability for child support starts (the 'effective date')**

The date a child support calculation first comes into force and liability begins is called the **'initial effective date'** and subsequent decisions commence on an 'effective date'.[27] The 'initial effective date' is specified in the notice issued to the non-resident parent (NRP) informing them that an effective application for child support has been made (see p25). The Child Maintenance Service (CMS) may telephone the NRP on or before the effective date and then confirm this in writing to the parent's last known postal address, or electronically. If the CMS does not telephone the NRP, it must send written notice to their last known postal address at least two days before the effective date, or electronically at least one day before the effective date.[28] The CMS will set the initial effective date and then make sure that the notice is issued at least two days before that date.

An alleged NRP cannot delay the effective date of a calculation by disputing parentage. The CMS does not make a calculation until the issue of parentage is resolved (see p40) but, if it later decides that the person is the NRP, the calculation is backdated to the initial effective date.

When making a decision, the CMS takes into account the information that applied at the date the decision would have effect.[29]

There are different rules for effective dates after a supersession or revision (see Chapter 9) and for calculations replacing default maintenance decisions (see p127).

6. When a calculation ends

A calculation continues until the Child Maintenance Service (CMS):

- cancels it at the request of the person who applied for child support (see below); *or*
- supersedes it after a change of circumstances means it has ceased to have effect (see below); *or*
- supersedes it for another reason (see p204); *or*
- revises it (see p199).

In some circumstances, this means that the calculation is replaced by another. In others, no further calculation is made. When the cancellation takes effect depends on the grounds on which the supersession or revision was made, or the nature of the request (see p131). Any arrears remaining after a calculation ends may still be collected (see Chapter 8). If an application is made for a child of the non-resident parent (NRP) who is not named in the existing calculation, the calculation is superseded and a new calculation replaces the old one.

Requesting a cancellation

A calculation must be cancelled when the applicant requests that the CMS ceases acting.[30]

Requests be made verbally or in writing. The CMS must then stop all action, including the collection and enforcement of arrears, although the applicant may specifically ask for this action to continue.

If the parents are living together

When the request to cancel a calculation is made, reasons need not be given. However, if the reason is that the parent with care (PWC) and NRP are living together, the CMS should be told. Once all the parties share a household, the NRP is no longer non-resident (see p11), so the child is no longer a qualifying child and the calculation ceases to have effect. Reconciliations not reported at the time may prevent the calculation being cancelled retrospectively.

The calculation ceases to have effect

Some changes of circumstances mean that the calculation is automatically terminated. The CMS must cancel a calculation (including a default decision) if the calculation ceases to have effect because:[31]

- the NRP or PWC dies; *or*
- the only, or all, child or children no longer qualify; *or*
- the NRP ceases to be a parent of the qualifying child(ren).

This means that the calculation is cancelled, for example, when:

- a child aged 16 or over leaves non-advanced education or becomes too old to count as a child (see p6); *or*
- the qualifying child, NRP and PWC start living together in the same household (see p11); *or*
- the qualifying child goes to live with someone else and, as a result, the PWC no longer counts as a PWC; *or*
- the qualifying child is adopted, in which case the NRP is no longer a parent; *or*
- the NRP is no longer considered a parent because of the results of a DNA test or a declaration/declarator of parentage.

Other cancellations

If the event leading to a possible cancellation requires investigation, cancellation of a calculation requires a formal decision by the CMS, either at its own initiative or following a request or application (see p130). The calculation remains in force until cancelled by a CMS decision (or until it ceases for some other reason).[32]

The CMS must cancel the calculation if the PWC, NRP or qualifying child is no longer habitually resident in the UK (see p14).[33]

If a NRP has successfully contested parentage, the calculation is cancelled and they may be able to obtain a refund of any child support paid (see p40).

If an applicant fails to provide the CMS with enough information to make a revision or supersession decision, the CMS *may* cancel the calculation.

When the cancellation takes effect

If a calculation is cancelled because it ceases to have effect or because of another relevant change (including the circumstances above), the cancellation takes effect from the date the change occurred.[34]

If the cancellation is because the NRP is not considered to be the parent because of a DNA test or declaration/declarator of parentage, the cancellation takes effect from the effective date of the original calculation (see p129).[35]

If a PWC requests that a calculation be cancelled, the cancellation normally takes effect from the date the request was received. A different date may apply, depending on the reason for the cancellation.[36]

Notification of the cancellation decision

When the CMS cancels a calculation or refuses to cancel one, it must notify the NRP, PWC and child applicant in Scotland, and must also provide information on revisions and supersessions and on the right of appeal.[37]

If the calculation was made following an application from a child in Scotland and that child is no longer a qualifying child, the CMS must notify the PWC, NRP and any other children aged 12 or over who are potential child applicants that the calculation has been cancelled.[38]

Notes

1. **Making decisions about child support**
1 s2 CSA 1991
2 CCS/1037/1995
3 s2 CSA 1991
4 *Brookes v SSWP* [2010] EWCA Civ 420
5 *R v Secretary of State for Social Security ex parte Biggin* [1995] 2 FCR 595, [1995] 1 FLR 851
6 s1(1) CSA 1991; *Brookes v SSWP* [2010] EWCA Civ 420
7 *Brookes v SSWP* [2010] EWCA Civ 420
8 *Smith v SSWP* [2006] UKHL 35

2. **The initial child support decision**
9 s11 CSA 1991
10 Reg 5 CSMC Regs
11 Sch 1 para 15 CSA 1991; regs 13 and 18(2)-(4) CSMC Regs
12 s11(2) CSA 1991
13 R(CS) 2/98
14 Reg 24 CSMC Regs

3. **Default maintenance decisions**
15 s12(1) CSA 1991
16 Reg 49 CSMC Regs
17 Reg 25(2) CSMC Regs
18 Reg 24(2) CSMC Regs
19 s16(1B) CSA 1991; reg 14(3) CSMC Regs

4. **Notification of decisions**
20 Regs 24 and 25 CSMC Regs
21 *R (Anufrijeva) v SSHD* [2004] 1 AC 604; *SSWP v AM (IS)* [2010] UKUT 428 (AAC)
22 Regs 24(1), 25(1) and 26 CSMC Regs
23 Reg 24(2) CSMC Regs
24 Regs 24(2) and 26(2) CSMC Regs
25 Reg 27A(3) CSMC Regs
26 Reg 25(3) CSMC Regs

5. **When liability for child support starts (the 'effective date')**
27 Reg 12 CSMC Regs
28 Regs 7, 11 and 12 CSMC Regs
29 Reg 5 CSMC Regs

6. **When a calculation ends**
30 ss4(5) and (6) and 7(6) and (7) CSA 1991
31 Sch 1 para 16 CSA 1991
32 *SM v CMEC* [2010] UKUT 435 (AAC); *GR v CMEC* [2011] UKUT 101 (AAC); *TB v SSWP and RB (CSM)* [2017] UKUT 218 (AAC)
33 s44(1) CSA 1991
34 Reg 18(3) CSMC Regs
35 s16(3) CSA 1991
36 s17(4) CSA 1991
37 Regs 24 and 27 CSMC Regs
38 Reg 27(2) CSMC Regs

Chapter 7

Collecting and paying child support

This chapter covers:

1. Introduction

Once a decision on liability for, and the amount of, child support has been made, payment can be made in different ways. The non-resident parent (NRP) can pay directly to the person with care (PWC) without the payment going through the Child Maintenance Service (CMS). Alternatively, the CMS can collect and enforce child support,[1] and certain other maintenance payments (see p143).[2] **Note:** the CMS usually refers to the NRP as the 'paying parent' and the PWC as the 'receiving parent'.

Fees are charged for using the CMS's collection service (see p136) and when some types of enforcement action are taken (see p188).[3]

A payment schedule is provided with any final maintenance calculation. If payments are not maintained according to the payment schedule, arrears accrue, and debt management or enforcement action may be taken. If child support is being paid direct to the PWC, they must report any missed or short payments to the CMS before any debt management action or enforcement action is taken. If the NRP has arrears, see Chapter 8.

The CMS does not have discretion about the amount of child support due.[4] The amount of child support cannot be altered, except by a revision, supersession, appeal or variation. The CMS does not suspend the current collection just because the NRP states that they cannot afford to pay. However, it may agree to lower payments if a decision on a revision, supersession, appeal or variation is pending (see p151).

Decisions on how payment is enforced *are* discretionary and should take into account all the circumstances of the individual case and the welfare of any child(ren) likely to be affected (see p124). This should allow scope for negotiation between the CMS and the individuals involved. Ask the CMS to investigate the circumstances fully in order to allow it to use its discretion appropriately.

2. **Payment of child support**

The Child Maintenance Service (CMS) can require the non-resident parent (NRP) to pay child support:[5]

- directly to the person with care (PWC); *or*
- directly to a child applicant in Scotland; *or*
- to, or via, the CMS, provided the PWC, NRP or child applicant in Scotland has requested this; *or*
- to, or via, another person.

The CMS has broad discretion to decide how payment is to be arranged. This includes the payment of any collection or enforcement fees.[6] Before making these decisions, the CMS must, as far as possible, give the NRP and the PWC an opportunity to make representations and must take these into account.[7]

Direct payment

The CMS prefers the parties to agree that child support should be paid by the NRP directly to the PWC. If direct payments are agreed, once the CMS has calculated the amount owed, the parties make their own arrangement about when and how payments will be made. This is known as **'direct pay'**. If the PWC (or child applicant in Scotland) requests a direct pay arrangement, the CMS must comply.

The CMS informs each parent about the amount of any initial arrears and regular payments due, and the date regular payments should start. The CMS will also inform the parties about the amount of collection fees they have avoided by using direct pay. It recommends payment by standing order or a money transfer service (such as PayPal or MoneyGram) if the PWC does not want to disclose financial details to the NRP. If the PWC does not provide bank details but the CMS still considers that a direct pay arrangement is appropriate, the NRP will be advised to store up the child support payments due until the PWC provides bank details.

Direct payments are not monitored by the CMS. Both parties should therefore keep careful records of the payments made. If the payment arrangement breaks down, the PWC can ask to use the collection service (see p135).

A NRP using direct pay must pay the full amount of child support due, according to the payment schedule. If the parties want to agree to lower payments, the CMS will encourage the parties to close the case and make a family-based arrangement.

Note: if the NRP in a closed '1993 rules' or '2003 rules' case who has transferred to the '2012 rules' was subject to enforced methods of payment (such as a deduction from earnings order) for the old case, the CMS offers a **'compliance opportunity'**. This is an opportunity to comply voluntarily (eg, by paying by direct debit or one of the other voluntary methods of payment – see p138) over the first six months of the '2012 rules' case. During this period, in most cases, half of the child support due is paid by voluntary methods, and half by a deduction from earnings order (see p161) or by deduction from a bank account (see p169) in order to safeguard some payment. The NRP is only then offered the option of 'direct pay' if payment is made on time and in full throughout the six-month period. If there is a refusal or a failure to comply, enforced methods of payment continue.[8]

If the NRP receives benefits at the start of this compliance opportunity, or during the period, the above does not apply. The case is administered by the CMS's collection service and child support payments are made by deductions from benefit in the usual way (see p139). A decision on whether the NRP is likely to pay, and should be allowed to make direct payments, is made on the information already available. If considered likely to pay, the case is administered under 'direct pay'. If not, it continues under the collection service, with the collection fees due (see p136).[9]

The collection service

The PWC (or child applicant in Scotland) can request that payment of child support be made via the CMS.[10] The CMS calls this collection service **'collect and pay'**. The NRP pays child support to the CMS, which then passes it on to the PWC. The CMS can only provide the collection service if the PWC (or child applicant in Scotland) requests the service.[11] It can only do so if the NRP agrees, or if the CMS thinks that payment is unlikely otherwise.[12] The NRP may at any time apply to switch to 'direct pay' without the agreement of the PWC, but the CMS will only agree to that if it considers it to be in the best interests of the qualifying child(ren). The CMS must agree if a PWC asks to switch to direct pay.[13]

If the NRP receives benefits, the PWC may want to use the collection service to obtain direct deductions from the benefits. This is particularly useful if a voluntary arrangement cannot be reached. However, there is a collection fee for direct deductions from benefits through the collection service (see p139).

The collection service can be requested at a later date – eg, if payments become irregular. The request can be made quickly through the online portal, verbally or in writing.

If the collection service is being used, the CMS has discretion to decide:

- the method by which the NRP pays;[14] *and*
- the person to whom child support is paid;[15] *and*
- the method by which payment is made to the PWC;[16] *and*
- the timing of payments;[17] *and*
- the amount of payments towards any arrears.[18]

The CMS must notify the NRP in writing of a payment schedule setting out the amounts and timing of payments due, to whom and how the payments must be made, and details of any overdue or outstanding sums. If a previous '1993 rules' or '2003 rules' case has been closed and outstanding arrears were transferred to the new computer system when the parties applied under the '2012 rules', this notice must also refer to those outstanding arrears.[19] The notice is sent as soon as possible after the child support calculation is made and again after any change in the details in the notice.[20] A copy is sent to the PWC.

Only payments actually received by the CMS can be passed on. The CMS aims to make the first payment to the PWC within six weeks of making the initial payment arrangements with the NRP. It also aims to transfer payments as soon as it receives them and no later than one week after receiving them from the NRP.

Using the collection service removes the need for direct contact between the NRP and PWC. It should also help ensure regular payments by starting enforcement action (see p159) as soon as payments are missed, although this does not always happen.

Even if the collection service is used, you should always keep your own records and evidence of payments in case you need to query the accuracy of arrears or the standard of service in handling payments. A payment statement is only issued on request, but only if there is reasonable doubt on the balance. Information about payments can be found through the online service (see p140).

Fees

Both the NRP and the PWC must pay regular fees if the 'collect and pay' service is used.[21] These are intended to encourage people to make direct payments instead.[22]

The following fees apply.[23]

- The NRP must pay an additional fee of 20 per cent of the child support liability for each day for which 'collect and pay' arrangements are in place. If child support is being paid to more than one PWC and not all are paid by 'collect and pay', the fee is only charged on those payments for which 'collect and pay' has been arranged.[24]
- Four per cent of the amount of child support due is deducted before paying the PWC.[25]

If the amount actually paid by the NRP is lower than the amount due, the CMS still deducts a fee of 4 per cent of the amount paid before making the payment of child support to the PWC; so the payment is split proportionately between child support and fees.[26]

Example

Greg is the NRP of four children who live with his former partner, Nicole. Greg has been assessed as liable to pay £35 a week in child support to Nicole. If the collection service is used, Greg must, in fact, pay £42 a week (£35 + (20% x £35)) to the CMS.

The CMS also deducts £1.40 (4% x £35) from the child support due to Nicole, so she receives £33.60 a week. The balance of £8.40 a week is retained by the CMS.

If the calculation of fees results in a fraction of a penny, this is disregarded if it is less than a half. If a half or over, it is rounded up to the next penny.[27]

In certain circumstances up until 21 May 2021, the CMS could waive the fees for cases which are related to previous '2003 rules' or '1993 rules' cases that were subject to enforced methods of payment (such as a deduction from earnings order) and which have now been closed (see p1). This power is used for a limited period to allow the NRP a 'compliance opportunity' (see p135) to determine whether it is appropriate to allow direct payment. In order to manage the 'compliance opportunity', payments must be administered by 'collect and pay'. Fees could be waived if:[28]

- the PWC, NRP and qualifying child in a '2012 rules' application are the same as in a previous '2003 rules' or '1993 rules' case; *and*
- a notice of ending of liability was issued on or after 23 May 2016 in relation to the previous case; *and*
- the previous case was one in which payment was being enforced on the date the notice of ending of liability was issued; *and*
- the new application under the '2012 rules' was made before liability in the previous case ended; *and*
- the CMS has specified that child support due under the new '2012 rules' calculation is to be paid by certain methods (eg, standing order, direct debit, automated credit transfer, credit card, debit card, cheque, postal order, banker's draft or cash), or by a combination of one of those methods and a deduction from earnings order (see p161), in order to allow the NRP to demonstrate that they are still likely to pay without an enforced method of payment; *and*
- the first payment made in accordance with these payment arrangements is the first payment of child support due under the '2012 rules' calculation.

In such cases, collection fees could only be waived from the effective date of the '2012 rules' calculation to the date the CMS decides that the payment arrangements are to end – ie, the end of the 'compliance opportunity', usually expected to be the first six months of the '2012 rules' calculation. The power for the CMS to waive fees in these cases ended on 22 May 2021.[29]

If someone is both a person with care and a non-resident parent

In some child support calculations, someone might be both a PWC and a NRP at the same time – eg, if the qualifying children from a relationship live with different parents after the relationship has ended. In this situation, both parents may be liable to pay child support to each other and a separate calculation is made for each. The CMS can offset their liabilities so that only the person liable to pay the higher amount pays, and the other person's liability is treated as having been satisfied. This can only be done if the collection service is being used[30] (where direct pay is used, parties could arrange between themselves to offset liabilities so that only one party pays the net amount due).

Example

Ali and Nazia have two children, Mohammed and Faisal. When they separate, Mohammed lives with Ali and Faisal lives with Nazia. Both parents apply to use the collection service. Ali works full time and is liable to pay child support of £60 a week. Nazia works part time and is liable to pay child support of £20 a week.

Instead of the CMS collecting and distributing two sets of payments, it deducts Nazia's liability from Ali's:

£60 – £20 = £40

Ali pays Nazia £40 per week. Nazia does not pay anything.

If someone's liability is offset in this way, collection fees are only calculated on the net amount paid, rather than on the actual liabilities – ie, in the above example, Ali pays £48 a week (£40 plus 20 per cent) and Nazia receives £38.40 a week (£40 minus 4 per cent).

If each party to a child support calculation is both a NRP and a PWC and each falls into arrears, these arrears can also be offset so that the CMS only has to pursue the party with the largest debt (see p153).[31] **Note:** any enforcement charges related to arrears must still be paid by each parent.

Method of payment

The CMS can specify that the NRP make payments by whichever of the following methods it considers appropriate:[32]

- standing order;
- direct debit;
- automated credit transfer;
- credit card;
- debit card;
- cheque;
- postal order;
- banker's draft;

- voluntary deductions from earnings (a deductions from earnings order can also be used as a method of enforcing payment if the NRP has arrears or fails to agree a payment method – see p161);
- cash.

If the collection service is being used, the CMS asks for payment to be made by standing order, direct debit or by deductions from earnings. The CMS can direct a NRP to take all reasonable steps to open a bank account for the purposes of payment of child support and any collection fees.[33] However, there is no penalty for failing to do so.

When deciding the method of payment, the CMS should give the parties the opportunity to make representations and must take these into account.[34]

If the NRP gets certain benefits, the CMS normally deducts the amount for child support directly from the benefits before the NRP receives them (see below).

If payment is made via the CMS, the PWC is usually paid by automated credit transfer, unless the CMS considers that it is necessary to use another method.[35] The PWC is asked to provide details of a bank, building society or post office account. If you do not have an account, or experience difficulty opening one, contact the CMS.

Deductions from benefit

If a NRP getting benefits is required to pay child support at the flat rate (see p58), this may pay be paid directly to the PWC. Direct pay is available in the same way as for other NRPs. However, the CMS prefers that NRPs getting benefits use 'collect and pay' (see p135).

If the collection service is being used, the CMS asks Jobcentre Plus to make a deduction of the child support liability from the NRP's benefit. Although child support is calculated weekly, the frequency of the deductions aligns with the frequency of the benefit payments.

Deductions can be made from the benefits that qualify a NRP for the flat rate, including from universal credit (UC) if the NRP has earned income (see p58).[36]

If someone should be paying at the flat rate but a variation has been made which results in the reduced or basic rate being applicable instead, deductions can be made towards the new amount of child support calculated.

If a NRP and their partner are get one of the means-tested benefits that qualify for the flat rate (see p58) and each is a NRP, the flat-rate deduction of £7 is split between them so that each contributes half the amount to their respective PWC.[37]

The CMS requests any deduction and Jobcentre Plus must make it in full wherever possible. The parent must be left with at least 10 pence a week (one penny for UC).[38] Partial deductions are not made. The deduction for child support is always made, whatever other deductions are due.

Note: deductions from benefit also cover any fees due, making the total deduction £8.40 a week (the amount received by the PWC therefore being £6.72

– ie, £7 minus 4 per cent). If the NRP was offered a 'compliance opportunity' at the start of the '2012 rules' case (see p135) and has been accepted as likely to pay voluntarily, deductions from benefits do not include an element for collection fees.[39]

Both the PWC and the NRP are notified that deductions are to be made.

If there are arrears of child support, see p152.

Timing of payments

Whether direct pay or collect and pay is used, the CMS calculates the total amount of child support (and any collection fees) due to be paid over a 'reference period' of 52 weeks, beginning on the effective date (see p129) or on the annual review date (see p73).[40] This total amount due is based on the assumption that the amount of child support will remain unchanged for the 52-week period. The NRP is then required to pay child support in equal instalments. The frequency of payments (usually weekly or monthly) is agreed with the NRP, and is usually at the same frequency as the wages are paid if they are employed. The NRP is sent a 'payment plan', showing how much is due to be paid, the start and end dates of the reference period and the frequency of payments. The PWC is sent an 'expected payment plan' showing the same information. New payment plans are issued if the amount due changes.

Unless undue hardship would be caused to any of the parties, the frequency of payments to the PWC is the same as the frequency set for the NRP's payments (but see p165 for deduction from earnings orders).[41]

Unless payments are to be by direct debit or standing order, the NRP is advised to make each payment three to four days before the due date in order to ensure that payments are received on time and to avoid arrears. Clearance times are allowed for each method of payment, but the CMS aims to make payments to the PWC within a week of receiving them from the NRP. If a delay in payments is caused by maladministration on the part of the CMS, the PWC may wish to complain and claim compensation (see Chapter 11).

Records and evidence of payments

It is important to keep records of both the payments made and received, in case mistakes are made. Records can be in the form of bank statements or receipts if payments are made in cash. If either party disputes the amount that the CMS says is owed, the reasons for the dispute can be presented to the CMS along with a request for a statement of transactions and calculations. If this is not provided, a complaint can be made (see Chapter 11).

Overpayments

An overpayment can arise because:

- a calculation has been changed and the amount of child support due for a past period has been reduced; *or*
- the NRP has paid more than the regular payment due for some other reason (including making voluntary payments in the initial payment period); *or*
- there has been a CMS error.

If the CMS receives an unexpected payment from the NRP, it should check to determine the reason for this – eg, it could be for an overdue collection to offset arrears or an amount towards a future collection.

If there is an overpayment, the CMS has discretion about how it deals with it.[42] The amount may be allocated to reduce arrears due under a previous calculation involving the same parties or, if there are no arrears, it can be used to reduce the amount payable under the current calculation.[43] Adjustments may also be made if there are overpayments of voluntary payments in the initial payment period (see p147) or if the NRP makes other payments to the PWC or to a third party (see p142) that can be treated as being in lieu of child support.[44] If this is the case, the CMS first makes adjustments to balance out the overpayment.

An adjustment of the amount due under the current child support calculation may reduce the amount to nil.[45] If it does, the PWC does not receive any more child support until the overpayment has been recovered.

If all, or some, of an overpayment made by the NRP remains after offsetting it against regular child support, arrears and other liability, the CMS can make a refund to the NRP.[46] That is a discretionary decision. Refunds are only usually made if there are no overdue collections or arrears on the case.

The CMS should refund overpayments made because of CMS error – eg, if a person was told to pay more than the calculation required or if the CMS failed to act on information that would have resulted in the child support liability being reduced or cancelled. If you are in a situation like that, you may also wish to complain and request compensation (see Chapter 11).

Recovery of overpayments from the person with care

Allocating overpayments against arrears or regular child support payments is a discretionary decision, and so the PWC may wish to negotiate with the CMS about the rate at which the amount is to be recovered, or for repayment to be made in a different way.

If it is not possible to reduce previous arrears or regular child support payments (perhaps because there is no current calculation and no arrears owed), or if the CMS decides that recovering arrears in this way is not appropriate, it can still decide to reimburse all or part of an overpayment directly to a NRP.[47] If the CMS reimburses the NRP, it can recover all, or part, of it from the PWC if they have benefited from being overpaid.[48] This also applies to reimbursing overpayments caused by the NRP making voluntary payments.[49]

The CMS aims to recover all overpayments, and contacts the PWC to ask for repayment and to discuss options for how repayment will be made. However, recovery of an overpayment from the PWC is not enforceable if there is no current child support calculation in force. If the PWC does not agree to make the repayment, recovery is suspended. An overpayment cannot be recovered from the PWC if they were receiving income support, income-based jobseeker's allowance (JSA), income-related employment and support allowance or pension credit (PC) at any time during the period in which the overpayment occurred or on the date the NRP was reimbursed.[50] Recovery of an overpayment also becomes temporarily unenforceable when a PWC starts to receive benefits, such as PC or income-based JSA, and it should be suspended. It may be reconsidered for recovery at a future date. In addition, the CMS cannot enforce the recovery of overpayments caused by its own administrative error, but the PWC will be asked whether they are prepared to repay them.

All decisions relating to recovery of overpayments are discretionary. The CMS must consider the welfare of any child(ren) likely to be affected by the decision (see p124). Before allocating overpayments against arrears or regular child support payments, the CMS must also consider, in particular:[51]

- the circumstances of the NRP and PWC; *and*
- the amount of the overpayment and the period over which it would be reasonable to adjust the child support payable in order to rectify the overpayment.

If you dispute whether an overpayment should be recovered from you, or if it appears to have been caused by an administrative error by the CMS, you should obtain advice. You may wish to complain (see Chapter 11) about any maladministration, taking into account all the loss and inconvenience caused. You should argue that a past overpayment caused by an error by the CMS should not have an impact on you and your child(ren) now.

Payments made to a third party

The CMS can treat certain payments made to a third party (eg, a mortgage lender) as payments of child support. This can include voluntary payments made between the effective date and the date of the calculation (used to offset any initial arrears – see p147) and payments made after the effective date.[52]

If the PWC agrees to receive payments from the NRP outside the usual child support collection service (eg, if a NRP agrees to pay an urgent utility bill on behalf of the PWC), these may be offset against the amount of child support owed by the NRP.[53] Payments can only be offset if child support is collected by the CMS's collection service.[54] The amount can be offset against any arrears owed, or from the ongoing liability if there are no arrears.

For a payment to be offset, it must have been agreed by the PWC and must be for one of the following, in relation to the home in which the qualifying child lives:[55]

- a mortgage or loan either to purchase the property or to pay for essential repairs to it;
- rent on the property;
- mains-supplied gas, water or electricity charges;
- council tax payable by the PWC;
- essential repairs to the heating system;
- essential repairs to 'maintain the fabric' of the home.

NRPs who pay child support directly can reach their own offsetting agreement, but the CMS does not monitor it.[56]

If the CMS intends to reduce ongoing payments of child support to the PWC, it should take into account the circumstances of both parties and the period over which it would be reasonable to adjust the payments.[57] If the current calculation is adjusted, the amount payable may be reduced to nil.[58]

The decision to offset payments made to third parties is discretionary and there is no right of appeal against it. If you are unhappy, you could complain about how the CMS has used its discretion (see Chapter 11).

Note: if parents make and accept voluntary 'non-scheme' payments, the CMS is likely to try to encourage them to make a private family-based arrangement rather than using the statutory scheme.

3. Collection of other payments

The Child Maintenance Service (CMS) can collect and enforce other forms of maintenance if child support is being collected.[59] Some parents may have, for example, 'top-up' maintenance under a court order in addition to child support (see p17).

The CMS's power to collect other maintenance is discretionary. The CMS can only collect other maintenance that falls due after it gives the non-resident parent (NRP) written notice that it will do so.[60]

The following payments under a court order can be collected by the CMS:[61]

- additional child maintenance in excess of the CMS maximum;
- maintenance for a child's education or training;
- maintenance paid to meet the additional expenses of a child with a disability;
- maintenance paid for a stepchild – ie, a child living with the person with care (PWC) who is not a qualifying child, but who was accepted by the NRP as a member of their family when the child used to live with them;
- spousal or civil partner maintenance for a PWC of a child for whom child support is being collected.

The methods used by the CMS for collecting and enforcing other types of maintenance are the same as for child support.[62] If a NRP is paying more than one type of maintenance and pays less than the total amount required, they should stipulate how the amounts are to be allocated. The CMS allocates as requested, except that if arrears of child support are specified, current child support is paid before arrears. If the NRP does not stipulate, the CMS has discretion on how to apportion the payments.[63]

Collection of court costs

If the CMS applies to a court to decide whether a person is a parent, the court can order them to pay the CMS's costs in bringing the case to court, including the costs of any DNA tests (see p45).

The CMS negotiates with the liable person about how these costs should be paid. It initially requests immediate payment of the full amount due, but may accept payment by instalments.

Payment of these costs can only be enforced through further court action – the rules for enforcement of child support (see p159) do not apply. The relevant court is the county court in England and Wales or the sheriff court in Scotland. If the case is contested, a hearing is arranged in the court with jurisdiction for the area in which the parent lives. The usual debt enforcement procedures can be applied by the court.

Notes

1. **Introduction**

1 s29(1) CSA 1991
2 s30(1) CSA 1991
3 DWP, *Supporting Separated Families: securing children's futures*, Cm 8399, July 2012; CSF Regs
4 R(CS) 9/98

2. **Payment of child support**

5 s29 CSA 1991; reg 2 CS(C&E) Regs
6 Reg 1(2A) CS(C&E) Regs
7 Reg 6 CS(C&E) Regs
8 Written ministerial statement by the Minister for State, DWP, House of Commons, *Hansard*, 20 May 2013, col 58WS; CS(DOF) Regs, Explanatory Memorandum
9 CS(DOF) Regs, Explanatory Memorandum
10 s29(1)(b) CSA 1991
11 s29(1)(b) CSA 1991
12 ss4(2) and (2A) and 7(3) and (3A) CSA 1991
13 DWP, *Supporting Separated Families: securing children's futures*, Cm 8399, July 2012
14 Reg 3 CS(C&E) Regs
15 Reg 2 CS(C&E) Regs
16 Reg 5 CS(C&E) Regs
17 Reg 4 CS(C&E) Regs
18 Reg 4 CS(MPA) Regs
19 Reg 7(1) CS(C&E) Regs
20 Reg 7(2) CS(C&E) Regs
21 s6 CMOPA 2008; CSF Regs 2014

22 DWP, *Supporting Separated Families: securing children's futures*, Cm 8399, July 2012
23 DWP, *Supporting Separated Families: securing children's futures*, Cm 8399, July 2012
24 Reg 7(2) CSF Regs 2014
25 Reg 7(3) CSF Regs 2014
26 DWP, *Government Response to the Consultation Supporting Separated Families: securing children's futures*, Cm 8742, November 2013; reg 7(3) CSF Regs 2014
27 Reg 7(5) CSF Regs 2014
28 Reg 12A CSF Regs 2014; CS(DOF) Regs, Explanatory Memorandum
29 Reg 1(2) CS(DOF) Regs
30 s41C(3) CSA 1991; reg 5 CS(MPA) Regs
31 Reg 7 CS(MPA) Regs
32 Reg 3(1) CS(C&E) Regs
33 Reg 3(2) CS(C&E) Regs
34 Reg 6 CS(C&E) Regs
35 Reg 5(1) CS(C&E) Regs
36 s43 CSA 1991; Sch 9B SS(C&P) Regs; Sch 7 UC,PIP,JSA&ESA(C&P) Regs
37 Sch 1 para 4(2) CSA 1991; reg 44(2) and (3) CSMC Regs
38 Reg 35(l) and Sch 9B SS(C&P) Regs; Sch 7 para 2(4) UC,PIP,JSA&ESA(C&P) Regs
39 CS(DOF) Regs, Explanatory Memorandum
40 s29(3)(ca) and (3A) CSA 1991; reg 4 CS(C&E) Regs, as substituted by reg 4(1) CS(MOC&NCR) Regs
41 Reg 5(3) CS(C&E) Regs
42 Regs 8 and 9 CS(MPA) Regs
43 Reg 8 CS(MPA) Regs
44 Reg 9 CS(MPA) Regs
45 Regs 8(3) and 9(3) CS(MPA) Regs
46 s41B(2) CSA 1991
47 s41B(2) CSA 1991
48 s41B(3) and (4) CSA 1991
49 s41B(7) CSA 1991
50 Regs 10A and 10B CS(AIAMA) Regs
51 Regs 8(2) and 9(2) CS(MPA) Regs
52 Regs 6 and 7 CS(MPA) Regs
53 Reg 6 (1) CS(MPA) Regs
54 s41C(3) CSA 1991
55 Reg 6(3)(a)-(f) CS(MPA) Regs
56 CS(MPA) Regs, Explanatory Memorandum
57 Reg 7(2) CS(MPA) Regs
58 Reg 7(3) CS(MPA) Regs

3. **Collection of other payments**

59 s30 CSA 1991; CS(CEOFM) Regs
60 Reg 5 CS(CEOFM) Regs
61 Reg 2 CS(CEOFM) Regs
62 Regs 3 and 4 CS(CEOFM) Regs
63 s30(3) CSA 1991

8

Chapter 8

Arrears

This chapter covers:

1. Arrears

The Child Maintenance Service (CMS) can only act on arrears if child support is being collected and paid through its collection service (see p135).[1] If the collection service is being used, the CMS can take enforcement action as soon as payments are missed.

If a non-resident parent (NRP) pays child support directly to the person with care (PWC), the PWC must notify the CMS that payments have stopped. The CMS is otherwise not aware of this. The CMS may then decide to take enforcement action. If it does, it also starts managing ongoing future payments through the collection service. It does not pursue arrears if payments are being made directly, even if they arose from a past period when the collection service was being used. However, it can add the arrears to the payment schedule.

If direct payment arrangements break down and the case is moved onto the collection service (see p135), the CMS will ask for payment records for the time direct payment was in place, pursue arrears due for this time and charge fees (see p136) on these arrears.

Alternatively, if a private family-based arrangement for child maintenance is made instead, the CMS closes the case. It then treats it as an 'arrears-only' case and pursues the arrears.

The CMS cannot take enforcement action on non-payment of maintenance in a private agreement. If a private agreement breaks down, the PWC can apply to the CMS for child support instead. The CMS can pursue all arrears of child support from the date the child support calculation is requested, but not any missed payments under the private agreement before that date.

The CMS's priority is to collect arrears in cases where child support is still in payment, so that children for whom child support is being paid can benefit from the arrears recovered. Historic arrears in cases where child support is no longer being paid are a lower priority, and may be written off (see p156).

When '1993 rules' and '2003 rules' cases closed as part of the case closure process (see p1), and a new application for child support was made, any outstanding arrears from the closed cases were verified at that point and any further action to recover the arrears was considered (see p158).[2]

Initial arrears

A minimal period may exist between a child support calculation being made and its initial effective date (see p129), but this may create initial arrears. The initial arrears may be reduced if a voluntary payment is made in that initial period (see below).

The CMS draws up a 'payment plan', which shows payments for the following 12 months, including initial arrears. Written confirmation of the collection schedule is issued once the final maintenance calculation has been completed.

The written notification states:[3]

- the amount due and to whom it is to be paid; *and*
- how it is to be paid – ie, method, day and interval between payments; *and*
- any amounts that are overdue and outstanding.

The CMS may request payment of the initial arrears as a lump sum. If a NRP cannot pay this all at once, they may negotiate an agreement to pay in instalments or a collection schedule to cover both the initial payment and the ongoing liability (see p149).

If you think the calculation is wrong, you may be able to challenge the decision (see Chapters 9 and 10). If you object to the way the CMS is dealing with collecting the amount you owe, you can make a complaint (see Chapter 11).

Note: if a court order made on or after 3 March 2003 has been in force for more than a year and there is an application to the CMS, any payments due under that order which the NRP has made after the effective date are treated as payments of child support.[4] This helps to avoid additional liability for child support accumulating if there is a gap between the effective date (at which point the court order ceases to have effect) and the date the calculation is actually made. If the payments made under the court order are at a higher rate than those due under the calculation, this is treated as an overpayment of child support and the calculation can be adjusted accordingly.

Voluntary payments made in the initial period

If the NRP makes voluntary payments through the CMS (or, if the CMS agrees, directly to the PWC or a third party) after the effective date, but before the calculation is made and notified, these may be offset against arrears of child support.[5] The CMS may seek the views of the parties when considering whether a payment should be classed as a voluntary payment.[6] By accepting a payment as a voluntary payment, the CMS can be deemed to have agreed to its being made directly to the PWC or a third party.[7] As these are discretionary decisions, the CMS must consider the welfare of any child likely to be affected (see p124). There is no right of appeal against these decisions.

Only the following types of payment can be offset:[8]

- in lieu of child support;
- in respect of a mortgage or loan on the child's home, or for repairs or improvements to the property;
- rent on the child's home;
- mains gas, water or electricity at the child's home;
- council tax payable at the child's home;
- repairs to the heating system at the child's home;
- repairs to the child's home.

Payments can be made by cash, standing order, cheque, postal order, debit card or other method or arrangement from an account of the NRP or on their behalf – eg, credit card.[9]

If the payments are made to the CMS, it passes them on to the PWC. Once the CMS has made the calculation, the voluntary payments are offset against the initial arrears.

If the payments are made directly to the PWC or a third party, the CMS checks with the PWC whether payments have been made.[10] This is normally done by telephone. If the PWC confirms the payments, this is usually accepted without any further need for proof. If there is a dispute about whether a payment has been made, the CMS asks the NRP to verify the payments by providing bank statements, duplicates of cashed cheques, receipts, paid bills or invoices, or a written or verbal statement from the PWC.[11] It is in the interests of both parties to ensure payments are recorded, and the CMS should explain to the NRP the importance of keeping a record and provide a form on which to do so.

If either party disagrees with a decision about offsetting, a complaint may be made (see Chapter 11). There is no right of appeal.

If offsetting means that the NRP has overpaid child support, the calculation may be adjusted to compensate them, or a refund may be made.[12]

If the NRP makes payments outside the usual collection service after the calculation is made (eg, if they pay an urgent bill on behalf of the PWC), see p142.

Arrears notice

The CMS may begin to consider action to recover arrears when:

- a payment from the NRP to the CMS is not received; *or*
- child support is being paid directly to the PWC and that person informs the CMS that a payment due has not been received.

The CMS aims to respond quickly when a payment is missed.[13] Once notified of the missed payment, the CMS contacts the NRP to discuss the issue. Although contact may be by telephone or in writing, the majority of contacts are through the online portal. It is important to check the portal regularly for any communications issued.

If the NRP has missed one or more child support payments, the CMS must send them an arrears notice stating the amount of all the outstanding arrears owed. The notice also explains the rules about arrears and requests payment of the outstanding amount.[14]

The arrears notice only shows the total amount of outstanding arrears, and not an itemised list of unpaid payments. A request for a full list of payments due but not received can be requested. The online portal also provides details of arrears and of payments made for each year.

If you have received an arrears notice, you should check that the amount owed is correct and tell the CMS of any mistakes. If you think that the balance is incorrect, ask for a payment statement and compare this with your own records. It is important to keep the CMS informed so that it does not start enforcement action in the meantime.

The NRP can contact the CMS to negotiate payment of arrears by instalments (see below). Once an arrears notice has been issued, another does not have to be sent if arrears remain uncleared, unless the NRP has made all the arranged payments for a 12-week period.[15]

The CMS does not send an arrears notice if direct pay arrangements are in place, or the collection service is being used but no enforcement action is being taken, and the CMS has notified the NRP during the previous 12 months that it will consider taking collection and enforcement action if payments are missed. In this case, the CMS can take enforcement action and start managing ongoing payments if the NRP has missed one or more payments.[16] In practice, the CMS notifies the NRP at each annual review about the possibility of collection and enforcement action if payments are missed.

Negotiating repayments

If you receive an arrears notice, you should contact the CMS to negotiate an agreement to pay the arrears. This is often best achieved by contacting the CMS by telephone.

You can contact the CMS before this point – eg, when you receive the collection schedule or if you have difficulty making ongoing payments. The CMS does not normally agree to defer payment of a current liability, although it may decide not commence enforcement action if a revision, supersession or appeal is pending (see p151).

If you intend to pay the arrears, the CMS may:

- accept a delayed payment, setting a time limit for the receipt of payment; *or*
- reschedule the amount to include it within the arrears.

If you indicate that a change of circumstances is causing you difficulty in making payments, the CMS may investigate whether there should be a supersession (see p204). In all cases, if you want to co-operate, try to renegotiate an agreement in good time before any anticipated change in circumstances – eg, redundancy. If you have paid regularly and the change would reduce the amount due, the CMS may accept a lower amount. You could also try to negotiate a suspension in payments if your personal circumstances make it difficult or insensitive to enforce recovery – eg, if you are unemployed, sick or in prison.

The CMS has the discretion to make an agreement with a NRP about how arrears will be recovered. To avoid other methods of recovery, you should come to an agreement as soon as possible and comply with it.

There are no set rules about the level of payments or how quickly the arrears must be cleared. Although CMS staff always begin by requesting full payment of the outstanding arrears, it may be possible to reach an agreement to pay the amount in instalments. The CMS aims to agree repayment plans that are affordable and that will be kept to.

In making these discretionary decisions, the CMS must take into account the welfare of any child likely to be affected (see p124) and should consider:

- the needs of the NRP and of any new family; *and*
- any representations from the NRP about hardship; *and*
- the needs of the PWC and the qualifying child.

If you have other financial priorities (eg, fuel) or other large debts, you should get independent money advice: preparing a financial statement and sending it to the CMS may assist in reaching an agreement. However, existing arrangements with other creditors may have to be renegotiated to take into account the child support calculation. As the CMS has several methods of recovery available, it is unlikely to agree to a NRP making low payments over a very long period. It is in your interests to come to an agreement in order to avoid further enforcement action, and to keep the CMS informed so that it does not assume that you are refusing to co-operate. For more information on preparing a financial statement and negotiating with creditors, see CPAG's *Debt Advice Handbook* (available free on AskCPAG.org.uk).

The CMS aims to make arrears agreements that will collect the arrears within two years, at a rate of up to 40 per cent of a NRP's net income, and also ensure that ongoing child support payments continue to be made.[17]

It may accept a plan to pay arrears by instalments over more than two years, but it may seek to obtain a liability order (see p180) if there will be more than £1,000 outstanding at the end of two years. A liability order gives the CMS the power to use a wide range of methods to enforce payment, should the plan not be completed. The CMS may also consider other methods of recovery.

Repayments spread over several years may help NRPs who are in financial hardship, but this means that the PWC receives payments very late and may want to make representations to the CMS. No interest is paid to the PWC in respect of arrears. If arrears have accrued because of CMS delay or error, you may wish to make a complaint and request compensation (see Chapter 11).

The PWC and qualifying children are not consulted about the level at which arrears are collected, but are informed when the decision has been made. This practice may be contrary to the European Convention on Human Rights' protection of private property,[18] but there has been no reported caselaw on this point (see also p190: a PWC cannot directly enforce the payment of child support).

If the non-resident parent does not reach an agreement or defaults

The CMS aims to take prompt action on arrears. If a repayment agreement is not reached, legal enforcement should begin. There is no set timescale for how quickly action should begin if no arrangement has been agreed, but it should begin as quickly as possible.[19]

If the NRP fails to reach or keep a repayment agreement:

- a penalty payment may be imposed,[20] although in practice, this power is not currently used; *and*
- a deduction from earnings order or other method of enforcement may be considered (see p159).

The CMS informs the NRP of its powers to collect and enforce child support. This information is also available through the online portal.

If there is a revision, supersession, variation or appeal pending

The CMS may suspend the collection of arrears if a decision on a revision, supersession, variation or appeal is pending. If the calculation is likely to be reduced, the CMS may agree to suspend collection of some of the ongoing payments. However, this does not happen often; the CMS prefers to speed up considering the case and aims to supersede calculations to reflect changes quickly in order to minimise arrears.[21]

If you are a NRP and have requested a revision, supersession or appeal and you are having problems paying current child support or any arrears, ask the CMS for lower regular payments.

Payment of arrears

Arrears do not have to be paid by the same method as ongoing child support payments – eg, they could be collected via the CMS, with ongoing payments made directly to the PWC. However, in practice, the CMS prefers to use the same method of payment for both.

Arrears of child support may be retained by the CMS and not passed to the PWC if they are in respect of a period before 12 April 2010 during which time the PWC (or their partner) was getting income support, income-based jobseeker's allowance, income-related employment and support allowance or pension credit (before this date, when considering means-tested benefits, child support payments were treated as income and so, had the arrears been paid before then, the benefits of the PWC would have been reduced accordingly).

The CMS can keep any arrears payments that would not have been passed to the PWC had the child support been paid when due[22] – ie, the CMS can retain an amount equal to the difference between the amount of benefit that was paid to the PWC and the amount that would have been paid had the NRP not been in arrears.[23] Payments of arrears are allocated between the CMS and the PWC in the same way as overpayments (see p141).

If the NRP makes a payment, the CMS normally allocates it first to paying off any fees or charges due to the CMS, then to paying ongoing child support liability, then to payment of arrears (firstly to '2012 rules' case arrears, then to any arrears on previous closed '1993 rules' or '2003 rules' cases).[24] When money is owed to more than one PWC and they are each due the same category of payment (eg, they are both owed ongoing child support or both owed '2012 rules' cases arrears), the payment is apportioned between the PWCs according to the amount owed to each. Priority is given to child support which became due first. These are discretionary decisions, and so the CMS should consider the welfare of any child likely to be affected by the decision (see p124).

Example

Justin is a NRP who owes Amira £400 and Bella £200 for arrears of child support. The debts are of the same category and became due on the same date when Justin missed payments. If Justin makes a payment of £300, this is apportioned between Amira and Bella based on the amount each is owed. Amira receives £200 and Bella receives £100.

If Amira's debt had become due before Bella's, the whole £300 payment would be made to Amira. Only when the debt to her had been cleared would payments be made to Bella.

If the non-resident parent is on benefit

If the NRP is in receipt of one of the benefits that would qualify them for the flat rate (see p58), a deduction of £8.40 a week may be made from the benefit towards any child support arrears. That also applies if the NRP or their partner gets universal credit (UC) and has earnings, provided their income level would otherwise qualify to pay the flat rate.[25] This deduction is a £7 payment towards arrears, plus a 20 per cent collection fee. The CMS retains that part of the deduction that is for fees.[26]

Deductions for arrears are separate to other deductions made from benefits and are not affected by the priority rules to decide which deductions should be made first. For more information on the priority rules on deductions from benefits, see CPAG's *Welfare Benefits and Tax Credits Handbook*.

The CMS cannot deduct an amount for both arrears and ongoing child support at the same time, so the maximum that can be deducted from a parent's benefits is £8.40 a week.

If you are a PWC and you believe that arrears owed by a NRP who gets benefits and is paying ongoing child support should be pursued in some other way, contact the CMS to explain your reasons. If the CMS is unwilling to take action, a complaint may be made (see Chapter 11).

Offsetting arrears

'Offsetting' is a way of balancing payments or arrears that are owed by a PWC and a NRP to each other, so that the CMS only has to pursue arrears from one of them. Similarly, the amount of child support a NRP is required to pay can be reduced to take account of arrears owed to them by the other person for a period when they were a PWC. Offsetting therefore reduces any arrears due under any current or previous child support calculation made in respect of the same relevant people – ie, a PWC and NRP (and child applicant in Scotland).[27]

Arrears may be offset if:

- a NRP becomes a PWC; *or*
- arrears are owed by both parties to a calculation.

Example

Ricky and Lara divorced five years ago. They have one child, Noah, who has lived with Lara since the divorce. Lara applied for child support and used the collection service. However, Ricky has not paid child support regularly for the past few years. Noah decides that he wants to live with Ricky, who becomes the PWC. Lara is now the NRP. If Ricky applies for child support, the amount that Lara must pay to Ricky each week can be reduced as a way of recovering the arrears still owed to her.

Noah has lived with Ricky for two years. Lara made regular child support payments for the first year, but when Ricky moves in with his new partner, she starts to miss payments. Noah then returns to live with Lara, who becomes the PWC again. At this time, Lara owes Ricky £1,000 in arrears. However, there are still £500 arrears that are yet to be recovered from when Ricky was the NRP and did not make regular payments. Rather than both sets of arrears being pursued, Ricky's arrears are deducted from Lara's. Lara has to pay Ricky £500 in arrears. Only Lara is pursued for arrears. Ricky's liability under the new calculation could be reduced to recover these.

Arrears can only be offset in this way if the collection service is being used. Those with an arrangement to pay child support directly can reach their own offsetting agreements, but the CMS does not monitor them.[28] Offsetting is a discretionary power. The decision to offset arrears does not require the agreement of either parent, but the CMS should notify all relevant parties to the calculation when it is considering offsetting and ask for their views. You are given 14 days in which to respond. The CMS should take into account parents' wishes and should also have regard to the welfare of any child likely to be affected by the decision (see p124).[29]

If there are no arrears of child support due, or an amount remains to be offset after any arrears have been taken into account, the CMS can reduce the amount payable under the current calculation. When reducing ongoing payments to the PWC, the CMS should take into account the circumstances of all the parties and the period over which it would be reasonable to adjust payments. Payments can be reduced to nil.[30]

If the current child support calculation is reduced, either the PWC or the NRP can contact the CMS at any time to ask that it be reviewed. The CMS should then discuss with both parties alternative ways of collecting any outstanding arrears.[31]

Suspending or pausing arrears

In certain circumstances, the CMS may consider suspending or pausing collection of arrears.[32] When collection is suspended or paused, the arrears still remain due and are collectable. They are not written off as may be the case with other child support arrears. The decision to suspend or pause action will be reviewed at intervals of no longer than 12 months. Suspending or pausing collection of arrears is a discretionary decision, and so the CMS must consider the welfare of any child likely to be affected by the decision (see p124).

If the CMS considers that it will not be possible to recover arrears but writing off the arrears (see p156) is not appropriate, it may suspend action. If the CMS considers that it is temporarily impossible or inappropriate to pursue arrears, it may pause action. Circumstances in which arrears might be suspended or paused include:

- a NRP being in residential care and getting a benefit that would otherwise mean they would pay the flat rate;
- a PWC owing money (eg, due to having received an overpayment) but there are no arrears due to that person against which the money owed can be offset;
- enforcement action not being appropriate because a NRP is seriously ill and has reduced income, is in hospital or is in prison;
- the difficulties of negotiating an arrears agreement where a NRP is on active military duty in a war zone.

Arrears that are suspended or paused are still included in a CMS arrears notice (see p148), but the CMS will explain that they are suspended or paused and that this will be reviewed.

Accepting part payment in full and final settlement

In certain circumstances, the CMS can treat a part payment of arrears of child support owed by a NRP as 'full and final settlement' of all the arrears owed.[33] This flexibility is intended to act as an incentive for the NRP to pay at least something, where they may not otherwise have done so. Part payment can only be accepted for arrears of child support, not for ongoing liability or for other debt, such as fees for a DNA test or fees for enforcement action.

Before accepting a part-payment offer from the NRP, the CMS must obtain the written consent of the PWC (or child applicant in Scotland, and PWC of that child).[34]

The decision to accept an offer of part payment is discretionary. The CMS only uses this power if an offer is made by the NRP or suggested by the PWC. It then investigates the circumstances of the NRP, and also considers the likely success of continued enforcement action in recovering the full arrears.[35] The CMS must also consider the welfare of any child likely to be affected (see p124). See also p156 for when arrears may be written off.

If the CMS intends to accept the offer, it prepares a written agreement setting out:[36]

- the name of the NRP; *and*
- the name of the PWC (or child applicant in Scotland) if their consent is required (but see below); *and*
- the amount of arrears and the period to which they relate; *and*
- the amount that the CMS proposes to accept as settlement of those arrears; *and*
- to whom the amount will be paid to and by what method; *and*
- the date by which the payment must be made.

A copy is sent to the NRP and to each PWC (or child applicant in Scotland) affected for their agreement.[37]

If the CMS considers the offer to be unreasonable, it may decide not to contact the PWC. In some circumstances, it may insist on the full amount of the arrears being paid – eg, if it thinks that the NRP has the ability to pay and there is a reasonable prospect of recovering the arrears.[38]

If there are arrears due both to a PWC and to the Department for Work and Pensions (DWP) (ie, because, for a period prior to 12 April 2010, the PWC would have received less benefit if the child support due had been paid), any part payment agreed is first allocated to pay the PWC. **Note:** if it is only the DWP that will not be paid in full if the offer is accepted, the CMS does not need the consent of the PWC (or child applicant in Scotland) before accepting the offer.[39] In such a case, the CMS has discretion to decide whether the amount offered is reasonable in the NRP's current financial circumstances.

If the NRP has arrears that are due to more than one PWC, these are treated as separate amounts.[40] The CMS does not ask the NRP to identify which PWC should receive the part payment.[41] If the NRP does not state a preference, the CMS apportions the payment between them. Each PWC is notified of how much of the part payment they will receive if they agree to accept this as a full and final payment. If one or more PWC rejects the offer, the CMS may apportion the amount between those who have accepted it. Arrears due to those who have rejected the offer remain outstanding and are pursued by the CMS.

If the offer is accepted and the agreed payment made, the PWC cannot change their mind and ask the CMS to reinstate and pursue the arrears. So a PWC may wish to accept an offer where, for example, they would rather receive some arrears than wait for the enforcement process to run its course. If the NRP pays all of the agreed amount, the liability for any outstanding arrears ends. The CMS notifies all parties of this and it cannot take further action on the outstanding arrears.[42] If the NRP fails to make all of the agreed part payment, a liability remains for the full amount of the outstanding arrears and the CMS pursues recovery.[43] The CMS can make a further proposed agreement for part payment in the future, even if the NRP has failed to keep to the terms of a previous agreement. A new agreement replaces any previous one.[44]

The part payment offered must be paid in one lump sum and should be paid to the CMS. At some point in the future, part payments may be able to be made by instalments.[45] However, there are no plans to introduce this at present.

Writing off arrears

The CMS has the power to write off certain arrears.[46] (**Note:** this is separate from the power to accept part payment of arrears.) Before 10 December 2012, a decision not to pursue recovery resulted in the arrears being suspended, but the liability still remained. Suspended arrears can be revived by the CMS in certain circumstances, but many arrears have remained on record, even though there is no prospect of their ever being collected.

The power to write off arrears is limited. The CMS cannot write off debts relating to DNA test fees, fees for enforcement action and court costs. The CMS can only write off arrears if it considers that it would be unfair or inappropriate for it to enforce the liability and:[47]

- the PWC (or child applicant in Scotland) has requested that the CMS stop taking action on the arrears; *or*
- the PWC (or child applicant in Scotland) has died; *or*
- the NRP died before 25 January 2010 and it is not possible to recover the arrears from their estate; *or*
- the arrears have accrued from an interim maintenance assessment (see previous editions of this *Handbook* for details of these) in force between 5 April 1993 and 18 April 1995. These arrears are not legally recoverable;[48] *or*
- the NRP has been advised that the arrears have been permanently suspended and that no further action would ever be taken to recover them. This may happen if, for example, the arrears resulted from a delay (which was not the NRP's fault) in establishing child support liability; *or*
- in Scotland, the arrears relate to debt that is subject to sequestration (Scottish bankruptcy) once the period of sequestration has ended. Debt in these circumstances is not legally recoverable;[49] *or*

- in Scotland, the NRP has been subject to a protected trust deed (a formal agreement between a debtor and creditors) that has expired.[50] Arrears in these circumstances are also not legally recoverable; *or*
- the arrears relate to liability for child support in a closed '1993 rules' or '2003 rules' case in certain circumstances (see p158).

A request to write off the arrears can be made at any time.

The CMS has discretion as to whether to use this power to write off arrears. Before doing so, it must consider all the circumstances of an individual case, the principles of child support law and the welfare of any child affected by the decision.

If the NRP has arrears that are due to more than one PWC, these are treated as separate amounts and separate decisions are made.[51]

If it is considering writing off arrears, the CMS must give written notice to the PWC and to the NRP (and a child applicant in Scotland).[52] The notice may be in writing or sent electronically and must set out:[53]
- the PWC (or child applicant in Scotland) who is owed the arrears; *and*
- the amount of arrears and the period to which they relate; *and*
- the reasons why the CMS believes that it would be unfair or inappropriate to enforce the arrears; *and*
- the effect of writing off the arrears; *and*
- an explanation of the right to make representations to the CMS within 30 days of receiving the notice about the proposal to write off the arrears.

The notice is treated as being received two days after it was sent by the CMS to the person's last known or notified postal address, or if sent electronically it is treated as being received at the end of the following day.[54]

The requirement for the CMS to give written notice does not apply if:[55]
- the person in question has died or cannot be traced; *or*
- the arrears relate to debt that is subject to sequestration; *or*
- in certain circumstances, the arrears arise from liability for child support in closed '1993 rules' or '2003 rules' cases (see p158).

When making its decision, the CMS must consider any written representations made by any relevant party.[56] If no written representations are made within 30 days, the CMS can decide to write off the arrears.[57]

If the CMS decides to write off arrears, the debt is extinguished. The CMS must give written notice of its decision to the PWC (and a child applicant in Scotland) and to the NRP (unless the person in question has died or cannot be traced or, in certain circumstances, the arrears arise from liability for child support in closed '1993 rules' or '2003 rules' cases – see p158).[58]

If the CMS does not write off the arrears, it may continue to pursue recovery. There is no right of appeal against its decision.

If the CMS writes off arrears due to a PWC and the case is closed, the CMS can also write off any collection fees due.[59]

Arrears in closed cases

The DWP has said that it will use the closure of existing '1993 rules' and '2003 rules' cases (see p1) to validate arrears and to prioritise recovery action.[60]

Arrears in historic cases are only transferred to the CMS computer system once the arrears have been validated and checked for accuracy. Existing enforcement action on the historic case is expected to continue while the validation process is ongoing. The parties are informed of any balance of arrears that is transferred to CMS.

Once arrears have been validated and transferred, no new enforcement action is started by the CMS unless the NRP has failed to pay an ongoing liability in the '2012 rules' case. This means that, once enforcement action in the historic case has ended, no further enforcement action will be started until the CMS accepts that a direct payment arrangement (see p134) is not suitable in the '2012 rules' case.[61]

If a historic case has been closed and there are arrears, but no ongoing liability for child support in a new '2012 rules' case, action to recover the outstanding arrears is expected to be treated as low priority.[62]

If all attempts at administrative recovery have been exhausted, the CMS can consider writing off arrears that arise from liability for child support in closed '1993 rules' or '2003 rules' cases.[63] It intends to do this proactively to address historic arrears as it considers it too costly to maintain records of these arrears on its computer systems.[64]

The CMS can consider writing off these arrears if they are:[65]

- over £1,000 and the effective date in the case was on or before 1 November 2008; *or*
- over £500 and the effective date was after 1 November 2008; *or*
- over £500 and arose in a closed '1993 rules' or '2003 rules' case which has been transferred to the CMS computer system.

If the NRP has not made any payments within the previous three months, the CMS can send written notice to the PWC (or child applicant in Scotland), inviting them to make representations as to whether the arrears should be written off. Representations must be made by post or electronically within 60 days of receiving the notice.[66] The CMS describes this as an opportunity for the PWC to ask for a last attempt to be made to collect the arrears. Representations could include information (eg, about a NRP's current whereabouts, employment or assets) that could help with successful collection of the arrears. The CMS only takes action to attempt collection if it is cost-effective to do so and it is reasonably certain that action may be successful.[67] If no representations are made within 60 days, the CMS can decide to write off the arrears. In such a case, it does not need to notify the parties of its decision.[68]

If the CMS receives written representations within 60 days saying that the PWC (or child applicant in Scotland) wants the arrears to be collected, it then considers whether it can successfully collect the arrears and it gives written notice by post or electronically to the NRP. Written representations may be made within 21 days of receipt of the notice.[69]

In these cases, the notice to each party must include the usual information about the arrears (see p157), except that it does not have to set out the period to which the arrears relate (or, if the arrears are over £1,000 and the effective date was on or before 1 November 2008, the amount of the arrears).[70]

The CMS can then decide whether to write off the arrears. When making its decision, the CMS must consider any written representations made by any relevant party.[71] It must give written notice of its decision to the PWC (and a child applicant in Scotland) and NRP (unless the person in question has died or cannot be traced).[72]

The CMS can also consider writing off smaller arrears amounts. That can be done if the NRP has not made any payments within the previous three months and the arrears are:[73]

- £1,000 or less and the effective date in the case was on or before 1 November 2008; *or*
- £500 or less and the effective date was after 1 November 2008; *or*
- £500 or less and arose in a closed '1993 rules' or '2003 rules' case which has been transferred to the CMS computer system.

The CMS is not required to invite representations from the parties before making its decision. It must, however, give written notice, either by post or electronically of its decision to the PWC (and a child applicant in Scotland) and to the NRP (unless the person in question has died or cannot be traced).[74]

If the arrears are under £65 and no payment has been received in the last three months, the CMS can write off the arrears without giving notice of its decision to the parties.[75] There is no right of appeal against a CMS decision to write off arrears.

2. Enforcement action to recover arrears

The Child Maintenance Service (CMS) should usually consider enforcement action as soon as it is clear that the non-resident parent (NRP) has failed to keep to the agreed payment arrangements for child support and any fees due and has not responded to warnings. The CMS allows the NRP seven days to respond to an arrears notice and to pay the arrears due. If no response is received within this time and a suitable payment agreement has not been made, the CMS will consider whether to start enforcement action.

The CMS will first try enforcement methods for which it does not need a liability order and so no court action is required. The CMS refers to these as 'administrative action'. A liability order is *not* required for:

- a deduction from earnings order. This is usually appropriate when the NRP is employed (see p161); *or*
- making deductions from bank accounts. This is likely to be used if the NRP is not an employee (see p169), or if a deduction from earnings order is not an effective method of clearing the arrears; *or*
- collecting arrears from a deceased person's estate (see p178).

If the NRP continues not to comply, the CMS can also pursue what it calls 'legal enforcement' options. To pursue these options, the CMS must first obtain a **liability order** from the magistrates court or, in Scotland, sheriff court (see p180). After a liability order has been granted, the CMS may take additional measures including:

- register the debt with a credit reference agency without the consent of the NRP, which will affect the parent's credit rating and their ability to obtain a mortgage and other credit (see p53);
- taking control of and selling goods (see p182);
- pursuing the disqualification of the NRP from driving or from holding or obtaining a passport or other travel authorisation (see p186);
- pursuing the imprisonment of the NRP (see p187).

Note: the rules concerning the collection and enforcement of payments of child support also apply to payment of any fees due for enforcement action, except that the CMS cannot seek disqualification of the NRP from driving or from holding or obtaining a passport or other travel authorisation, or their imprisonment, when enforcement action is being taken solely to recover fees.[76]

Decisions about collection and enforcement are discretionary and so the CMS must take into account the welfare of any child likely to be affected by the decision (see p124). A decision concerning collection and enforcement cannot be challenged by seeking a revision and then appealing to the First-tier Tribunal.[77] However, certain enforcement decisions can be appealed in the courts. A deduction from earnings order can be appealed to a magistrates' court (England or Wales) or the sheriff court (Scotland). Orders to deduct amounts from bank accounts can be appealed in the family court (England and Wales) or the sheriff court (Scotland). Decisions of the courts on disqualification from driving or from holding or obtaining a passport can also be appealed. It may be possible to challenge other decisions by judicial review (see p198). A complaint can also be made about the way the CMS has exercised its discretion (see Chapter 11).

Note: child support arrears are *not* covered by the Debt Respite Scheme (Breathing Space).[78]

Enforcement where a non-resident parent is outside the UK

In some cases where the NRP is habitually resident outside the UK, the CMS can assist a PWC to obtain a court order for ongoing maintenance, which can then be enforced by applying (in England and Wales) to the Reciprocal Enforcement of Maintenance Orders (REMO) Unit via the local Maintenance Enforcement Business Centre[79] or (in Scotland) the Scottish government's Central Authority and International Law Team. It can also assist with enforcing an existing order and with enforcement where a NRP is habitually resident in the UK but has income or assets abroad.[80] These arrangements relate to a range of countries with which the UK has reciprocal agreements.[81] The details of the powers depend on the nature of the agreement in each case.

If arrears were accrued when the parties were habitually resident in the UK, the CMS can use its usual enforcement powers in relation to any assets that the NRP has retained in the UK if they now live abroad.

If a NRP is habitually resident in an EU country, where any proceedings were started before the end of the transition period after the UK left the EU (ie, started before 31 December 2020), the CMS can enforce certain arrears that accrued while both parents were resident in the UK. The CMS can also make enquiries about assets a NRP may own in a EU state. Such enforcement between EU member states is under the EU Maintenance Regulation.[82] This framework took precedence over, but was compatible with, the 2007 Hague Convention.[83] The EU Maintenance Regulation has now been revoked in UK law at the end of the transition period. However, the UK has now ratified the 2007 Hague Convention as an individual state and so continues to be bound by its terms for the cross-border recovery of child maintenance and systems for recognition and enforcement of maintenance obligations.

Deduction from earnings orders

When a deduction from earnings order is made

The CMS may make a deduction from earnings order, instructing the NRP's employer to make deductions from wages or salary and pay them to the CMS.[84] The CMS does not need a court order to do this and it is the first enforcement option that is likely to be used against an employed NRP who cannot provide a good reason for the arrears, or who has failed to agree a method of payment with the CMS. If the full amount requested by the CMS cannot be deducted from earnings, the CMS may use other methods to collect and enforce the remainder.

A NRP can also choose a voluntary deduction from earnings order as the method of making regular child support payments, even if there are no arrears (see p138).

Earnings

'Earnings' include wages, salary, fees, bonuses, commission, overtime pay, occupational pension or statutory sick pay, any other payment made under an employment contract and a regular payment made to compensate for loss of wages.[85] Earnings do not include working tax credit, any social security benefit or disabilty benefit, a payment by a foreign government or the government of Northern Ireland, or a payment to a special member of a British reserved armed force.[86] 'Net earnings' is the amount remaining after income tax, national insurance (NI) and contributions towards a pension scheme have been deducted.[87]

A deduction from earnings order cannot be made if there is a good reason not to use one.[88] For what is considered 'good reason', see p168.

The best way for a NRP to avoid a deduction from earnings order being made is to negotiate an arrears agreement (see p149) and keep to it wherever possible. However, making ongoing payments in full may be enough to prevent an order from being made. If a NRP objects to an order, this is likely to be rejected if they are unlikely to make regular payments using a different method.

The decision to make a deduction from earnings order is discretionary and the welfare of any children must be considered (see p124).[89] If the NRP is advised that the CMS intends to make an order, they should inform the CMS, preferably in writing, how any children would be affected. If a deduction from earnings order is made, the NRP can appeal against it to the magistrates' court in England and Wales, or the sheriff court in Scotland (see p168).

A deduction from earnings order can be made while the NRP is waiting for a decision on a revision, supersession or appeal, but the CMS should consider the grounds of the revision, supersession or appeal before making one. A NRP can also make representations about the amount and method of payments (see p138 and p146). The CMS may accept lower payments, but may still impose an order.

A deduction from earnings order cannot be made if the employer is based outside the UK and has no place of business in the UK, but can be made in Great Britain against an employer in Northern Ireland and vice versa.[90]

A deduction from earnings order cannot be made if the NRP is in the armed forces. Instead, the CMS can request the armed forces to make deductions for child support under armed forces law, known as a deduction from earnings request, which sets limits on the amounts that can be deducted.[91] The CMS has a memorandum of understanding with the Ministry of Defence on the use of deduction from earnings requests. They are always expected to be made unless the parent is on active military operations.

Note: a deduction from earnings order may also have been made as part of 'compliance opportunity' arrangements (see p135) offered to a NRP when a previous '2003 rules' or '1993 rules' case closed. If a child support application was made under the '2012 rules' before the date the existing case closed, the CMS may have allowed the NRP to pay a portion of the '2012 rules' child support liability by a voluntary method of payment for a period of time and make a deduction from earnings order for the remainder. In this situation, the CMS does not have to consider whether there is a good reason not to make an order, and there is therefore no right of appeal on this ground against the order being made.[92]

Information the non-resident parent must provide

The NRP must provide the name and address of their employer, the amount of their earnings and anticipated earnings, their place of work and the nature of their work within seven days of being asked to do so in writing by the CMS.[93] Once a deduction from earnings order is in force, the NRP must inform the CMS within seven days of leaving employment, becoming employed or being re-employed.[94] Failure to take all reasonable steps to comply with any of these requirements is an offence, punishable with a fine of up to £500.[95]

For these purposes, information sent to the CMS is treated as having been given or sent on the day that it is received.[96] Any notice sent from the CMS is treated as though it was given or sent on the day that it was posted[97] or, if sent electronically, as having been given or sent at the end of the first day after the day it was sent.[98]

What the employer must do

A copy of the deduction from earnings order must be 'served' on the employer and the NRP.[99] The employer must comply with it within seven days of receiving it,[100] and can be fined up to £1,000 for providing false or misleading information, or deliberately withholding information from the CMS.[101]

The order must state:[102]

- the name and address of the NRP; *and*
- the name of the employer; *and*
- the NRP's place of work, employee number and NI number (if known by the CMS), and the nature of their work; *and*
- the normal deduction rate(s) (see p164) and the date on which each takes effect; *and*
- the 'protected earnings proportion' (see p164); *and*
- the address to which the deductions must be sent.

An employer must inform the CMS in writing within 10 days of being served with an order if it does not, in fact, employ the NRP.[103]

If a parent who is subject to a deduction from earnings order leaves their job, the employer must notify the CMS within 10 days.[104] If an employer finds out that an order is in force against an employee, it must notify the CMS within seven days of becoming aware of this.[105] Failure to take all reasonable steps to comply with any of these requirements is an offence, punishable by a fine of up to £500.[106]

The employer must inform the NRP in writing of the amount of each deduction no later than the date of the deduction or, if not practicable, by the following payday.[107] If the deduction will always be the same amount, this can be done by a statement given at least annually.[108] If the employer does not give you notice, you can complain to an employment tribunal, which can order the employer to pay you a fine up to the total amount of the unnotified deductions, even if paid to the CMS.[109] This fine does not affect any deductions already paid to the CMS.

For other duties about providing information, see p34. The CMS and the child maintenance section of the gov.uk website provide further information for employers.

Employers can manage deduction from earnings orders online.[110]

If an employer implements a deduction from earnings order incorrectly and you dispute this, you should ask the CMS to intervene.

For these purposes, information sent by post to the CMS is treated as having been given or sent on the day that it is received.[111] Any notice sent by from the CMS is treated as though it was given or sent on the day that it was posted. Any notice sent or received electronically is treated as been given or sent at the end of the day following the day it was sent.[112]

How much is deducted

The deduction from earnings order states a 'normal deduction rate' and a 'protected earnings proportion'.[113]

The **'normal deduction rate'** is the amount that will be deducted each payday, provided it does not bring the NRP's net earnings below a certain amount (the protected earnings proportion). The normal deduction rate can include the current child support liability and an amount for any arrears, penalty payments (see p151) and any fees due. There are no special rules on how quickly the CMS should aim to clear the liability, although often the maximum deduction rate of 40 per cent of net earnings is applied (see p149). You may wish to discuss with the CMS how it has chosen to apply its discretion.

Note: more than one normal deduction rate can be set, each applying to a different period.[114]

The **'protected earnings proportion'** is 60 per cent of net earnings.[115] Deductions must not reduce earnings below this level.

The CMS does not know the NRP's net earnings or pay frequency, as it receives only gross income information from HM Revenue and Customs. The employer is therefore responsible for calculating the protected earnings proportion. The CMS provides employers with pay frequency options for weekly, fortnightly, four-weekly and monthly pay, from which the employer selects the normal deduction rate corresponding to the parent's pay frequency.[116] If the parent is paid at a different frequency, the CMS must cancel the order (see p167).[117]

These amounts also apply to deduction from earnings orders made after 10 December 2012 in 'arrears only' cases under the '1993 rules' and '2003 rules' (ie, cases where there are arrears outstanding but no regular ongoing child support liability), provided the CMS gives written notice to the NRP. Any deduction from earnings order made before this date continues under the previous rules until it is cancelled or lapses.[118]

Note: if an order is made as part of a 'compliance opportunity' (see p162), payments under the order do not need to be made in equal instalments.

Payment

The employer must pay the CMS monthly by the 19th of the month following the month in which the deduction is made.[119] This means that there is always a delay before the PWC receives the first payment from the CMS. The PWC receives monthly payments, even if the NRP is having weekly deductions made. These monthly payments may not always be for the same amount (see p166).

The payment by the employer may be made by credit transfer, cheque or any other method to which the CMS agrees.[120] The deduction from earnings order reference number must be given so that the CMS can identify the PWC.

It is an offence, punishable by a fine of up to £500, for an employer to fail to take all reasonable steps to pay the CMS on time.[121]

Administration of the deductions

An employer can deduct a charge for administrative costs each time a deduction is made under a deduction from earnings order. This means that employees paid weekly can be charged more for administrative costs. The charge must not exceed £1 per deduction and can be made even if this would bring someone's earnings below the protected earnings proportion.

Each payday, the employer should make a deduction from net earnings at the normal deduction rate plus any administration charge. If deducting the normal deduction rate would reduce net earnings below the protected earnings proportion, the amount of the deduction should be adjusted to ensure the protected earnings proportion is not breached.[122]

If the employer fails to make a deduction, or it is less than the normal deduction rate, arrears build up and are deducted at the next payday in addition to the normal deduction, applying the same rules for protected earnings.[123]

If, on a payday, the NRP is paid for a longer period than that for which the normal deduction rate is set, the deduction is increased in proportion to the length of the pay period.[124]

Such fluctuations in deductions may mean that the PWC receives irregular payments.

Example

Edward is due to pay child support of £48 a week and has net earnings of £240 a week. When a deduction from earnings order is considered, there are arrears of £432. The order shows a normal deduction rate of £60 (child support due plus £12 towards arrears) and a protected earnings proportion of £144. The employer can deduct £1 administrative costs for weeks in which a deduction is made.

Payday	*Net pay*	*Child support due*	*Deduction*	*Pay*	*Unpaid*
5/7	£240	£60	£61	£179	
12/7	£250	£60	£61	£189	
19/7	£160	£60	£17	£143	£44
26/7	£160	£104	£17	£143	£88
2/8	£240	£148	£97	£143	£52
9/8	£250	£112	£107	£143	£6
16/8	£250	£66	£67	£183	
23/8	£240	£60	£61	£179	
30/8	£120	£60	Nil	£120	£60
6/9	£240	£120	£97	£143	£24
13/9	£240	£84	£85	£155	
20/9	£250	£60	£61	£189	
27/9	£240	£60	£61	£179	

In the week of 19/7, the full deduction cannot be made, as this would take income below the protected earnings proportion. A deduction is made of £16 plus a £1 administration fee. The amount of the deduction from earnings order outstanding is added to the next amount due on 26/7. As earnings are again low, the full deduction cannot be taken and is carried forward.

In the week of 30/8, earnings are too low for a deduction to be made and therefore there is no deduction and no administrative charge.

Payment to the person with care

When payments under the order have reached the CMS, they should be passed on to the PWC within approximately 10 days. If the PWC was receiving income support or income-based jobseeker's allowance in the period to which the arrears relate, some of the payments may be retained in lieu of benefit paid.[125] This only applies to arrears of child support payments that were due to be made before 12 April 2010 (when child support was taken into account as income for means-tested benefits).

Example

Following on from the previous example, Edward's ex-wife Lowri will receive the following payments.

Month	*Payment by the 19th of the month*	*Current liability paid (£48 a week due)*	*Arrears paid (assigned to oldest debt)*
July		Nil	Nil
August	£156	£156	Nil
September	£328	£192	£136
October	£300	£192	£108

By the time Lowri gets the first payment from the deduction from earnings order in August, the amount owing is £624 (£432 + £192 (July)), but because of Edward's fluctuating earnings, Lowri receives less than the amount due. It is only in September that Lowri begins to receive arrears of child support, even though the order was made in July.

Priority of orders

A deduction from earnings order takes priority over an attachment of earnings order made by a county court and any arrestment of earnings under Scottish law.[126] In England and Wales, if a deduction from earnings order is served on an employee who is already subject to an attachment of earnings order made by a magistrates' court to recover a fine, council tax or maintenance, the earliest order has priority.[127]

Any deductions under a lower priority order are taken from the net earnings left after deductions under the first order have been made.

Reviews, cancellations and lapsed orders

The CMS must **review** a deduction from earnings order if there is a change in the amount of the calculation, or if any arrears, penalty payments and any collection or enforcement fees included have been paid off.[128] This does not apply if a normal deduction rate that takes into account the change has already been specified (see p164). An order may be changed on this review.[129] An employer must comply with the change within seven days of the new order being served on it.[130]

If the NRP is paid at a frequency other than weekly, fortnightly, four-weekly or monthly, the CMS *must* **cancel** the order.[131]

The CMS *can* cancel the order if:[132]

- no further payments are due under it; *or*
- liability in a '1993 rules' or '2003 rules' case has ended; *or*
- it is ineffective or there appears to be a more effective way of collecting the payments; *or*
- it is defective (see p168) or does not comply with a procedural requirement; *or*
- the CMS did not have, or has ceased to have, jurisdiction to make it; *or*
- using it to enforce a default maintenance decision or interim maintenance decision, and any requirement to pay collection fees, is no longer appropriate, given the compliance or attempted compliance of the NRP; *or*
- it has agreed with the NRP an alternative method for payment of the child support and any fees due, and it considers that it is reasonable to discharge the order.[133]

If the order was made as part of a 'compliance opportunity' (see p162), the CMS can also cancel it if:[134]

- the NRP receives a benefit that means the flat rate applies (see p58); *or*

- the NRP has made payments by the agreed voluntary method for the agreed period and the CMS considers that it is reasonable in the circumstances to cancel the order.

If an order was in force for a '1993 rules' or '2003 rules' case and there were outstanding arrears when that case closed and an application was made under the '2012 rules', the order is treated as cancelled when the arrears are transferred to the '2012 rules' computer system. The order therefore continues until the arrears are validated. If there are no outstanding arrears, the order is treated as cancelled on the date the first deduction is made under an order under the '2012 rules'.[135]

The CMS must send written notice of cancellation to the NRP and employer.[136]

A deduction from earnings order **lapses** when a NRP leaves the employment.[137] The CMS can **revive** it if the NRP finds a new job with the same or a different employer.[138] If it is revived, copies of the notice must be served on the parent and new employer.[139] Any shortfall under the order before the revival cannot be carried over to the revived order.[140]

Appeals

A NRP can appeal against a deduction from earnings order to the magistrates' court in England and Wales or the sheriff court in Scotland.[141] The appeal must be made within 28 days of the order being made (56 days if the parent is not resident in the UK).[142] An appeal may only be made on the grounds that:
- the order is 'defective' (see below); *or*
- the payments made to the parent are not earnings (see p162);[143] *or*
- unless the order is made as part of a 'compliance opportunity' (see p162), there is 'good reason' not to use an order (see below).[144]

A deduction from earnings order is **defective** if it is impracticable for an employer to comply with it because it does not include the correct information required.[145] Many orders may include incorrect information (such as errors in names, addresses and dates), but an appeal will not succeed on this basis if the employer can still comply with it. Although some early appeals were upheld because the order was unsigned, a signature is not legally required.

When determining whether there is a **good reason** not to use an order, the CMS must consider whether making the order is likely to result in the disclosure of the parentage of a child and the likely impact of this on the NRP's employment or on any relationship between the NRP and a third party.[146] The impact of a third party becoming aware of the NRP's deduction from earnings order is not considered to be a good reason in any other circumstances.[147]

A good reason for not imposing an order may also exist if a relative of the NRP or PWC is employed by the same employer as the NRP and they are likely to find out about the order. If employment or family relationships may be adversely affected as a result, this should be a good reason not to impose an order.[148]

The fact that a NRP may prefer a different method of payment or would prefer the employer not to be informed about their child support liability are not considered good reasons to refrain from using a deduction from earnings order.[149]

In England and Wales, there is no specific application form for the appeal. In Scotland, the form of the application for an appeal is laid out in the sheriff court child support rules.[150]

Once the application is made, the court notifies the CMS. The CMS checks the deduction from earnings order and contacts the employer to check the earnings. If the order is based on incorrect amounts, the CMS varies and reissues it. If the case gets as far as a court hearing, the magistrates/sheriff may quash the order or specify which payments, if any, constitute earnings.[151] The court cannot question the child support calculation itself.[152]

Even if the court quashes the order, it cannot order the CMS to repay deductions to the NRP.[153] For this reason, if deductions are being made from payments that are not earnings, or on the basis of an incorrect normal deduction rate or protected earnings proportion, it may be better to challenge the order by way of judicial review.

Either party may be represented by a lawyer. The CMS appoints its own staff to conduct deduction from earnings order appeals and appear at related court hearings.[154] The NRP may also be represented by a lay person, if the magistrate or sheriff deems them suitable. An authorised lay representative does not have the full rights of a legal representative, but may be entitled to expenses.

Note: if you think the CMS has not properly exercised its discretion in making a deduction from earnings order, you can make a complaint (see Chapter 11) and/or consider judicial review (see p198).

Deductions from bank accounts

If a NRP has failed to pay child support, the CMS can make an order requiring a bank or building society to make deductions from their account and pay the CMS. The CMS can make an order without the NRP's consent, and without applying to court or obtaining a liability order.[155] The deductions can either be regular (see p171) or be made as a lump-sum payment (see p173).[156] As soon as a NRP is in arrears, a deduction order becomes possible as a method of enforcement.

An order is most commonly made if a NRP is self-employed and a deduction from earnings order is therefore not possible. It may also be used if a deduction from earnings order is unlikely to collect arrears at an acceptable rate. The CMS will consider the reasonableness and proportionality of making an order in each case. For example, as the fee for making a lump-sum deduction order is £200 (see p188), it may not be proportionate for the CMS to consider making such an order if the arrears are less than £500.[157]

The decision to make such an order is a discretionary one and so the CMS must take into account the welfare of any children likely to be affected by the decision (see p124).

To make an order, the CMS must be aware that the NRP has an account with a specific bank or building society. The CMS has discretion to choose the most suitable account from which to make deductions. Generally, regular deduction orders are directed at current accounts and lump-sum deduction orders at savings accounts. The use of deduction orders on more complex accounts, such as notice accounts or stocks and shares accounts, may also be considered.[158]

Since 14 December 2018, deduction orders can also be made in respect of a joint account.[159] This may be a personal joint account or an account used by a partnership in England and Wales in which the NRP is a partner without limited liability.[160] This does not apply to partnerships in Scotland.

A regular deduction order and, since 14 December 2018, a lump-sum deduction order can also be made in respect of an account which is used by a NRP as a sole trader. Deduction orders cannot be made in respect of any other accounts (ie, apart from partnership accounts in England and Wales and sole trader accounts) which are used wholly or partly for business purposes.[161]

The CMS always attempts to make deductions from a NRP's individual accounts first. If there are insufficient funds, it then considers deductions from any joint accounts. Joint personal accounts are considered before any partnership accounts. In order to protect the interests of other partners, deductions are not made from a partnership account if the account balance is less than £2,000.[162]

Before making a deduction order on a joint account, the CMS can require the bank to provide information on:[163]

- the name and home address (or correspondence address) of each account holder; *and*
- the type of account, account number and sort code; *and*
- the balance in the account; *and*
- details of any transactions on the account in the previous six months.

The bank must provide this information within 14 days of the request. If the information does not allow the CMS to establish the proportion of the funds in the account belonging to the NRP, the CMS assumes that each account holder owns an equal share.[164]

When a bank is sent a deduction order, it must notify the CMS of certain matters within seven days – eg, if the account does not exist, has been closed or is in a different name from that specified in the order. It must also notify the CMS within seven days if the name of a joint account holder is changed, provided the order remains in force at any time during that seven-day period.[165]

It is an offence, punishable by a fine of up to £500, for a bank not to comply with the requirements of a regular deduction order or to fail to provide information when required to do so, unless it can show that all reasonable steps were taken to comply.[166]

The bank can take an amount from the account to cover its administrative costs. The maximum amounts that can be charged are:[167]

- £10 for each deduction made under a regular deduction order; *or*
- £55 for each deduction made under a lump-sum deduction order.

Regular deduction orders

A regular deduction order can be used to collect both arrears and ongoing child support payments.[168] The CMS does not intend to use regular deduction orders as an ongoing method of collecting child support and arrears. The CMS imposes these orders to negotiate a preferred method of collection with the NRP.[169]

Before a regular deduction order is made on a joint account, notice must be given to each account holder, giving each of them an opportunity to make representations on the proposed order and the amounts to be deducted.[170]

Each account holder must be told:

- the name of the NRP and that the order is in respect of their child support liability; *and*
- the number and sort code of the account; *and*
- the proposed dates on which deductions will be made; *and*
- that they can make representations about the proposed order, the amounts to be deducted and the dates on which deductions will be made. Representations must be made within 14 days of receiving the notice, although the CMS may allow longer if it is reasonable in the circumstances. An order cannot be made until this period has expired; *and*
- that the order is likely to be made in the terms set out in the notice unless representations are received.

The CMS may also provide any further information about the NRP that it considers essential to allow joint account holders to make representations.[171]

When a regular deduction order is made, a copy is sent to the bank, the NRP and, if it concerns a joint account, each of the other account holders. The order must specify the amount of the regular deduction and the dates on which deductions are due to be made.[172]

The maximum that can be deducted is 40 per cent of the NRP's gross weekly income (net weekly income in '1993 rules' and '2003 rules' cases). The weekly income is to be calculated as at the date of the current child support calculation or, if arrears are being collected for a calculation no longer in force, at the date of the most recent previous calculation. If a default maintenance decision has been made, the maximum that can be deducted is £80 a week.[173]

Priority of payments

If the NRP's account is subject to other deduction orders, such as a third-party debt order, these are generally paid first before a regular deduction order is dealt with. The exception to this is if a third-party debt order is served on the bank after the regular deduction order, but on or before the date a payment is due to be made under the deduction order. In this case, the deduction order is paid first on that occasion, unless the bank has already taken steps to process the other orders. For future payments, it is assumed that the other orders take priority.[174]

Minimum amounts

A deduction cannot be made if the amount of credit in the relevant account is below a certain level on the date a deduction is due to be made. The minimum amounts are:

- £40, if deductions are made monthly; *or*
- £10, if deductions are made weekly; *or*
- if deductions are made for any other period, £10 for each whole week in that period, plus £1 for each additional day in that period.

In addition to these amounts, there must be sufficient funds in the account to pay the administrative costs.[175] Deductions are not made from a partnership account if the account balance is less than £2,000.

Reviews and variations

A NRP, a bank or, if the order concerns a joint account, any other account holder can apply to the CMS for a **review** of a regular deduction order if:[176]

- the parent does not have a beneficial interest in some, or all, of the money in the account; *or*
- there has been a change in the amount of the child support calculation; *or*
- any amount payable under the order has been paid; *or*
- there has been a change in the NRP's current income (net weekly income in '1993 rules' and '2003 rules' cases);[177] *or*
- because of an official error, an incorrect amount has been specified in the order; *or*
- the order does not contain the correct information or exceeds the maximum deduction rate; *or*
- in the case of an order concerning a joint account:
  - another account holder satisfies the CMS that the amount contributed by the NRP to the account has decreased, or will decrease within three months of the date of the application for review; *or*
  - another account holder who did not make representations within the 14-day period before the order was made (see p171) satisfies the CMS that they had a reasonable excuse for not doing so and applies for a review within three months of the expiry of that period.

A regular deduction order can be **varied** to change the amount that is deducted if:[178]

- the CMS accepts that the NRP has made a payment of child support arrears, or a payment towards an enforcement fee, and no alternative method of payment is in place; *or*

- there has been a successful appeal against a child support calculation; *or*
- the order has been changed following a successful review or appeal to the family court (sheriff court in Scotland); *or*
- there are arrears that are not included in the order; *or*
- in the case of an order on a joint account, the CMS believes that the amount contributed by the NRP to the account has changed, or will change within three months of the date of the order being made or varied.

The CMS has discretion to vary the deduction period or the deduction dates at any time.[179]

Before varying a regular deduction order concerning a joint account to increase the amount deducted or to change the deduction dates, the CMS must serve a notice on each account holder.[180] This notice must contain the same types of information about the account as the notice served before an order is first made (see p171). It must also explain:

- why the CMS proposes to vary the order; *and*
- that each account holder can make representations about the proposal to vary the order, the amounts to be deducted and the dates on which deductions will be made. Representations must be made within 14 days of receiving the notice, although the CMS may allow longer if it is reasonable in the circumstances. The order cannot be varied until this period has expired; *and*
- that the order is likely to be varied in the terms set out in the notice unless representations are received.

Lump-sum deduction orders

If it is established that the NRP owes arrears of child support, the CMS considers whether a lump-sum deduction order is the most appropriate method of recovering them. That is likely to be the preferred approach if the NRP has an account balance sufficient to make a single payment to clear arrears.

Once the CMS has decided to make a lump-sum deduction order, it serves an interim order on the NRP's bank. This acts as an instruction to secure funds up to the amount of the order in a specified account until further notice. The bank is expected to prevent these from being moved or reduced below the amount that is ordered or, if funds are already below this amount, not to allow them to decrease further (unless the CMS permits it to do so – eg, because of hardship).[181]

Once funds have been secured, a copy of the interim order is served on the NRP. The bank and the parent each have 14 days (unless it is a joint account – see below) in which to make representations to the CMS.[182] In the case of a joint account, the notice must tell each account holder:[183]

- the name of the NRP and that the order is in respect of child support liability; *and*
- that the interim order is an instruction to the bank to secure the funds and that the CMS proposes to make a final order; *and*

- the earliest proposed date on which a deduction under the final order will be made; *and*
- that each account holder can make representations about the proposal, the proposed amount to be deducted and the earliest date proposed for deducting the amount. Representations must be made within 28 days of receiving the notice, although the CMS may allow longer if it is reasonable in the circumstances; *and*
- that the order is likely to be made in the terms set out in the notice unless representations are received.

The CMS can also provide any further information about the NRP that it considers essential to allow joint account holders to make representations.[184]

Once an interim order has been made, the CMS can issue a final lump-sum deduction order. It must not do this until the period for making representations (14 days or, for an order on a joint account, 28 days) has expired and it has considered any representations made. The order is served on the bank, on the NRP and, in the case of an order concerning a joint account, on each of the other account holders.[185]

A final order instructs the bank to pay to the CMS either the amount due or, if less, the amount in the account. The bank must pay the amount to the CMS once the period for appealing has expired (see p178) or, if an appeal has been made, once the appeal has been concluded and any period for further appealing has expired.[186]

The amount sought by the CMS in the final order must not be more than the amount specified in the interim order.[187] The CMS must ensure that the amount deducted from a joint account does not exceed an amount that is fair, given all the circumstances. In considering what amount to deduct, the CMS must pay particular attention to the amounts contributed to the account by each of the account holders.[188]

An order is treated as having been 'served' on a person at the end of the day on which the copy is posted to their last known address or at the end of the first working day after the day it was sent, if sent electronically.[189]

The NRP, a bank or, in the case of an order concerning a joint account, another account holder can ask the CMS not to instruct the bank to secure funds – ie, to allow money in the account to be moved or reduced. The CMS can agree to this if:[190]

- the NRP, their partner or any relevant other child is experiencing hardship in meeting their ordinary living expenses; *or*
- in the case of an order concerning a joint account, another account holder, their partner or any child for whom they are a PWCis experiencing hardship; *or*
- the NRP (or a joint account holder) has any written, contractual obligations regarding the money that were made before the order was made; *or*

- the NRP (or a joint account holder) has made an agreement with the bank and the availability of an amount in the account is required as security for that agreement; *or*
- there are any other circumstances that the CMS considers appropriate in the particular case.

In deciding whether to allow funds to be moved or reduced, the CMS must take into account:[191]

- any adverse impact the decision may have on the NRP or anyone else; *and*
- any alternative arrangements which may be made by the parent, any other account holder and the bank or building society.

If it agrees, the CMS serves a notice on the bank instructing it to move or to remove the funds.

Priority of payments

In **England and Wales**, if there is a final lump-sum deduction order and another interim third-party debt order, a bank must comply with them in the order in which they were served on it. If an interim lump-sum deduction order is served after an interim third-party debt order, the final versions of these other orders take priority.[192]

In **Scotland**, a bank or must give priority to the lump-sum deduction order and any other orders, according to the order in which they were served on it.[193]

Minimum amounts

A deduction should not be made if the amount of credit in the relevant bank account is below a minimum level. The current minimum level is £55 plus the amount of administrative costs charged by the bank.[194] The administrative costs must not be more than £55.[195] Deductions are not made from a partnership account if the account balance is less than £2,000.

Variations

In certain circumstances, a NRP, their bank or a joint account holder can ask the CMS to use its discretion to vary the order. A variation reduces the amount specified in the order.[196] The circumstances include if:[197]

- the CMS accepts the parent's agreement to make a payment;
- there has been a revision or supersession of, or a successful appeal against, the child support calculation;
- there has been an appeal to the family court (sheriff court in Scotland) against making an order, or against a refusal by the CMS to consent to funds being moved or reduced;
- the CMS allows money in the account to be moved or reduced because it agrees that otherwise hardship may be caused (see p174);

- the parent is under a written contractual obligation made before the lump-sum deduction order was made.

Lapsed, discharged and revived orders

A regular deduction order lapses if the CMS considers it reasonable and:[198]

- an alternative method of payment of the child support due, including any fees, has been agreed between the CMS and the NRP; *or*
- on two consecutive deduction dates (or more if the CMS decides this is appropriate), there have been insufficient funds in the account to make the deduction; *or*
- in the case of an order concerning a joint account, the CMS is satisfied that the NRP has stopped making contributions to the account or will stop making contributions to the account in the next deduction period.

If the order lapses, this takes effect on the day the bank receives notification of this from the CMS.

A lapsed regular deduction order is treated as remaining in force for certain purposes. It can be **revived** if:[199]

- the NRP fails to comply with an agreement about an alternative method of payment; *or*
- the CMS has reason to believe that there are now sufficient funds in the account to make a deduction; *or*
- in the case of an order concerning a joint account, the NRP has started to make contributions to the account again.

Before reviving a lapsed regular deduction order on a joint account, the CMS must serve a notice on each account holder and consider any representations received. The CMS must provide the same information as for varying a regular deduction order, and the process and timescale for representations are the same (see p173).[200]

A **regular deduction order may be discharged** by the CMS if it considers it appropriate and *must* be discharged if:[201]

- the account specified in the order has been closed; *or*
- the child support calculation is no longer in force and the amount due, including any fees, has been paid in full; *or*
- the NRP has complied with any alternative method of payment agreed with the CMS for a period it considers appropriate; *or*
- the CMS has reviewed the order and the amount to be deducted has been reduced to nil or a court has set aside the order on appeal; *or*
- six months have passed since the order lapsed (and, in the case of an order on a joint account, the account holders have not been informed that the CMS is considering reviving the order), unless an appeal has been made (see the bullet point below); *or*

- an appeal has been made against a lapsed order and one month has passed since either the appeal was concluded or the time limit for a further appeal has expired, whichever is the later; *or*
- the NRP has died; *or*
- in the case of a joint account, the NRP is no longer an account holder.

A lump-sum deduction order lapses if the CMS considers it reasonable and:[202]
- there is no money in the account (including if the amount has reduced to nil because the CMS has given permission for money to be used, for instance, in cases of hardship – see p174); *or*
- an alternative method of payment of the child support due, including any fees, has been agreed between the CMS and the NRP.

If the order lapses, this takes effect on the day the bank society receives notification of this from the CMS.

A lapsed lump-sum deduction order is treated as remaining in force for certain purposes. It can be **revived** if:[203]
- there was no money in the account specified in the order, but the bank has informed the CMS that there is now money in the account (even if it is not sufficient to pay the whole amount specified in the order); *or*
- the order lapsed because there was no money in the account because the CMS had given permission for money to be used (eg, in cases of hardship) and the bank has informed the CMS that there is now money in the account (even if it is not sufficient to pay the whole amount specified in the order); *or*
- money is still due under the order and the NRP has failed to comply with an agreed alternative method of payment of the child support due.

A lump-sum deduction order may be discharged by the CMS if it considers it appropriate in all the circumstances, and *must* be discharged if:[204]
- the account specified in the order has been closed; *or*
- in the case of an order concerning a joint account, the NRP is no longer an account holder in relation to that account; *or*
- the amount of arrears specified in the order, including any fees, has been paid in full; *or*
- the NRP has paid the total amount of arrears due, including any fees, by an alternative method of payment agreed with the CMS; *or*
- after considering representations about making an interim order, the CMS has decided not to make a final order; *or*
- six months have passed since the order lapsed, or since a deduction was made if the amount of the deduction was for all of the funds in the account but less than the amount due under the order (unless an appeal has been made – see the next bullet point); *or*

- an appeal has been made against a lapsed order and one month has passed since the appeal was concluded or the time limit for a further appeal expired, whichever is the later; *or*
- the NRP has died.

If the order is discharged, this takes effect on the day the bank receives notification of this from the CMS.

Appeals

A NRP and, in the case of an order concerning a joint account, another account holder have the right to appeal against a regular deduction order or a lump-sum deduction order and related decisions made by the CMS. The appeal is made to the family court in England and Wales or the sheriff court in Scotland. Once the appeal is made, the NRP should notify the CMS immediately.

You can appeal against:[205]

- the making of a regular deduction order;
- any decision by the CMS on a request to review a regular deduction order;
- a refusal to allow funds which are the subject of an interim lump-sum deduction order to be moved or used – eg, in the case of hardship (see p174). In this case, the NRP, their partner and any relevant other child (and, in the case of an order concerning a joint account, another account holder, their partner and any child for whom the other account holder is a PWC) all have the right of appeal;
- the making of a final lump-sum deduction order.

An appeal must be made within 21 days of the date you receive notice of the order or decision. In England and Wales, this time limit cannot be extended by the court. In Scotland, an appeal may be accepted late if the court accepts that there are special reasons.[206] A NRP or another account holder is considered to have received the notice of the order or decision at the end of the day on which it was posted to their last known address, or if sent electronically the end of the first working day after the day it was sent.[207]

Depending on the decision made by the court on an appeal, the order may be maintained as it is, or the CMS may be required to review, vary, or discharge the order or let it lapse.

Recovery of arrears from an estate

Most types of enforcement action stops when a NRP dies. However, if a NRP has died on or after 25 January 2010, any arrears for which they were liable immediately before death become a debt, payable to the CMS from the estate.[208] The CMS can request the payment of arrears of child support (and any collection fees – but not fees for enforcement action or for a DNA test) from an estate without having to apply to court or obtain a liability order. The decision to recover arrears is a discretionary one. The CMS can contact the administrator or executor of the estate to request payment.

The CMS aims to avoid legal action where possible when using this power and to avoid delaying or obstructing the administration of an estate.[209]

The CMS is notified automatically when other government departments are informed of the death of a NRP. However, the PWC may also wish to inform the CMS that the NRP has died.

The administrator or executor has the same rights of appeal, following the same procedures and time limits, as the NRP had before death.[210]

The CMS must disclose relevant information to enable the administrator or executor to make a decision about whether to pay or to appeal the arrears. The CMS has discretion to decide whether the information requested is essential and therefore whether it should be disclosed.[211] The CMS should not disclose the address of any person involved in the case unless there is written consent, and should also prevent the disclosure of any information that could lead to the PWC, or any other relevant person, being located.[212]

It is intended that child support arrears will be treated in the same way as other debts – eg, unpaid utility or council tax bills. It does not appear that they take priority over other payments.

Before making a claim on an estate, the CMS should check thoroughly the amount of outstanding debt, including completing any outstanding reassessments relating to periods before the death.[213] Administrators of the estate should check that the CMS has carried out this process and that the amount of debt to be recovered is accurate.

When arrears should not be recovered

The CMS should not pursue arrears from an estate without the consent of the PWC. If the PWC does not wish to pursue the arrears, the CMS should not take any further action unless the arrears are owed only to the CMS.[214] For further details on when arrears may be written off, see p156. The CMS will not consider it cost-effective to seek recovery from an estate if the arrears are less than £65.[215]

The CMS also has a duty to take into account the welfare of any child likely to be affected (see p124). This includes children of the NRP who may not have been the subject of the child support calculation, or other dependent children who would otherwise benefit from the estate. When the CMS registers its claim against the estate, it may not be aware of other children or the potential implications for them. If the CMS later becomes aware of any potentially adverse impact on other children, it should reconsider whether to pursue the arrears.[216] The CMS also takes into account the administrative cost of recovering arrears in this way.[217]

If the arrears recovered from an estate would be retained by the CMS in lieu of any benefit paid, they should not be pursued if this would have a detrimental effect on a PWC or a qualifying child. This only applies to arrears relating to a period before 12 April 2010, when child support was counted as income for means-tested benefits. The CMS should contact the PWC to establish what impact the recovery would have before approaching the administrators of the estate.[218]

Obtaining a liability order

If enforcement methods, such as a deduction from earnings order, are inappropriate (eg, because the NRP is not employed) or have been tried but have proven ineffective, the CMS may apply to the magistrates' court in England and Wales, or the sheriff court in Scotland, for a liability order.[219] The CMS may also seek a liability order in parallel with the pursuit of other administrative enforcement methods (eg, if a deduction from earnings order is being used but will be insufficent to clear arrears or if a repayment arrangement would still leave more than £1,000 of arrears after two years).

The CMS does not normally seek a liability order if the arrears are less than £500, or less than £1,000 if they relate to arrears from a closed '1993 rules' or '2003 rules' case. The CMS also does not seek a liability order if there is an outstanding review or appeal that may affect the amount of the arrears due.

A liability order has no effect in itself on collection of child support. It provides legal recognition of the debt, and allows the CMS to take further enforcement measures. More than one liability order can be in force in respect of the same NRP for arrears that cover different periods. A liability order is required before the CMS can take action to:

- register the debt with a credit reference agency without the consent of the NRP, which will affect the parent's credit rating and ability to obtain a mortgage and other credit (see p53);
- take control of and sell goods (see p182);
- disqualify the NRP from driving or from holding or obtaining a passport or other travel authorisation (see p186);
- imprison the NRP (see p187).

The CMS will always seek the agreement of the PWC to enforcement action being taken before it seeks a liability order.[220] The CMS must give the NRP seven days' notice of its intention to seek a liability order (28 days, if they are not resident in the UK).[221] The notice must state the amount of child support outstanding, including any collection or enforcement fees.

If the court decides that the payments are due but have not been made, it must make the order.[222] The court cannot question the child support calculation itself.[223] When making a liability order, the court can take into account payments made by the NRP by a method other than that specified by the CMS.[224]

An order (including one made in Northern Ireland) granted in any part of the UK can be enforced anywhere in the UK.[225]

If the court makes the liability order, it usually orders the NRP to pay the CMS's legal costs.

Time limits

Since 12 July 2006, there has been no time limit for applying for a liability order. Debts that were older than six years on 12 July 2006 (ie, that became due on or before 12 July 2000) and were not subject to a liability order cannot be enforced through a liability order and will be recovered by other methods.[226] The six years do not begin to run until the NRP is notified of the calculation. Although a calculation can be backdated, liability does not exist until it is made.[227]

The CMS does not need to act on a liability order immediately after it is granted. If an order is made, there may be a long delay before the CMS takes any further action. Action that directly aims to recover money (eg, taking control of goods) must be taken within six years from the date of the order.[228] The six-year time limit does not apply to action that does not, in itself, recover money, such as imprisonment or disqualification from driving.[229]

England and Wales

The NRP is sent a summons, giving 14 days' notice of the hearing. The magistrates' court decides whether or not to issue the liability order, but cannot consider whether the parent is liable or the calculation has properly been made.[230] If an appeal against a decision of the CMS on those issues is pending, however, the court may decide to adjourn.

The court may decide not to issue an order if the NRP appears to be co-operating. However, the CMS may still ask for the order to be granted on the understanding that it will not be enforced if the NRP continues to co-operate. If the NRP does not attend the court, the CMS may still obtain the order, unless the application has not properly been made.

It is unusual for a NRP to attend a liability order hearing, but they may do so if they wish. This may be necessary if they wish to make representations to the court to challenge the application. In some instances, the court must be notified of the intended attendance before the court date. This will allow the court to adjourn and to arrange another hearing with a sufficient time estimate. A lawyer or another person may represent the NRP.

Note: from 19 July 2021, the CMS can apply for numerous liability orders at the same time on a bulk basis (previously it was required to use a prescribed form for each liability order, which meant that the magistrates had to sign each individually). This is intended to speed up enforcement action.[231]

Scotland

The NRP is sent a notice of the application for a liability order and has 21 days to object to its being made. This should be done in writing by returning the notice stating the grounds of the objection and enclosing evidence. If objections are received, a court hearing is held. Even if the parent does not attend, the sheriff must still consider the objections.[232] The court cannot question the NRP's liability for child support, or the calculation itself. An extract of the liability order may be issued 14 days after the order is actually made.

Taking control of goods and other enforcement action

If a liability order has been made, in England and Wales, the CMS can instruct enforcement agents to take control of the NRP's goods or to take court action. In Scotland, a liability order can be enforced by 'diligence' (the term for various processes of debt enforcement in Scottish law).[233] The law on taking control of goods and diligence can be complex. The following is not a full statement of the law, but a summary of the processes that can be used by the CMS.[234] If you are subject to enforcement action by the CMS, get help from a money adviser.

The CMS aims to use the full range of sanctions available, including taking control of goods, removing a driving licence, disqualifying the NRP from holding or obtaining a passport, and imprisonment, where appropriate.[235] The CMS uses these enforcement methods to encourage the NRP to comply with an agreement to make payments for child support and arrears. If you are not satisfied with enforcement action taken, you can complain (see Chapter 11).

England and Wales

If a liability order has been made, the amount on the order can be enforced in England and Wales by **taking control of and selling the NRP's goods.**[236] The enforcement agent (a private bailiff) carrying this out must, at least seven clear days before taking action, give the person written notice. The notice must include details of the liability order and the debt.[237] It must also explain how payment of the debt in full can be made to avoid the taking and subsequent sale of goods.[238]

Certain items cannot be taken. These include:[239]

- tools, books, vehicles and other items necessary for work, up to a total value of £1,350; *and*
- clothing, bedding, furniture, household equipment and provisions reasonably required to meet the basic domestic needs of the NRP and every member of their household.

Fees can be charged at each of the stages involved in the process.[240]

For more information about bailiffs, including how to complain about them, see CPAG's *Debt Advice Handbook* (available free at AskCPAG.org.uk).

Once a liability order has been made, the CMS can **register the order as if it were a judgment debt.**[241] This record is publicly available and damages the NRP's credit rating (see also p53 for when the CMS can disclose information directly to credit reference agencies). If payment is made within one month of the registration, the entry is cancelled and no record remains. If payment is made outside of one calendar month, the record will remain for a period of six years, even if the debt is satisfied in full.[242] The CMS can also use the county court to recover any amount that remains unpaid.[243]

A charging order allows a debt to be registered against the NRP's property (and certain other assets, such as land, stocks, shares and any interest arising from a trust). When the property is sold, the debt due under the liability order can be recovered from the proceeds of the sale. In some cases, it may not be possible to register a charge, in which case a caution against dealings may be obtained to prevent the property from being sold without the CMS's knowledge. Once a charge or caution has been registered, the CMS can consider applying to the court for an **order of sale**, forcing the NRP to sell the property and to pay the debt.

A third-party debt order can be obtained by the CMS if it is aware that the NRP has a bank account or is owed money by a third party. The order freezes funds in the account and requires that person to release funds to the CMS up to the amount of the liability order. In practice, the CMS is likely to apply for a lump sum or regular deduction order (see p169) before making any application for a third-party debt order.

Scotland

In Scotland, the CMS can ask sheriff officers to issue a 'charge for payment', a formal request in writing demanding that the NRP pay the debt within a specific period, usually 14 days. If payment is not made, various enforcement processes (known as 'diligence') can be used.

The CMS can ask the sheriff court to freeze money or goods through an **arrestment**. This prevents money in an account being used, and prevents any money owed to the NRP from being paid into the account. A company holding any goods owed to the parent can be required to cancel the transaction and to transfer the money used to pay for the goods to the CMS instead.

The sheriff court can also make an **attachment order**, preventing the NRP from selling or transferring belongings. If the NRP still does not pay the arrears, the goods can be seized and sold at public auction and the proceeds paid to the CMS.

The CMS can instruct sheriff officers to register the debt against any heritable property – eg, a house, garage, land or business premises. This is known as **inhibition**, and prevents the NRP selling or transferring the property until the debt has been paid.

Orders preventing the disposal of assets

In England, Wales and Scotland, the CMS can take action in the High Court and family court (England and Wales) or the Court of Session and sheriff court (Scotland) to prevent a NRP disposing of assets or transferring them out of the UK in order to avoid paying child support arrears.[244]

If the asset has already been disposed of, the court can make an order to 'set the transaction aside' or, in Scotland, to 'reduce the disposition' – ie, to reverse the disposal.[245] If the NRP is about to dispose of an asset, the court can make an order to prevent this.

The court can review any disposal of assets by the NRP, except if the asset was given as part of a contract with an innocent party who acted in good faith.[246] For example, if the parent disposes of a sum of money to purchase goods from an individual who had no knowledge of the intention to avoid paying child support, the transaction cannot be reversed. An asset transferred to another as part of a marriage agreement or the formation of a civil partnership can, however, be reviewed by the court.[247] Assets transferred under a will are not treated as having been disposed of.

If the court is satisfied that the CMS would be able to take action to recover arrears from the asset in question, the burden of proof is on the NRP to show that they did not dispose of, or were not about to dispose of, the asset with the intention of avoiding paying child support.[248] If an order is made in Scotland, the parent can apply to the court to have it reviewed, varied or recalled at any time.[249]

Bankruptcy

A NRP may have child support arrears when they are made bankrupt. Child support arrears are not a debt provable in (ie, not a debt that can be included in) bankruptcy.[250] The CMS is not a creditor that can be bound by an individual voluntary arrangement (IVA) in England and Wales, this being a binding compromise agreement with creditors to avoid the consequences of bankruptcy) made by a NRP and so any liability for arrears of child support cannot be reduced by means of an IVA.[251]

The courts may intervene to stay enforcement when a bankruptcy is pending or has been decided.[252] However, CMS policy is that it cannot take enforcement action while a NRP is being made bankrupt.[253] Therefore, if the CMS is notified of bankruptcy, any ongoing enforcement action ceases until the bankruptcy order has been made.

In this case, the CMS may decide not to enforce the liability order because it may not be practical – eg, a charging order/inhibition of sale may not be effective, because any property may already have been sold to pay creditors.

As part of bankruptcy proceedings, the NRP can inform the court of their child support liabilities. The administrator of the bankruptcy should take this into account when deciding how much money the parent needs to meet their basic living expenses. This decision is made before any available funds are distributed among creditors.

The CMS may still consider further enforcement measures, such as disqualification from driving or imprisonment, against a NRP who is bankrupt, particularly if they have a steady income. In these circumstances, the NRP must show that they cannot afford to meet their child support liability. That may be more difficult if the administrator of the bankruptcy has already made provision for the current child support payments when deciding how much money is needed to meet basic living expenses. In the vast majority of cases, the CMS still pursues child support.[254]

If a NRP is granted sequestration (bankruptcy) in Scotland, any child support debt up to the date of sequestration is no longer legally recoverable and may be written off (see p156).[255] A new deduction from earnings order may be sought for the payment of any child support and arrears that have become due since the date of sequestration.

A NRP in Scotland can apply for a trust deed (a formal voluntary agreement to repay all or part of a person's debts) if £5,000 or more is owing (to all creditors, not just to the CMS). A trust deed can become 'protected' in certain circumstances. In this case, child support arrears up to the day before the trust deed was granted are no longer collectable and any ongoing enforcement action must be cancelled.[256] Money collected by the trustee (known as a 'dividend') will be distributed amongst creditors when the trust deed is discharged, and may pay off some of the child support arrears.[257] Other child support arrears included within the trust deed can be written off. A new deduction from earnings order may be sought for the payment of any child support and arrears that have become due since the date the protected trust deed was granted.

3. Sanctions for non-payment

If other methods of recovery have failed, the Child Maintenance Service (CMS) may apply to the courts, or sheriff court in Scotland to impose sanctions on the non-resident parent (NRP) to try to force payment of debts secured by a liability order. The CMS can apply:[258]

- to disqualify the NRP from driving for up to two years; *or*
- to disqualify the NRP from holding or obtaining a passport or other UK travel authorisation for up to two years; *or*
- to imprison them for up to six weeks.

Only one of these sanctions can be imposed on the NRP at a time. **Note:** the CMS can only take these actions if the other enforcement proceedings have been tried unsuccessfully. It is not enough that other mechanisms have been considered, but not pursued.[259]

Before taking action, the CMS must attempt to contact the parent. This is usually by letter detailing the sanctions that may be considered if payment is not made. These powers are only used as a last resort where all other methods of recovery have failed. The CMS has said that this action will be used only in exceptional circumstances and where a liability order is in place and arrears of over £1,000 remain outstanding.[260] Suspended prison sentences and suspended disqualifications from driving are more common than actual committals and disqualifications.[261] Disqualification from holding or obtaining a passport can also be suspended.[262]

These powers are discretionary, and when deciding whether to take these types of action, the CMS must consider the welfare of any child likely to be affected (see p124).

The CMS must apply to the magistrates' court (or, in Scotland, sheriff court) for an order disqualifying the NRP from driving or a warrant committing them to prison.[263] A committal order will not be made against an NRP under the age of 18.[264] The CMS makes one application to the court, and the court decides whether either disqualification from driving or committal to prison is appropriate. The CMS can make representations to the court on which it thinks is more appropriate, and the parent can respond to any such representations.[265]

The CMS can also apply to the court for an order disqualifying the parent from holding or obtaining a passport or other UK travel authorisation. The court cannot disqualify the parent from holding or obtaining a passport *and* commit them to prison.[266] **Note:** the power to disqualify a parent from holding or obtaining a passport does not apply in Northern Ireland.

The NRP must attend the hearing.[267] The court can summon them to appear in court and to produce their driving licence or passport (if they have one).[268] If the NRP does not appear, the court may issue a warrant for their arrest.[269]

The court must enquire into the parent's means, whether a driving licence or passport is needed to earn a living and whether there has been 'wilful refusal or culpable neglect' to pay the child support due.[270] It cannot question the child support calculation or the liability order. The court can only disqualify the NRP from driving or from holding or obtaining a passport, or commit them to prison, if there has been 'wilful refusal or culpable neglect'.[271] The decision as to whether to make the order is at the court's discretion. The CMS must prove 'beyond reasonable doubt' that the NRP has the ability to pay and has wilfully refused.[272]

A written statement from an employer is accepted as proof of earnings.[273]

Disqualification from driving or holding a passport

If the court decides that there has been wilful refusal or culpable neglect and that it is appropriate to disqualify the NRP from driving or from holding a passport, it makes an order.[274] If the CMS applied for an order but the court did not make one, the CMS can apply again if the parent's circumstances have changed.[275]

In England and Wales, there is no longer a prescribed form for the order. The law in Scotland requires that the order states the amount outstanding, including child support, collection and enforcement fees and the expenses incurred by the CMS in making the application.[276] If an order is made, the NRP must give up their driving licence and counterpart or any passport or travel authorisation to the court.

The implementation of the order may be suspended for a particular period or on particular conditions – eg, that the parent makes regular payments (or, in the case of an order concerning the holding of a passport, if the court is satisfied that exceptional circumstances justify the order being suspended).[277]

The maximum period of disqualification from driving or from holding a passport is two years.[278] If, after the order has been issued, part payment is made, either the NRP or the CMS can apply to the court to have the order revoked or the period of disqualification reduced.[279] The CMS can make representations to the court as to how much of the outstanding arrears should be paid before it would be appropriate for the court to revoke the order. When the court makes an order on holding a passport, it can order that the NRP be searched and that any money found can be paid towards the arrears due. If part payment is made this way, the court then has discretion to decide whether to reduce the period of disqualification or to revoke the order.[280]

If the amount is paid in full, the order must be revoked.[281] The NRP will have to apply to the DVLA and pay a fee for the driving licence to be reinstated. If the arrears have not been paid in full at the end of the period of disqualification, the CMS may apply again for disqualification.[282]

You may appeal against the court's decision. An appeal should be made within 21 days of the court's decision (28 days in Scotland, where the court can accept a late appeal if it considers that there are good reasons).[283]

Imprisonment

If the court decides that there has been 'wilful refusal or culpable neglect' and it is appropriate, a warrant for imprisonment is issued.[284] If the CMS has applied for the court to consider disqualification from driving or committal to prison, the court should explain the reasons why that is preferred. The CMS is likely to prefer pursuing commital to prison if it does not have sufficient information about the NRP's finances to judge the likely effect that pursuing disqualification would have on them.

A warrant for imprisonment cannot be issued against a NRP who is under 18.[285]

Instead of immediate committal to prison, the court usually fixes a term of imprisonment and suspends it (usually for a period of two years) on conditions.[286] The condition is usually that regular payments are made. A warrant of commitment is issued and, although there is in England and Wales no longer a prescribed form for this, in Scotland it will state the total amount outstanding, including child support, collection and enforcement fees and the expenses incurred by the CMS in making the application.[287] If the amount is paid in full, the NRP will not be imprisoned.

The maximum period of imprisonment is six weeks.[288] If, after the warrant has been issued, part payment is made, the period of imprisonment is reduced by the same proportion as that by which the debt has been reduced.[289]

If the NRP is imprisoned, release can be immediate if the liability order debt is paid in full. If part of the debt is paid, the prison sentence can be reduced.[290] Advisers should check whether the payment needs to be made to the prison or to the CMS.

The court cannot write off the arrears, so if full payment is not made, arrears still exist following the period of imprisonment. If a warrant is not issued or the court does not fix a term of imprisonment, the CMS can renew the application at a later date on the grounds that the NRP's circumstances have changed.[291]

If the NRP builds up a new debt (eg, by not keeping up with current child support payments), the CMS can go back to court to request a warrant in respect of each new debt.

4. Fees for enforcement action

If the Child Maintenance Service (CMS) takes certain enforcement action, fees are imposed on the non-resident parent (NRP) as follows:[292]

- £50 for making a deduction from earnings order (see p161);
- £50 for making a regular deduction order (see p171);
- £200 for making a lump-sum deduction order (see p173);
- £300 for applying for a liability order (see p180).

Enforcement fees may be waived by the CMS if:[293]

- an additional fee would otherwise be due because:
  - more than one deduction from earnings order is sought by the CMS because the NRP has more than one employer or has recently changed jobs; *or*
  - more than one regular deduction order or lump-sum order is sought because the NRP has more than one bank or building society account, or has recently changed accounts; *or*
  - the amount being collected under a deduction from earnings order or regular deduction order has changed; *or*
- the CMS has sought a liability order, but it was not granted; *or*
- the CMS's action to impose a deduction from earnings order, regular deduction order or lump-sum deduction order has been successfully challenged by the NRP by appeal or judicial review; *or*
- due to error or maladministration by the CMS, the deduction from earnings order, regular deduction order or lump-sum deduction order has lapsed or been discharged; *or*
- a deduction from earnings order is made because the NRP has chosen to use this as the method of paying the child support liability; *or*
- a deduction from earnings request (see p162) is made for a NRP in the armed forces when that parent is deployed on operational duty.

Note: there are no fees for enforcement action on outstanding arrears in cases under the '2003 rules' and '1993 rules'.

From 23 May 2016, enforcement fees can also be waived in certain circumstances (see p137) while the NRP is being offered a 'compliance opportunity' (see p135) to prove that they will pay voluntarily in order to be allowed to use 'direct pay' in a '2012 rules' case. In such cases, if a deduction from earnings order is imposed during the compliance period to cover a portion of the payments due, the fee for the order can be waived.[294] At the end of the compliance opportunity, if the order is varied (ie, because the NRP has not complied and it has to be varied to cover the full amount of child support due), an enforcement fee of £50 is due. This fee is only due the first time the deduction from earnings order is varied, and can be waived by the CMS for one of the usual reasons listed above.[295] The power to impose and waive these fees in these circumstances ended on 22 May 2021.[296]

The decision to waive an enforcement fee is a discretionary one and so the CMS must take into account the welfare of any child likely to be affected by the decision (see p124). There is no right of appeal against the decision, but if you are unhappy with the decision you should ask the CMS to look at it again and consider making a complaint (see Chapter 11).

An enforcement fee is payable to the CMS, not the person with care (PWC). It becomes due when the action is taken. Fees are recovered by the CMS from any arrears owed by the NRP before the balance is paid to the PWC.[297] If an enforcement fee is charged, the CMS must send the NRP a notice as soon as possible stating the amount of the fee and the enforcement action in respect of which it has been imposed.[298] The fees will then be included in any future statement of arrears.

Note: the rules on collecting and enforcing payments of child support also apply to payment of fees, except that the CMS cannot seek to disqualify a NRP from driving or from holding or obtaining a passport or other travel authorisation, or seek their imprisonment, where enforcement action is being taken against them solely to recover fees.[299]

5. **Delays in collection and enforcement**

Many cases accumulate arrears. In recent years, the Child Maintenance Service (CMS) has said that it has been pursuing a more vigorous approach to enforcement and taking enforcement action more quickly in response to a non-resident parent (NRP) failing to pay.

If you are a person with care (PWC) and concerned about the speed of pursuit, contact the CMS and explain the effects of this on the welfare of the child(ren). In particular, you may want to request that a deduction from earnings order be made. If a deduction from earnings order or another form of enforcement is refused, the reasons for this should be explained.

Note: enforcement action was suspended during the coronavirus pandemic, but has recommenced now. If the CMS is not pursuing enforcement action, you can make a complaint (see Chapter 11).

Note: enforcing the obligation to pay child support is at the discretion of the CMS.[300] This means that a PWC cannot decide which method of enforcement is used. If you believe that there has been undue delay by the CMS, or that it has not used its discretion reasonably or rationally, you can make a complaint (see Chapter 11). Judicial review (see p198) could also be considered. Get specialist advice before considering an application for judicial review.

If arrears have built up because of CMS maladministration, you may be eligible for compensation (see p245).

Enforcement by the person with care

Although there is no provision in child support legislation for the PWC to bring their own court action against the NRP for the child support due, it may be possible to do so. In practice, however, such action may be difficult. The European Court of Human Rights has confirmed that only the CMS has the legal standing to enforce child support, and that a lack of direct access to the courts by a PWC to enforce child support payments from a NRP does not breach the right to a fair hearing under the European Convention on Human Rights.[301]

In certain circumstances, legal action against the CMS may be possible if there has been a serious breach of statutory duties (such as discrimination). If you are considering legal action, get legal advice. However, it is not possible to sue the CMS for negligence in the way it deals with your case.

Using the complaints procedure is more likely to be an effective means of obtaining redress within a reasonable timescale (see Chapter 11).

Notes

1. **Arrears**

1 ss4(2)(b) and 7(3)(b) CSA 1991
2 DWP, *Supporting Separated Families: securing children's futures*, Cm 8399, July 2012; DWP, *Preparing for the Future, Tackling the Past: child maintenance – arrears and compliance strategy 2012-2017*, January 2013
3 Reg 7 CS(C&E) Regs
4 Reg 8A CS(MAJ) Regs
5 s28J CSA 1991
6 Reg 2(2) CS(VP) Regs
7 *DP v CMEC (CSM)* [2012] UKUT 63 (AAC)
8 Reg 3(b) CS(VP) Regs
9 Reg 3(a) CS(VP) Regs
10 Regs 2(2) and 4(b) CS(VP) Regs
11 Reg 4(a) CS(VP) Regs
12 s41B(1A) and (2) CSA 1991; reg 9 CS(MPA) Regs
13 Written Q&A UIN 266704, 19 June 2019; DWP, *Preparing for the Future, Tackling the Past: child maintenance – arrears and compliance strategy 2012-2017*, January 2013
14 Reg 3(3) CS(MPA) Regs
15 Reg 3(4) CS(MPA) Regs
16 Reg 3A CS(MPA) Regs

17 DWP, *Child Maintenance Frequently Asked Questions,* August 2012; para 53003 DMG
18 First Protocol, Art 1 European Convention on Human Rights
19 DWP, *Preparing for the Future, Tackling the Past: child maintenance – arrears and compliance strategy* 2012-2017, January 2013
20 s41A CSA 1991 and reg 7A CS(C&E) Regs; Sch 7, para 3(1) UC,PIP,JSA&ESA(C&P) Regs
21 DWP, *Preparing for the Future, Tackling the Past: child maintenance – arrears and compliance strategy 2012-2017*, January 2013
22 s41(2) and (2A) CSA 1991; reg 8 CS(AIAMA) Regs
23 Reg 8 CS(AIAMA) Regs
24 para 51005 DMG
25 Regs 3-8 CS(MA) Regs 2019 and Explanatory Memorandum
26 Sch 9B para 3(1) SS(C&P) Regs
27 Reg 7(1) CS(MPA) Regs
28 Child Maintenance and Enforcement Commission, *Child Maintenance and Other Payments Act: Summary of Responses to the Consultation on Draft Regulations*, November 2009, para 3
29 Child Maintenance and Enforcement Commission, *Child Maintenance and Other Payments Act: Summary of Responses to the Consultation on Draft Regulations*, November 2009, para 3
30 Reg 7(3) CS(MPA) Regs
31 Child Maintenance and Enforcement Commission, *Child Maintenance and Other Payments Act: Summary of Responses to the Consultation on Draft Regulations*, November 2009, para 3.5
32 Chapter 57 DMG
33 s41D CSA 1991
34 s41D(3) and (5)-(7) CSA 1991
35 DWP, *The Draft Child Support Management of Payments and Arrears (Amendment) Regulations 2012: government response to consultation on draft regulations*, October 2012
36 Reg 13D(1) and (2) CS(MPA) Regs
37 Reg 13D(3) CS(MPA) Regs
38 DWP, *The Draft Child Support Management of Payments and Arrears (Amendment) Regulations 2012: government response to consultation on draft regulations*, October 2012
39 Reg 13C(1) CS(MPA) Regs
40 Reg 13B CS(MPA) Regs
41 DWP, *The Draft Child Support Management of Payments and Arrears (Amendment) Regulations 2012: government response to consultation on draft regulations*, October 2012
42 Reg 13E(1) and (2) CS(MPA) Regs
43 Reg 13E(3) CS(MPA) Regs
44 Reg 13E(4) and (5) CS(MPA) Regs
45 DWP, *The Draft Child Support Management of Payments and Arrears (Amendment) Regulations 2012: government response to consultation on draft regulations*, October 2012
46 s41E CSA 1991
47 s41E(1) CSA 1991 and reg 13G CS(MPA) Regs
48 DWP, *Preparing for the Future, Tackling the Past: child maintenance – arrears and compliance strategy 2012-2017*, January 2013
49 CS(MA) Regs 2018, Explanatory Memorandum, para 7.30
50 Reg 9 CS(MA) Regs 2019 and Explanatory Memorandum
51 Reg 13F CS(MPA) Regs
52 The duties on the CMS to give written notice do not apply to someone who cannot be traced or who has died: regs 13(2) and 13H(2) CS(MPA) Regs
53 Reg 13H CS(MPA) Regs
54 Reg 13H(5) and (6) CS(MPA) Regs
55 Reg 13H(2) CS(MPA) Regs
56 Reg 13I CS(MPA) Regs
57 Reg 13H(4) CS(MPA) Regs
58 Reg 13J CS(MPA) Regs
59 para 63006 DMG
60 DWP, *Supporting Separated Families: securing children's futures*, Cm 8399, July 2012; DWP, *Preparing for the Future, Tackling the Past: child maintenance – arrears and compliance strategy 2012-2017*, January 2013
61 DWP, *Supporting Separated Families: securing children's futures*, Cm 8399, July 2012
62 DWP, *Preparing for the Future, Tackling the Past: child maintenance – arrears and compliance strategy 2012-2017*, January 2013
63 Regs 13G(g) and (h) and 13K CS(MPA) Regs
64 CS(MA) Regs 2018, Explanatory Memorandum, paras 7.21-7.23
65 Regs 13G(g) and (h) and 13K(1)(c) and (e) and (2)(c) CS(MPA) Regs
66 Reg 13H (3)(da)(I) CS(MPA) Regs
67 CS(MA) Regs 2018, Explanatory Memorandum, para 7.23

68 Reg 13J(2) CS(MPA) Regs
69 Reg 13H(1A) and (3)(da)(ii) CS(MPA) Regs
70 Reg 13H(3)(b) CS(MPA) Regs
71 Reg 13I CS(MPA) Regs
72 Reg 13J CS(MPA) Regs
73 Regs 13G(g) and (h) and 13K(1)(b) and (d) and (2)(b) CS(MPA) Regs
74 Regs 13H(2) and 13J CS(MPA) Regs
75 Regs 13G(g) and (h), 13K(1)(a) and (2)(a) and 13J(2) CS(MPA) Regs

2. **Enforcement action to recover arrears**

76 Reg 13 CSF Regs
77 *KA v CMEC* [2009] UKUT 99 (AAC)
78 Reg 5(4)(f) The Debt Respite Scheme (Breathing Space Moratorium and Mental Health Crisis Moratorium) (England and Wales) Regulations 2020 No.1311
79 gov.uk/child-maintenance-if-one-parent-lives-abroad/other-partner-lives-abroad
80 *Child maintenance: overseas cases and income (UK),* House of Commons Library briefing paper 7775, December 2020
81 Details available at gov.uk/child-maintenance-if-one-parent-lives-abroad
82 Council Regulation (EC) No 4/2009 of 18 December 2008 on jurisdiction, applicable law, recognition and enforcement of decisions and cooperation in matters relating to maintenance obligations
83 Convention of 23 November 2007 on the International Recovery of Child Support and Other Forms of Family Maintenance
84 s31 CSA 1991
85 Reg 8(3) and (4) CS(C&E) Regs
86 Reg 8(4) CS(C&E) Regs
87 Reg 8(5) CS(C&E) Regs
88 s29(4)(a) CSA 1991; reg 3(3) CS(C&E) Regs 1992
89 *R v Secretary of State for Social Security ex parte Biggin* [1995] 2 FCR 595, [1995] 1 FLR 851
90 Sch 1 para 10 CS(NIRA) Regs
91 CSA(CA)O; s342(1)(e)(ii) Armed Forces Act 2006; reg 10 Armed Forces (Forfeitures and Deductions) Regulations 2009 No.1109; *Commanding Officers Guide: Manual of Service Law,* Ministry of Defence, 2011 (updated March 2021), *Chapter 20: Forfeitures and Deductions,* para 45
92 Regs 3(3) and 6 CS(DEOAMMA) Regs
93 Reg 15 CS(C&E) Regs
94 Reg 15(1) CS(C&E) Regs
95 s32(8) and (11) CSA 1991; reg 25(ab) and (b) CS(C&E) Regs
96 Reg 1(3)(a) CS(C&E) Regs
97 Reg 1(3)(b) CS(C&E) Regs
98 Reg 1(3)(c) CS(C&E) Regs
99 s31(6) CSA 1991
100 s31(7) CSA 1991
101 s14A CSA 1991; reg 4(2)(b) CSI Regs; CMS, *Make Child Maintenance Deductions From an Employee's Pay,* gov.uk/child-maintenance-for-employers
102 Reg 9 CS(C&E) Regs
103 Reg 16(1) CS(C&E) Regs
104 Reg 16(2) CS(C&E) Regs
105 Reg 16(3) CS(C&E) Regs
106 s32(8) and (11) CSA 1991; reg 25(aa), (b) and (c) CS(C&E) Regs
107 Reg 13 CS(C&E) Regs; s8(2)(b) ERA 1996
108 s9 ERA 1996
109 s12(3)-(5) ERA 1996
110 childmaintenanceservice.direct.gov.uk
111 Reg 1(3)(a) CS(C&E) Regs
112 Reg 1(3)(b) CS(C&E) Regs; reg 1(3)(c) CS(C&E) Regs
113 Reg 9 CS(C&E) Regs
114 Reg 9(d) CS(C&E) Regs
115 Reg 11(2) CS(C&E) Regs
116 Regs 10(1) and (2) and 11 CS(C&E) Regs, as substituted for '2012 rules' cases and other 'arrears only' cases by reg 4(4) CS(MOC&NCR) Regs
117 Reg 10(3) CS(C&E) Regs, as substituted for '2012 rules' cases by reg 4(4) CS(MOC&NCR) Regs
118 Regs 1(4), 11 and 12 CS(MOC&NCR) Regs
119 Reg 14(1) CS(C&E) Regs
120 Reg 14(2) CS(C&E) Regs
121 s32(8) and (11) CSA 1991; reg 25(aa) CS(C&E) Regs
122 Reg 12(2) CS(C&E) Regs
123 Reg 12(4) CS(C&E) Regs
124 Reg 12(3A) CS(C&E) Regs
125 Reg 8 CS(AIAMA) Regs
126 Reg 24(2)(a) and (4) CS(C&E) Regs
127 Reg 24(2)(b) CS(C&E) Regs
128 Reg 17 CS(C&E) Regs
129 Reg 18 CS(C&E) Regs
130 Reg 19 CS(C&E) Regs
131 Regs 10(3) and 20(1)(g) CS(C&E) Regs, as substituted for '2012 rules' cases and other 'arrears only' cases by regs 4(4) and (6) and 11 CS(MOC&NCR) Regs
132 Reg 20(1) CS(C&E) Regs
133 Reg 20(1A) CS(C&E) Regs

134 Reg 36 CS(C&E) Regs, as inserted by reg 3(3) CS(DEOAMMA) Regs, modifying reg 20 by inserting paras (1)(i) and (1B) until 21 May 2021
135 Reg 4 CS(DEOAMMA) Regs, amending reg 12 CS(MOC&NCR) Regs until 21 May 2021
136 Reg 20(2) CS(C&E) Regs
137 Reg 21(1) CS(C&E) Regs
138 Reg 21(4) CS(C&E) Regs
139 Reg 21(5) CS(C&E) Regs
140 Reg 21(6) CS(C&E) Regs
141 Reg 22(1) CS(C&E) Regs
142 Reg 22(2) CS(C&E) Regs
143 Reg 22(3) CS(C&E) Regs
144 Reg 22(3A) CS(C&E) Regs
145 Reg 8(1) CS(C&E) Regs
146 Reg 3(4) CS(C&E) Regs
147 Reg 3(6)(c) CS(C&E) Regs
148 Reg 3(5) CS(C&E) Regs
149 Reg 3(6) CS(C&E) Regs
150 r5 and Sch Forms 5 (for appeal against the order) and 5AA (for appeal about whether 'good reason' applies) AS(CSR)
151 Reg 22(4) CS(C&E) Regs
152 s32(6) CSA 1991
153 *Secretary of State for Social Security v Shotton* [1996] 2 FLR 241
154 ss48 and 49 CSA 1991; r6 AS(CSR)
155 ss32A and 32F CSA 1991
156 Reg 25A CS(C&E) Regs
157 para 56012 DMG
158 Child Maintenance and Enforcement Commission, *Deduction Order Review*, Research Report No.2, March 2011, p16
159 Reg 25XA CS(C&E) Regs
160 Reg 25A(1), definition of 'joint account', CS(C&E) Regs
161 Reg 25X CS(C&E) Regs
162 DWP, *Child Maintenance: changes to compliance measures*, December 2018
163 Reg 25XC CS(C&E) Regs
164 CS(MA) Regs 2018, Explanatory Memorandum, para 7.11
165 Regs 25E(5A) and 25O(5A) CS(C&E) Regs
166 ss32D and 32K CSA 1991; regs 25E, 25O and 25AC CS(C&E) Regs
167 Reg 25Z CS(C&E) Regs
168 s32A CSA 1991
169 para 56068 DMG
170 s32B(1) CSA 1991; reg 25A1 CS(C&E) Regs
171 Reg 25XB CS(C&E) Regs
172 s32A(5) and (7) CSA 1991; reg 25B(1) CS(C&E) Regs
173 Reg 25C CS(C&E) Regs, as amended by reg 4(7) CS(MOC&NCR) Regs for '2012 rules' cases
174 Reg 25H CS(C&E) Regs
175 Reg 25D CS(C&E) Regs
176 Reg 25G CS(C&E) Regs
177 Reg 25G(2)(d) CS(C&E) Regs
178 Reg 25I CS(C&E) Regs
179 Reg 25I(3) CS(C&E) Regs
180 Reg 25IA CS(C&E) Regs
181 ss32E and 32G CSA 1991; reg 25N CS(C&E) Regs
182 s32E(6) CSA 1991; reg 25M CS(C&E) Regs
183 Reg 25MA CS(C&E) Regs
184 Reg 25XB CS(C&E) Regs
185 s32F CSA 1991; reg 25MA(4) CS(C&E) Regs
186 ss32G(5) and (6) and 32H(1) CSA 1991
187 s32F(3)(a) CSA 1991
188 s32F(3)(b) and (4) CSA 1991
189 Reg 25A(3)(b) CS(C&E) Regs
190 s32I CSA 1991; reg 25N(1) and (2) CS(C&E) Regs
191 Reg 25N(3) and (4) CS(C&E) Regs
192 Reg 25P(1) and (2) CS(C&E) Regs
193 Reg 25P(6) CS(C&E) Regs
194 Reg 25Q CS(C&E) Regs
195 Reg 25Z(b) CS(C&E) Regs
196 s32J(3) CSA 1991; reg 25R CS(C&E) Regs
197 Regs 25R and 25N CS(C&E) Regs
199 Reg 25K CS(C&E) Regs
200 Reg 25KA CS(C&E) Regs
202 Reg 25S CS(C&E) Regs
203 Reg 25T CS(C&E) Regs
204 Reg 25U CS(C&E) Regs
205 Reg 25AB CS(C&E) Regs
206 **EW** paras 9.17 and 9.19 *Practice Direction 30A: appeals*, Family Procedure Rules 2010; *AH v SSWP (CSA)* [2017] EWFC 9
S rr5AB and 5AC AS(CSR); r2.6 Act of Sederunt (Summary Applications, Statutory Applications, Appeals etc. Rules) 1999 No.929
207 Reg 25A(3)(b) and (4) CS(C&E) Regs
208 s43A CSA 1991; reg 11 CS(MPA) Regs
209 Child Maintenance and Enforcement Commission, *Child Maintenance and Other Payments Act: Summary of Responses to the Consultation on Draft Regulations*, November 2009, para 4.9
210 Reg 12 CS(MPA) Regs
211 Reg 13 CS(MPA) Regs
212 Reg 13(3) CS(MPA) Regs

213 Child Maintenance and Enforcement Commission, *Child Maintenance and Other Payments Act: Summary of Responses to the Consultation on Draft Regulations*, November 2009, para 4.11
214 Child Maintenance and Enforcement Commission, *Child Maintenance and Other Payments Act: Summary of Responses to the Consultation on Draft Regulations*, November 2009, para 4.6
215 para 61027 DMG
216 Child Maintenance and Enforcement Commission, *Child Maintenance and Other Payments Act: Summary of Responses to the Consultation on Draft Regulations*, November 2009, para 4.8
217 DWP, *Preparing for the Future, Tackling the Past: child maintenance – arrears and compliance strategy 2012-2017*, January 2013
218 Child Maintenance and Enforcement Commission, *Child Maintenance and Other Payments Act: Summary of Responses to the Consultation on Draft Regulations*, November 2009, para 4.7
219 s33 CSA 1991
220 para 73023 DMG
221 Reg 27 CS(C&E) Regs
222 s33(3) CSA 1991
223 s33(4) CSA 1991
224 *Bird v SSWP* [2008] EWHC 3159 (Admin)
225 Reg 29 CS(C&E) Regs; r3 AS(CSR)
226 Reg 28(2) and (2A) CS(C&E) Regs; DWP, *Preparing for the Future, Tackling the Past: child maintenance – arrears and compliance strategy 2012-2017*, January 2013
227 *R (Sutherland) v SSWP* [2004] EWHC 800 (Admin)
228 s9 Limitation Act 1980
229 *CMEC v Mitchell* [2010] EWCA Civ 333
230 *Farley v CSA and another* [2006] UKHL 31
231 *Explanatory Memorandum* to the Child Support (Collection and Enforcement and Maintenance Calculation) (Amendment No.2) Regulations 2021 No.763
232 *Secretary of State for Social Security v Nicol* [1996] SLT 34
233 ss35(1) and 38(1) CSA 1991
234 s38 CSA 1991
235 DWP, *Preparing for the Future, Tackling the Past: child maintenance – arrears and compliance strategy 2012-2017*, January 2013
236 s35 CSA 1991; Part 3 TCEA 2007
237 Regs 6-8 TCG Regs
238 Sch 12 para 58 TCEA 2007
239 Reg 4 TCG Regs
240 Taking Control of Goods (Fees) Regulations 2014 No.1
241 s33(5) CSA 1991
242 Reg 11(2) and (3) RJOF Regs 2005
243 s36 CSA 1991
244 s32L CSA 1991
245 s32L(2) CSA 1991
246 s32L(5) CSA 1991
247 s32L(5) CSA 1991
248 s32L(7) CSA 1991
249 s32L(11)(b) CSA 1991
250 r14.2(2)(c)(iii) Insolvency (England and Wales) Rules 2016 No.1024
251 *CMEC v Beesley* [2010] EWCA Civ 1344; s382(5) Insolvency Act 1986, as amended by s142 WRA 2012
252 s285(1) and (2) Insolvency Act 1986
253 para 77015 DMG
254 DWP, *Preparing for the Future, Tackling the Past: child maintenance – arrears and compliance strategy 2012-2017*, January 2013
255 s145 Bankruptcy (Scotland) Act 2016
256 ss162, 163 and 172 Bankruptcy (Scotland) Act 2016
257 s176 Bankruptcy (Scotland) Act 2016

3. **Sanctions for non-payment**

258 ss39A, 39B, 40, 40A and 40B CSA 1991
259 ss39A(1) and 39B(1)(a) and (b) CSA 1991; *Karoonian v CMEC and Gibbons v CMEC* [2012] EWCA Civ 1379
260 DWP, *Preparing for the Future, Tackling the Past: child maintenance – arrears and compliance strategy 2012-2017*, January 2013; DWP, *Child Maintenance: changes to compliance measures*, December 2018
261 National Tables; child maintenance service statistics data to December 2021
262 s39C(2)-(4) CSA 1991
263 ss39A(2), 39B, 40 and 40A CSA 1991
264 ss40(5) and 40A (3) CSA 1991
265 s39A(4) CSA 1991
266 s39B(1) and (6) CSA 1991
267 ss39A(3) and 39B(4) CSA 1991
268 **EW** Regs 35(1) and 35A(1) CS(C&E) Regs
S rr5A and 5AZA and Forms 5A and 5AZA AS(CSR)
269 **EW** Reg 35(1) CS(C&E) Regs
S r5B(1) AS(CSR)
270 ss39A(3) and 39B(4) CSA 1991
271 ss39B(5), 40(3), 40A(1) and 40B(1) CSA 1991
272 *Karoonian v CMEC and Gibbons v CMEC* [2012] EWCA Civ 1379

273 **EW** Regs 35(2) and 35A(2) CS(C&E) Regs
S r5C AS(CSR)
274 ss39B and 40B CSA 1991
275 **EW** Regs 35(3) and 35A(3) CS(C&E) Regs
S r5F AS(CSR)
276 **EW** Regs 35(4)-(5), 35A(4)-(5) and Schs 4 and 5 CS(C&E) Regs (omitted as from 19 July 2021 by CS(CEMC) Regs)
S Regs 35(5) and 35A(5) CS(C&E) Regs; rr5E and 5EA and Forms 5E and 5EA AS(CSR)
All ss39B(8) and 40B(3) CSA 1991
277 ss39C(2)-(4) and 40B(1)(b) CSA 1991
278 ss39C(1) and 40B(1) CSA 1991
279 ss39E(1) and (3) and 40B(5)(a) CSA 1991
280 ss39D and 39E(4) CSA 1991
281 ss39E(2) and 40B(5)(b) CSA 1991
282 ss39C(5) and 40B(7) CSA 1991
283 **EW** s111A Magistrates Court Act 1980
S r6.3 Act of Sederunt (Sheriff Appeal Court Rules) 2015 No.356
All ss39B(11)(b) and 40B(8)(c) CSA 1991
284 ss40 and 40A CSA 1991
285 ss40(5) and 40A(3) CSA 1991
286 ss40(3)(b) and 40A(1)(b) CSA 1991
287 **EW** as Sch 3 CS(C&E) Regs was omitted as from 19 July 2021 by CS(CEMC) Regs
S Reg 2 Child Support (Civil Imprisonment) (Scotland) Regulations 2001 No.1236; r5D and Form 5D AS(CSR)
288 ss40(7) and 40A(5) CSA 1991
289 **EW** Reg 34(5) and (6) CS(C&E) Regs
S Reg 3 Child Support (Civil Imprisonment) (Scotland) Regulations 2001 No.1236
290 ss40(8) and 40A(6) CSA 1991; reg 34 CS(C&E) Regs
291 **EW** Reg 33(3) CS(C&E) Regs
S r5F AS(CSR)

4. **Fees for enforcement action**

292 Reg 10 CSF Regs 2014
293 Reg 12 CSF Regs 2014
294 Reg 12A CSF Regs 2014; CS(DOF) Regs, Explanatory Memorandum
295 Regs 10(2) and 12(1A) CSF Regs 2014
296 Reg 1(2) CS(DOF) Regs
297 Reg 11 CSF Regs 2014
298 Reg 7(1B) and (4) CS(C&E) Regs
299 Reg 13 CSF Regs 2014

5. **Delays in collection and enforcement**

300 *Kehoe v UK* [2009] 48 EHRR, [2008] 2 FLR 1014
301 *Kehoe v UK* [2009] 48 EHRR, [2008] 2 FLR 1014

Chapter 9

Challenging a decision: revisions and supersessions

This chapter covers:

1. Changing a decision

Most decisions can be changed or challenged by a revision or supersession. However, there are some decisions that cannot (see p198).

Correcting an accidental error

The Child Maintenance Service (CMS) can also correct an accidental error in a decision or in the record of a decision at any time.[1] An 'accidental error' may include an obvious administrative or clerical error, such as an income figure being recorded incorrectly on the CMS computer system because of a typing error. The correction of an accidental error can be requested by a party to the decision, or initiated by the CMS. The correction is then treated as part of the record of the decision.[2]

An 'accidental error' differs from an 'official error' (see p202).

When a correction is made, the parties must be notified of the corrected decision and provided with the usual details (see p128). The corrected decision can be revised, subject to the usual time limits (see p200) which begin on the day notice of the correction was given.

A revision or supersession is a decision that changes an earlier decision.

- **A revision** means that the decision which is wrong is itself changed. The revised decision usually takes effect from the date the original decision had effect.
- **A supersession** means that the original decision is replaced by a new decision, which takes effect from a later date.

As with all decisions, revisions and supersessions are made by officials who work for the CMS and who make decisions on behalf of the Secretary of State for Work and Pensions. A revision or supersession usually happens because the CMS is told that something is wrong or has changed since the initial decision was made. The CMS may also itself initiate a revision or supersession.

If a decision is challenged within 30 days, it may be revised. Outside this time period, a decision can only be revised if the CMS accepts a late application (see p201), or in special circumstances where the original decision was wrong in such a way that it can be revised at any time – eg, if there has been an official error (see p202). If these special circumstances are not met, the decision may be superseded instead. A decision may also be superseded if circumstances have changed since it was made. The table below shows when decisions may be revised or superseded.

If the original decision is not incorrect, but the CMS has not dealt with the case properly in some way (eg, there has been intimidating or unnecessarily intrusive questioning, or unwarranted demands for evidence and documentation), a complaint can be made at any time (see Chapter 11).

In some cases where the original decision is wrong (eg, where maladministration has led to an official error), it may be appropriate to make a complaint as well as applying for a revision.

Revisions and supersessions

Why is the decision being challenged?	*When?*	*What can be done?*
The decision is wrong for any reason.	Within 30 days of being told the decision.	Revision.
The CMS made a mistake (an 'official error'), or it was misled or did not know about something that would have affected its decision, or someone is not a parent of a child to whom a calculation relates.	At any time.	Revision. If the CMS did not know something or was misled, the decision may only be revised in certain circumstances (see p200). If these do not apply, the decision may be superseded.
The decision is wrong for any reason (other than one of the above reasons).	More than than 30 days after being told the decision.	Supersession. A late application for revision may also be made (see p201).
Something that affects the decision has changed.	At any time.	Supersession.

A variation is an element of the child support calculation. This means that if an application for a variation is made after a calculation is in force and the CMS accepts it, it will then revise or supersede the original calculation so as to include the variation. See Chapter 5 for details.

For how to change a decision on deductions of child support from benefits, see CPAG's *Welfare Benefits and Tax Credits Handbook*.

If you believe that the other parent is fraudulently claiming a benefit, you cannot directly challenge this decision, but you may raise the issue with the CMS, which contacts another part of the Department for Work and Pensions, which then investigates.

Decisions of the First-tier Tribunal and the Upper Tribunal (see Chapter 10) may also be superseded or revised, but only in certain circumstances (see p204 and p205).

Note: most decisions are now about '2012 rules' cases. However, some decisions may still be made about previous '1993 rules' or '2003 rules' cases, even if made after ongoing liability for child support in those cases has ended. Nothing in the rules about ending liability on those cases prevents decisions from being made on liability before the cases ended. Any such decisions may be challenged as explained in this chapter.[3]

Challenging a decision that cannot be revised or superseded

Some decisions cannot be revised or superseded. These are mainly about information gathering, collection and enforcement (including decisions about fees), and refusals to make an interim or default maintenance decision.

If you want to challenge such a decision, provide the CMS with further information and ask it to reconsider. If the decision involved the CMS exercising its discretion, there may be further information that could be provided to the CMS about the welfare of any children affected (see p124). If the CMS refuses to change the decision, you could make a complaint. An accidental error in a decision or in the record of a decision can also be corrected at any time (see p196).

Some decisions on the enforcement of arrears cannot be revised or superseded, but may be appealed in court (see p161).

Judicial review

Judicial review is the legal procedure that allows a court to examine the way in which a public body has exercised its decision-making power to ensure that it has done so lawfully.[4] A person affected by a decision or action of a public body or one of its officers may ask the High Court (or the Court of Session in Scotland) to carry out a judicial review of the decision or action. Unlike tribunals, these courts have the power to order you to pay the other side's costs as well as your own.

A judicial review looks at the validity of the process by which a decision was made, rather than the actual result of the decision.

The court can 'set aside' the decision and can also order the public body which made the decision to consider it again in a lawful way. Judicial review is a 'last resort' process and is not usually possible if there is a right to raise the issue in an appeal to the First-tier Tribunal, Upper Tribunal or the court. If you are considering a judicial review of a CMS decision, you should seek legal advice as soon as possible after the decision is made.

In England and Wales, before you can apply for a judicial review in the High Court you must usually follow a 'pre-action protocol'. This is designed to avoid expensive litigation, and the majority of straightforward cases are resolved at this stage. It is therefore a valuable way of procuring the changing of a decision when there is no right of appeal. This protocol does not apply in Scotland, but it is generally good practice to avoid litigation and the sending of a 'letter before claim' may achieve a satisfactory outcome.

Judicial review may be used to challenge a decision of the Upper Tribunal to refuse permission to appeal against a First-tier Tribunal decision, and occasionally to challenge First-tier Tribunal decisions in the Upper Tribunal.

In England and Wales, an application must be made to the High Court promptly and, in any event, within three months of the decision being challenged.[5] In Scotland, an application must be made within three months (or a longer time if the Court of Session considers it equitable in the circumstances).[6] The court's permission must be obtained before making an application.[7]

Judicial review of a child support decision may succeed if:[8]

- the CMS makes an error in law – eg, it does something it has no power to do; *or*
- the CMS fails to take into account a relevant matter or takes an irrelevant matter into account, or where a decision is 'so outrageous in its defiance of logic or of accepted moral standards that no sensible person who had considered the question could have arrived at it'[9]; *or*
- there has been procedural unfairness.

For more details about judicial review, see cpag.org.uk/jr and CPAG's *Welfare Benefits and Tax Credits Handbook.*

2. Revisions

The Child Maintenance Service (CMS) can revise a decision:[10]

- on its own initiative; *or*
- if requested by a person with care (PWC), non-resident parent (NRP) (or child applicant in Scotland); *or*
- if a person applies for a variation.

Decisions that can be revised

Most child support decisions can be revised, including:[11]

- a decision to make a calculation (including a variation on a calculation), an interim maintenance decision or a default maintenance decision;
- a decision not to make a calculation, unless the CMS has made an interim or default maintenance decision instead (in which case, this decision may be revised). A refusal to make an interim or default maintenance decision may not be revised (but you may ask the CMS to reconsider its refusal);
- a decision of the First-tier Tribunal to make, or to refuse to agree to, a variation to a calculation following a referral by the CMS;
- any supersession decision made by the CMS (see p204);
- a decision which has previously been revised.

A decision can only be revised on the basis of the circumstances at the time the decision took effect. It cannot be revised because of a change in circumstances after the date the decision was made, or because of an expected change.[12] Instead, the decision can be superseded (see p204) or a new child support application can be made.

For revisions of default maintenance decisions, see p128.

Note: under the 'test case' rules (see p237), the CMS can postpone the revision of a decision until the outcome of an appeal in the test case is known.

When a decision can be revised

A decision can be revised:

- on any grounds, provided an application for a revision is made within the time limit or a late application is accepted (see below); *or*
- at any time if there are specific grounds (see p202).

Time limits for a revision on 'any grounds'

The CMS can revise a decision on any grounds if:

- a person applies within 30 days of the decision (or of the date an accidental error in the decision, or in the record of the decision, was corrected); *or*
- a person applies for a variation within 30 days, provided the grounds for a variation existed from the date of the decision being revised; *or*
- the CMS initiates the revision within 30 days of the original decision.

To apply for a revision on any grounds, you do not have to provide a reason for challenging the decision. It is enough that you believe the decision to be wrong.

If you apply within the 30-day time limit, but the CMS refuses to carry out a revision because there is insufficient information or evidence, it may allow you more time to provide this if requested (the CMS generally allows 14 days to provide information and extends this to 16 days to allow for the time taken to reach the CMS by post). If the CMS does not allow this extra time to provide information and evidence, it may still revise the decision at a later date if it accepts a late application for a revision (see below).

If you miss the time limit, it may be possible to make a late application (see below). In addition, check whether there are specific grounds to apply for a revision at any time (see below). Using the facility to upload documents on the online portal avoids any delay with postal services.

Late applications

The CMS can extend the 30-day period for applying for a revision on any grounds if it considers that:[13]

- the application has merit; *and*
- there are 'special circumstances' which mean that it was not practicable to apply within the time limit; *and*
- it is reasonable to allow the application.

'Special circumstances' are not defined. Any special circumstances can count. Include as much detail as possible to explain why an application is late. The application for an extension must identify the decision you want revised and explain why an extension should be granted.[14] There is no absolute time limit for seeking a revision on any grounds. However, the longer the delay in applying for a revision, the more compelling the special circumstances must be.[15] Not being aware of, or misunderstanding, the law is not usually accepted as special circumstances.

When the CMS is considering whether to accept a late application, any days prior to the correction of an accidental error in a decision or in the record of a decision are not counted towards the time limit.[16]

An application that is refused may not be renewed,[17] although the CMS may have power to reconsider a refusal to extend.[18] If a late application for a revision is refused, the CMS should then consider whether the decision can be revised on one of the specific grounds on which a decision may be revised at any time (see p202) or whether it can be superseded.[19]

If the CMS refuses to accept a late application for an 'any grounds' revision, this means it has considered whether to revise the original decision. There is no right to appeal any decision not to extend the time limit, but you can appeal to the First-tier Tribunal against the original decision.[20]

Judicial review of a refusal to extend the time limit for making a revision may also be possible (see p198).

Note: because a supersession (see p204) cannot usually lead to a decision being backdated to the original effective date, if possible you should make a late application for a revision. However, in case this is not accepted, an application for a supersession can be made at the same time, if appropriate. For example, a decision may be based on the wrong information about a child's education. If you have missed the deadline for applying for a revision, you may make a late application (giving special reasons) and you may also apply for a supersession if there has been a mistake about a fact (see p205).

'Any time' revisions on specific grounds

The CMS can revise a decision at any time if:[21]

- an appeal has been made in time (or within the time allowed for late appeals) and it has not yet been determined. If an appeal is lodged, the CMS checks whether the decision should be revised. This allows the CMS to take into account any new information that has come to light in the appeal process. If a decision is revised in these circumstances, the appeal may lapse (see p204); *or*
- there has been an 'official error' (see below); *or*
- the decision is wrong because of a misrepresentation or failure to disclose a material fact (see p203) and, because of this, the decision is more advantageous to the person who misrepresented or failed to disclose than it would otherwise have been; *or*
- it is an interim maintenance decision or default maintenance decision; *or*
- the information about historic income (or unearned income for a variation) given to it by HM Revenue and Customs (HMRC) has since been amended; *or*
- the decision is wrong because a child support calculation has been made for someone who was not, at the time it was made, a parent of the qualifying child.

If the CMS makes a decision which is then appealed and, while that appeal is pending, the CMS makes a second decision on the same case, when the First-tier Tribunal decides the appeal on the first decision, the CMS can revise its second decision at any time if it would have been made differently had the CMS known about the tribunal's decision.[22]

Official error

'Official error' is a mistake made by an officer of the CMS, another part of the Department for Work and Pensions or HMRC, which was not caused, or contributed to, by anyone outside these bodies.[23] This includes mistakes of law (see p205), except those only shown to be an error by a decision of the Upper Tribunal or court. It also includes mistakes of fact, such as:

- a mistake of arithmetic;
- a wrong assumption about a person's circumstances where there was no evidence for it;
- a mistake made because CMS staff failed to ask something that was relevant, failed to take specific evidence into account, or did not forward information or evidence, when they should have done, to the officer who made the decision.

Note: if the official error appears to be accidental (eg, a mistake of arithmetic), you can ask the CMS to correct this. The CMS can correct an accidental error in a decision, or in the record of a decision, at any time (see p196). If the CMS does so, the time limit for requesting a revision of the decision begins from the date of the correction.[24]

Misrepresentation and failure to disclose

A **'misrepresentation'** is a written or spoken statement of fact which is untrue.[25] This applies to an untrue statement, even if the person making it believes it to be true.[26]

There is only a **'failure to disclose'** a fact if there is a legal duty to report that fact to the CMS.[27] Therefore, a person who is asked to give information, but does not, has failed to disclose that information. However, if a person is not asked for the information, there can be no failure to disclose unless it is one of the facts that a PWC or NRP must always report. There is no general duty to report all changes of circumstances to the CMS, but there are some changes which must be reported (see p50).

The CMS can only consider a revision if the original decision was more advantageous to the person who misrepresented or failed to disclose.[28]

How to apply for a revision

The notification of a decision (see p128) explains how to ask for a revision of that decision.[29] The request for a revision may be made by telephone or through the webchat facility or by uploading a written request online. Unless the issue is straightforward, it is best to follow up any telephone call to the CMS in writing, confirming the reason for the request.

The CMS is neither required to notify the parties that it is considering a revision nor required to inform one party that the other has applied for a revision. However, if there is an application for a variation that has had a preliminary consideration[30] or a request for a revision of a calculation with a previously agreed variation,[31] the other parties are usually contacted and asked for their representations.

There are rules about what information the CMS should disclose (see p51).

If you request a revision, you must show that there are grounds for so doing,[32] unless you are applying within the time limit or a late application is accepted (see p201) (in which case, it is enough that you simply think that the decision is wrong).

Provide a full explanation of your reasons for seeking the revision, and any supporting information or evidence.

If you do not provide sufficient information or evidence for the CMS to make a decision, the CMS may permit you more time in which to do so (see p200).

The CMS can decide to:

- revise the decision; *or*
- make a default maintenance decision (see p127); *or*
- refuse to revise the decision.

If someone has lodged an appeal (see Chapter 10), the CMS can still consider whether the decision should be revised. If it is revised and the revised decision is more advantageous to the person appealing, the appeal lapses (see p215).[33]

If the revised decision does not benefit the person appealing, the appeal goes ahead against the decision as revised. The person who appealed is given one month to make any further representations on the appeal.[34]

The revised decision

All the parties must be notified of the decision and provided with the usual details (see p128).[35] If there is more than one PWC in relation to a NRP, all must be notified. The normal rules on disclosure of information apply (see p51).[36]

If the decision is revised, this normally has the same effective date as the decision it replaces,[37] unless the effective date was wrong, in which case the revised decision has the effective date it should have had.[38]

If a revision is refused, the notification of the decision must include the reasons for the refusal and details of how to appeal.

The time limit for appealing against a decision that has been revised runs from the date of the notice of the revised decision.[39]

3. Supersessions

The Child Maintenance Service (CMS) can supersede a decision at any time, with or without an application, if certain rules are met. Usually a decision is superseded because of a change in circumstances since the decision was made. There is no general duty to tell the CMS of all changes of circumstances. See p50 for the changes that you must tell the CMS about. A decision can also be superseded if it was wrong in law (see p205).

The main difference between a revision and a supersession is that a superseded decision generally takes effect from the date on which it is made (see p208), whereas a revision generally takes effect from the effective date of the decision that is being revised. However, there are exceptions to this general rule.

A child support calculation is likely to be subject to regular supersessions. See p73 for the rules about annual reviews and p75 for the rules about periodic current income checks.

Decisions that can be superseded

Most child support decisions (whether made by the CMS, the First-tier Tribunal or the Upper Tribunal) can be superseded.[40] Decisions that can be superseded include:

- a decision to make a child support calculation (including a variation of a calculation), an interim maintenance decision or a default maintenance decision (see p128);
- a decision of a First-tier Tribunal on a CMS referral of a variation application;
- a revised decision (see p200).

When a decision can be superseded

The CMS can normally supersede a decision if:[41]

- there has been a relevant change of circumstances since the decision had effect, or it is expected that there will be such a change. In some circumstances, there must be a significant change in the amount of the calculation as a result (see p206); *or*
- it was made in ignorance of, or was based on a mistake about, a material fact; *or*
- there is an application for a variation of the calculation.

A decision made by the CMS may also be superseded if it is wrong in law (see below).

If the CMS is notified of a change of circumstances, it does not have to consider anything apart from that change when it is considering whether to supersede the decision. If the CMS is acting on its own initiative to supersede the decision, it does not have to consider anything other than the change that caused it to act.[42] It does not have to investigate whether all the other circumstances are still correct. However, the CMS might decide to incorporate the supersession process into a 'case check', which could result in other changes or errors being identified, and subsequent revisions or supersessions being carried out.

Under the 'test case' rules, the CMS may delay superseding a decision until the outcome of an appeal in another test case is known (see p237).

Wrong in law

If a decision is wrong in law, it may be superseded. However, this could also constitute an official error and therefore be grounds for a revision at any time (see p202). This may be more advantageous than a supersession, as a revised decision normally takes effect from the date that the original decision took effect.

A decision is wrong in law if:[43]

- when making it, the CMS misinterpreted or overlooked part or all of an Act of Parliament, a regulation or relevant caselaw; *or*
- there is no evidence to support it; *or*
- the facts are such that no reasonable person applying the law could have come to such a conclusion; *or*
- there is a breach of 'natural justice' – ie, the procedure used has led to unfairness, or the officer who took the decision appeared to be biased;[44] *or*
- the CMS has not given sufficient reasons for the decision; *or*

- when exercising its discretion, the CMS took something irrelevant into account or ignored something relevant – eg, the welfare of a child (see p124).[45]

A decision is also wrong in law if the regulation under which it is made was not made lawfully.

When a decision cannot be superseded

The CMS cannot supersede a decision:[46]
- which may be revised instead (see p199);
- refusing to make, or cancelling, a child support calculation. A further application for a calculation should be made instead.

In a case in which gross income is determined on the basis of current income (see p69), a decision cannot be superseded on the basis that there has been, or it is anticipated that there will be, a change in the current income of the non-resident parent (NRP), unless the new income level is at least 25 per cent different from the previous income.[47] This 'tolerance level' does not apply if the superseding decision:[48]
- is made by the CMS as part of an annual review of gross income or a periodic check of current income; *or*
- is made because of an error of law; *or*
- supersedes a calculation decision that was based on an estimate of current income.

The CMS intends calculations to remain in place for a reasonable period. In many cases, the calculation is likely to remain in place for the year ahead.

Deciding whether to request a supersession

Before requesting a supersession because of a change of circumstances, you may wish to establish whether a fresh calculation would be to your advantage. Unless it is a change that must be reported (see p50), you need only tell the CMS about the changes in your favour. If the change only relates to one party, the CMS may not tell the other person. However, if it does, that person might tell the CMS about other changes. These may cancel out the effect of the changes which led you to ask for a supersession.

If you believe that the other parent's circumstances have changed (eg, a NRP no longer has relevant other children living with them), you may ask for a supersession and for the CMS to investigate (see Chapter 3). The CMS does not have to investigate other aspects of the case, but any changes of which it is aware must be taken into account when it decides whether or not to supersede.

How to apply for a supersession

A party to the calculation may apply for a supersession at any time. There are no time limits. If an application is made, the CMS must consider it and supersede it if the conditions on p205 are met.

The CMS can also initiate a supersession. It must take into account the welfare of any children affected (see p124) when considering whether or not to do so. The CMS learns of some changes automatically from Jobcentre Plus and of others from third parties.

If the supersession is in relation to an application for a variation that has had a preliminary consideration (see p108),[49] or is a supersession of a previously agreed variation,[50] the other relevant parties are contacted and notified of the grounds of the application and of any relevant information or evidence the applicant has given. They are not given details of any long-term illness or disability of a relevant other child (if the application for variation was made on that basis), of harmful medical evidence or of the address of a relevant person or qualifying child if that would cause a risk of harm or undue distress.[51]

Otherwise, perhaps surprisingly, the other parties are not notified of the application for a supersession. The normal rules about disclosure apply to the information given in any notification (see p51).[52]

The CMS does not have to check all the facts again and need not consider any issue that is not raised by the application or which did not lead to its decision. It can just consider the issues raised in the application.[53] There are no limits on the length of time for which issues need not be considered.[54] You should therefore include all available information and evidence that supports your case for the decision to be changed in the application. Information provided may need to be verified in the normal way (see Chapter 3).

The superseding decision

The CMS may decide that:

- there are no grounds for a supersession to be made; *or*
- there are grounds for a supersession, but the calculation remains unchanged; *or*
- there are grounds for a supersession and the calculation should be changed; *or*
- the calculation should be cancelled.

If the decision results in a supersession, whether or not a new calculation is made (including an interim maintenance decision (see p110) or default maintenance decision – see p127), the parties must be notified of the decision and provided with the usual details (see p128).[55] The notice must also state how to apply for a revision or supersession, and how to appeal.[56]

If a supersession is refused, notification is also given, including the reasons for the refusal and the right to challenge the decision.[57]

You can ask for a supersession decision to be revised and may then, if the decision is one against which there is a right of appeal, appeal to the First-tier Tribunal (see Chapter 10).

If the CMS intends to cancel the case, it must notify each party. If the reason for cancellation is a child applicant in Scotland's ceasing to be a qualifying child, the CMS must inform any other potential child applicants in the case.[58]

Effective date of the superseding decision

The general rule is that a supersession takes effect from the day on which the decision is made or the application for the supersession/variation was made.[59] However, the effective date may be different in certain circumstances (see the table below, but note that this does not cover all the circumstances in which a calculation is cancelled – see p130).

Note: the CMS discourages an application for a supersession via the webchat facility. Instead, you are directed to report the changes through the online portal.

Circumstances	*Effective date*[60]
Gross income is based on current income and the NRP is required to report a change because their current income has changed by at least 25 per cent.	The day on which the change occurred.
There is a new qualifying child in relation to the NRP.	The day that would be the initial effective date (ie, two days after the day on which written notification would be sent to the NRP) if a new application were made for that child, if there were no calculation already in force.
The application is made by one of the parties.	The day the application is received by the CMS.
The CMS has acted on its own initiative.	If the CMS acts on the basis of information provided by a third party, the day that information is provided. In any other case, the day on which the decision is made.
There is an anticipated change in circumstances.	The day on which the change is expected to occur.
There is an expected change in circumstances which is a ground for a variation.	The day on which the change is expected to occur.

A qualifying child dies or ceases to be a qualifying child.	The day on which the change occurred.
A relevant other child (or a child supported under other maintenance arrangements) dies or ceases to be a qualifying child for child support purposes.	The day on which the change occurred.
A person with care (PWC) ceases to be a PWC in relation to a qualifying child.	The day on which the change occurred.
A PWC, NRP or a qualifying child ceases to be habitually resident in the UK.	The day on which the change occurred.
A NRP (or their partner) becomes or stops being entitled to a benefit that qualifies them for the flat rate.	The day on which the change occurred.
The CMS is superseding a decision given by the First-tier Tribunal or the Upper Tribunal following the CMS's having served notice that a test case which could have affected that decision was pending before the Upper Tribunal or a court.	The day on which the decision of the First-tier Tribunal or Upper Tribunal would have taken effect had it been decided in accordance with the decision in the test case.
The CMS is superseding a decision of the First-tier Tribunal or the Upper Tribunal on the ground that it is wrong because of a misrepresentation about, or a failure to disclose, a material fact, and the decision is more advantageous to the person who misrepresented or failed to disclose than it would otherwise have been but for that error.	The date on which the First-tier Tribunal or Upper Tribunal decision took, or was to take, effect.
A decision of the CMS is superseded because it is shown to have been wrong by the Upper Tribunal or by a court.	The date of the relevant Upper Tribunal or court decision.

Notes

1. **Changing a decision**

1 Reg 27A CSMC Regs
2 Reg 27A CSMC Regs
3 *TR v SSWP and PR (CSM)* [2020] UKUT 339 (AAC)
4 *West v Secretary of State for Scotland*, 1992 SC 385, 1992 SLT 636, reported as *West v Scottish Prison Service*, 1992 SCLR 504
5 r54.5 CRP
6 s27A Court of Session Act 1988
7 s27B(1) Court of Session Act 1988, r54.4 CRP
8 *Council of Civil Service Unions v Minister for the Civil Service* [1984] 1 WLR 1174, [1984] 3 All ER 935
9 ie, '*Wednesbury* unreasonable' – per Lord Diplock in *Council of Civil Service Unions and Others v Minister for the Civil Service* [1985] AC 374 at 410

2. **Revisions**

10 ss16 and 28G CSA 1991; reg 14(1)(a) and (d) CSMC Regs
11 s16 CSA 1991
12 Reg 14(2) CSMC Regs
13 Reg 15(4) CSMC Regs
14 Reg 15(3) CSMC Regs
15 Reg 15(5) CSMC Regs
16 Reg 27A(4) CSMC Regs
17 Reg 15(7) CSMC Regs
18 See CIS/93/1992
19 DWP, *Mandatory Consideration of Revision Before Appeal: government response to public consultation*, September 2012
20 *R (CJ) and SG v SSWP (ESA)* [2017] UKUT 324 (AAC); *AO v SSWP and JA (CSM)* [2017] UKUT 499 (AAC)
21 Reg 14(1) and (3) CSMC Regs
22 Reg 14(3A) CSMC Regs
23 Reg 14(4) CSMC Regs
24 Regs 14(1)(a) and 27A CSMC Regs
25 R(SB) 9/85
26 R(SB) 2/92 (*Page and Davis v CAO*)
27 CCS/15846/1996
28 Reg 14(1)(b) CSMC Regs
29 Reg 24(2) CSMC Regs
30 Reg 57 CSMC Regs
31 Reg 61 CSMC Regs
32 R(I) 1/71
33 s16(6) CSA 1991; Sch para 1(1) CSMC Regs
34 Sch para 1(2) CSMC Regs
35 Reg 26(1) CSMC Regs
36 Reg 25(3) CSMC Regs
37 s16(3) CSA 1991
38 Reg 16 CSMC Regs
39 r22(2) TP(FT) Rules

3. **Supersessions**

40 s17(1) CSA 1991
41 Reg 17(1)-(3) CSMC Regs
42 s17(2) CSA 1991; reg 17(6) CSMC Regs
43 R(A) 1/72; R(SB) 11/83
44 *R v Gough* [1993] AC 646, [1993] 2 WLR 883, [1993] 2 All ER 724
45 *Wednesbury Corporation v Ministry of Housing and Local Government (No.2)* [1965] 3 WLR 956, [1965] 3 All ER 571
46 Reg 17(4) and (5) CSMC Regs
47 Reg 23(1) and (2) CSMC Regs
48 Reg 23(3) CSMC Regs
49 Reg 59 CSMC Regs
50 Reg 61(1) CSMC Regs
51 Reg 59(1)(a) and (5) CSMC Regs
52 Reg 25(3) CSMC Regs
53 s17(2) CSA 1991; reg 17(6) CSMC Regs
54 Under s17(2) CSA 1991 – see *CA v SSWP & TB* [2020] UKUT 205, para 153
55 Reg 26(1) CSMC Regs
56 Reg 24(2) CSMC Regs
57 Regs 24(2) and 26(2) CSMC Regs
58 Reg 27 CSMC Regs
59 s17(4) CSA 1991
60 Reg 18 CSMC Regs

Chapter 10

Challenging a decision: appeals

This chapter covers:

1. Considering an appeal

Most decisions made by the Child Maintenance Service (CMS) can be appealed to an independent appeal tribunal: the First-tier Tribunal (Social Entitlement Chamber).

Before you can appeal, you must apply for a revision, asking the CMS to reconsider its decision. This is called a **'mandatory reconsideration'**. In order to be sure of having a right to appeal, you should request a mandatory reconsideration and should do so within the time limit for a revision (see p200).

If you appeal without first seeking a mandatory reconsideration, the CMS can treat the appeal as if it were a request for a mandatory reconsideration.[1] If the CMS does not do this, ask for a mandatory reconsideration as soon as possible, explaining why it is late, if necessary.

The CMS issues a letter, outlining its response to your request (a 'mandatory reconsideration notice'). Two copies are sent – you must send one of them to the First-tier Tribunal with the appeal.

Note: the CMS can correct an accidental error in a decision or in the record of a decision at any time (see p196). A mandatory reconsideration of the corrected decision must be requested before an appeal to the First-tier Tribunal can be made.

Who can appeal

Usually, anyone who is a party in a child support calculation (ie, a person with care, a non-resident parent and, in Scotland, a child applicant) has the right to appeal.[2] A party can also appoint a representative to represent them in the appeal (see p223).

Regardless of who appeals, all the parties in a child support calculation are also parties in the appeal and have the same rights, except that only the person making the appeal (the 'appellant') can ask to withdraw the appeal. Because an appeal can be withdrawn without the consent of any other party (see p223), it is best for each person who wishes to challenge a decision to bring their own appeal. The appeals can be heard together.

The CMS may also refer an application for a variation to the First-tier Tribunal in certain cases (see p111).

If a person with a right of appeal dies, the executor or administrator of their estate can continue with any appeal that is already underway.[3]

Decisions that cannot be appealed

Only decisions and, in some cases, refusals to make decisions, can be appealed. It is not possible to appeal if no decision has been made – eg, because of a delay. Similarly, decisions about fees and some decisions about the method of collection or the enforcement of payment cannot be appealed. Appeals about some enforcement decisions (eg, about decisions to impose a deduction from earnings order or a regular or lump sum deduction order – see Chapter 8) can be made to the courts.

Decisions about the ending of liability in '1993 rules' and '2003 rules' cases as part of the transition to the '2012 rules' scheme (see p1) also cannot be appealed.[4] However, a decision about that liability before it ended *can* be appealed, even if the decision is made after liability ended.[5]

If you are uncertain whether you can appeal against a decision, get advice straight away. If a decision cannot be appealed, you can ask the CMS to reconsider and send any further information if appropriate. However, the CMS is not required to reconsider. Your only legal remedy is judicial review (see p198). If there is a delay in making a decision, or some other kind of poor service from the CMS, you may also wish to complain (see Chapter 11).

Parentage disputes

If someone denies at the time of, or during the course of, an appeal, being the parent of a child named in the child support application, the appeal is not dealt with by the First-tier Tribunal, but by the family court (in England and Wales) or the sheriff court (in Scotland).[6] Any other grounds of appeal are dealt with by the tribunal. If the appeal is sent to the tribunal and it involves a denial of parentage, the tribunal should transfer that issue to the court.[7] For more information about parentage disputes, see p40.

2. Appealing to the First-tier Tribunal

When the Child Maintenance Service (CMS) makes a decision, each party (ie, the person with care (PWC) and non-resident parent (NRP), and, in Scotland, any child applicant) must be sent a notice of that decision and information on the right to challenge it.[8] The CMS may send notice of the decision electronically through the online portal.

If you are unhappy with a decision, you must first ask the CMS to reconsider it (see p211). Once you have the mandatory reconsideration notice, if you are still unhappy you can appeal by sending a notice of appeal directly to the First-tier Tribunal. Form SSCS2 should be used, if possible, which is available from gov.uk (updated 26 January 2022).[9] It is accompanied by a 28-page help sheet (Form SSCS2A) which also provides guidance about the conduct of remote (telephone or video) hearings. Take care to provide all the information required by Form SSCS2.

The notice of appeal must include:[10]

- the appellant's name and address; *and*
- the name and address of any representative (see p223); *and*
- an address to which documents about the appeal may be sent or delivered; *and*
- the name and address of any 'respondent' (ie, the other party), if known; *and*
- the grounds of the appeal – ie, the reasons for disagreeing with the CMS.

The appellant must also send a copy of:[11]

- the mandatory reconsideration notice; *and*
- any statement of reasons sent by the CMS for the decision; *and*
- any available documents supporting the appeal that have not already been supplied to the CMS or to the other party.

Form SSCS2 also enables you to provide your email address and that of your representative, if you have one. You can manage your appeal online and receive emails and text message updates. The new form asks whether you wish to take part in an oral hearing by telephone, by video or face to face, although how the hearing is conducted remains at the discretion of the tribunal. Your availability to attend court may be indicated on an interactive calendar, for the period of between three and eight months in the future. You also indicate whether you can accept a hearing at short notice (14 days or fewer) – the tribunal will call you if a cancellation enables your case to be brought forward.

The appeal may not be accepted by the First-tier Tribunal unless the mandatory reconsideration notice is included. Documents supporting the appeal are normally accepted by the tribunal after the notice of appeal has been sent, but should be sent as soon as practicable. The updated appeal form states that evidence can either accompany the form or be sent in later, with a reminder that it should be provided as early as possible.

If there was a long delay before the CMS sent you the mandatory reconsideration notice and you think you have been placed at a disadvantage (eg, if it is now more difficult to obtain evidence), tell the tribunal.[12]

There are strict time limits for making an appeal, which may be extended in certain circumstances.

Time limits

An appeal must normally be received by the First-tier Tribunal within one month of your being sent the mandatory reconsideration notice.[13] The tribunal can extend this time limit, but there is still an absolute time limit within which you must appeal.

Time limits

'Month' means a complete calendar month from the day of notification.[14]

When calculating time, if something has to be done by a certain day, it must be done by 5pm that day. If a time limit ends on a day other than a working day, it must be done by the next working day to meet the time limit.[15] A notice of a decision counts as having been sent on the second day after the day it was posted or if sent electronically the end of the day following the day it was sent.[16]

If you are appealing against a refusal to revise a decision following a late application for a revision (see p201) where time was not extended, this one-month time limit runs from the date of notification of the original decision, not the date on which the CMS notified you of its refusal to revise. However, if the CMS refused to revise a decision following an application for a revision that was made within the time limit (see p200) or the extended time limit, the one-month time limit runs from the date on which the notice of refusal to revise was issued.

Note: if you had difficulty meeting a time limit for any reason related to the coronavirus pandemic, explain that to HM Courts and Tribunals Service (HMCTS) as soon as possible. Tribunals are instructed to look sympathetically on any requests for extension of time for reasons related to the pandemic.[17]

Late appeals

If an appeal is not made within the one-month time limit, the First-tier Tribunal can extend the time limit, provided neither the CMS nor the other party objects.[18]

The time limit can only be extended by 12 months – ie, there is an **absolute time limit** of 13 months from the date of the mandatory reconsideration notice being sent in which to appeal.[19]

Note:

- in very exceptional circumstances (eg, if you did not receive notice of the decision), it may be possible to argue that the tribunal has discretion to accept an appeal outside this absolute time limit. You must show that you did everything you could have done to appeal in time;[20]
- previous, more generous provisions for late appeals can no longer by relied upon in most cases.[21]

If you appeal outside the one-month time limit and the CMS or the other party objects, the tribunal decides whether the appeal should go ahead. It should bear in mind the overriding objective that appeals should be dealt with fairly and justly (see p218). It does not have to be satisfied that there are special reasons for the delay.[22] There is no guarantee that the tribunal will admit a late appeal, so make sure you appeal in time wherever possible.

If a notice of appeal is submitted outside the time limit, in addition to the information listed on p213, it must also include the reasons why it is late and a request for it to be accepted.[23] It is best to include as much detail as possible about why there may be special reasons for the appeal being late and why it would be fair for it still to be admitted. There is a box in section 2 of Form SSCS2 for the provision of any such information.

If the First-tier Tribunal decides that an appeal cannot go ahead because it was made outside the time limit, you can appeal to the Upper Tribunal (see p232) against this decision.[24]

After an appeal is made

When the First-tier Tribunal receives your appeal, the regional office of HMCTS sends you an acknowledgement. This advises you that HMCTS has also sent a copy of the appeal and any accompanying documents to the CMS and any other parties.[25] HMCTS checks that the appeal is validly made – ie, that the correct information has been included, the appeal has been made on time and the form has been signed. If the appeal is not validly made, HMCTS returns it to you and you have 14 days to complete it properly or provide the required information. If you do not do so, the appeal may be 'struck out' (see p221).

HMCTS informs you that the hearing can be arranged either by telephone, video or face to face at the nearest appeals venue. If it is face to face and the venue is not convenient for you, request that it be changed to a different one. There are over 100 venues which are in most cities and towns in England, Wales and Scotland. Any request should be made promptly, as the later the request is left the more likely it is to be refused. In general, a request for a change of venue made in good time is likely to be agreed to by HMCTS.

When the CMS receives a copy of the appeal, it may revise the decision. If it is revised and the revised decision is more advantageous to the person appealing, the appeal lapses.[26] All parties should be notified that the appeal has lapsed. A 'lapsed appeal' brings an end to the tribunal's jurisdiction to consider the original decision, as that decision is now replaced. It does not lapse because parties now agree on an issue, or because the issue no longer exists: in such circumstances the tribunal may still consider the appeal. You cannot appeal a decision to lapse an appeal or ask for it to be reinstated. However, either party may lodge a fresh appeal against the revised decision within the usual time limits. You do not have to submit an application for a mandatory reconsideration of the revised decision. The fresh appeal application can be on the same grounds or on different grounds to the original appeal application. Once lodged, the fresh appeal application is processed in the normal way, and all parties should receive a revised response from the Secretary of State taking into consideration the changes within the revised decision. The CMS should try to inform all the relevant people that the appeal has lapsed. See p203 for further information.

If the CMS does not revise the decision (or revises the decision but the revised decision is not more advantageous to the person appealing), it should prepare a 'response' to the appeal. This should be sent to the tribunal, and copied to you and the other parties as soon as reasonably practical. Before sending the response, the CMS should check with each party whether they would like their address, or any information that could lead to identification, to be removed from the papers (see p217).

The CMS must send the response to the tribunal within 42 days of receipt of the notice of appeal.[27] The CMS should only request an extension to this deadline in exceptional circumstances. At the time of writing, anecdotal evidence is that the response can be delayed for around four to six months. The response should state:[28]

- the name and address of the official who made the decision; *and*
- the name and address of that official's representative (if any) – known as a 'presenting officer'; *and*
- an address where documents for the CMS can be sent or delivered; *and*
- the name and address of the other parties and their representatives (if any).

The response should explain which of the grounds of appeal the CMS disagrees with, and why.[29] The response may also indicate whether the CMS thinks the case requires a hearing or could be decided by just considering the papers.[30]

The response must have the following attached to it:[31]

- a copy of any written record of the decision being appealed, and any statement of reasons for it, if not already sent with the appeal; *and*
- copies of all documents the CMS has that are relevant to the case.[32]

If any delay in the CMS sending the response to the tribunal is causing hardship, you can apply to the tribunal for a direction instructing the CMS to provide the response.

Once all parties receive the copy of the response from the CMS, any party may make a written submission and supply any further documents in reply. This is your opportunity to explain your case in detail, and to provide any documents or other evidence to back it up. Your written submission should be sent to the tribunal within one month of receiving the CMS's response. The tribunal sends a copy of any written submission to the CMS and to any other respondent.[33]

Although this one-month time limit is in the rules, it is unlikely that the tribunal will refuse to accept further evidence and submissions after this, especially if there is to be an oral hearing at which submissions and further evidence may be expected to be presented. It is more helpful to the tribunal to send evidence ahead of the hearing, even if this is late, than to present it on the day of the hearing, especially if there is a large quantity of evidence (which is likely to lead to an adjournment of the hearing and further delay). Where a hearing is to be held by telephone or video, all evidence must be provided in good time as it cannot be provided on the day of the hearing.

Confidentiality

If either the PWC or NRP wants their address, or the address of the child, to be kept confidential, they should inform the CMS or tribunal on the notice of appeal, or within 14 days of receiving an appeal enquiry form.[34] The CMS and tribunal must take appropriate steps to ensure that this information (or any information that would help identify this) is not revealed to another party.

3. Tribunal procedures

Both the First-tier and Upper Tribunal have procedural rules setting out their powers and how they should deal with appeals. There are also practice directions and practice statements, which set out how they should conduct themselves. The rules are similar for both the First-tier and the Upper Tribunal and so this section applies to both (and explains where there are differences). The rules about hearings and decisions are also part of the procedural rules (see p226 and p229). Caselaw has also established principles on how appeals should be conducted.

If the tribunal fails to follow the correct procedure, this may be a ground for appealing against its decision, as a breach of the procedural rules could mean that the decision is based on an error of law.[35] A complaint may also be made to HM Courts and Tribunals Service (HMCTS). For details of how to complain to HMCTS, see CPAG's *Welfare Benefits and Tax Credits Handbook*. A failure to follow procedure could also be challenged by judicial review (see p198).

If a party to the appeal fails to comply with any rule, practice direction or direction given by the tribunal, the tribunal may take any action which it considers 'just' (including striking out the appeal – see p221).[36] The Upper Tribunal has more extensive powers to deal with failure to comply with the rules.

The First-tier Tribunal may refer a person to the Upper Tribunal for it to deal with the issue.[37]

Legally qualified members of HMCTS staff ('registrars') and other appropriately trained staff ('legal officers', formerly 'caseworkers'[38]) can make many of the decisions about a case and how it is handled (but not final decisions on an appeal). They must act under the supervision of a judge and in accordance with relevant guidance. A party to the appeal can, within 14 days of being sent a notice of any decision made by a member of staff, apply in writing for the decision to be considered again by a judge.[39]

The overriding objective: fair and just

The overriding objective of the procedural rules is to enable the tribunal to deal with appeals 'fairly and justly'.[40] Whenever the tribunal exercises a power under the rules (eg, to admit or not admit a late appeal, or to strike out an appeal), it must consider whether it would be fair and just. Similarly, when the tribunal interprets what the rules mean or what the practice directions say, it must try to come to the interpretation which enables an appeal to be dealt with in a way which is fair and just.[41]

It is important to bear this overriding objective in mind in any dealings with the tribunal.

The rules set out some of the things that must be taken into account in the giving of effect to the overriding objective in the exercise of any power under the rules or in the interpretation of any rule or practice direction.[42] The tribunal should:

- deal with the case in a way which is proportionate to its importance, the complexity of the issues, the anticipated costs and the resources of the parties; *and*
- avoid unnecessary formality and be flexible in the proceedings; *and*
- ensure, so far as practicable, that all the parties are able to participate fully in the proceedings; *and*
- use any special expertise of the tribunal effectively; *and*
- avoid delay, so far as so doing is compatible with proper consideration of the issues.

Note: this list is not exhaustive. Other matters can still be taken into account when considering what is fair and just in a particular case.[43]

The parties to an appeal also have a duty to assist the tribunal in dealing with cases fairly and justly.[44]

Directions

Tribunals may give a wide range of directions in order to manage an appeal. These must be consistent with the overriding objective.

The tribunal can give directions:

- extending or shortening the time for compliance with any rule or direction;
- consolidating or hearing together two or more appeals that raise common issues, or treating one as the lead case;
- permitting or requiring a party to amend a document;
- permitting or requiring a party or another person to provide documents, information, evidence or submissions. There are more specific powers to obtain evidence (see p220);
- dealing with an issue in the proceedings as a preliminary issue – eg, deciding precisely what decision is under appeal or whether the tribunal has jurisdiction;
- holding a hearing to consider any matter. This could include, for example, a preliminary hearing to decide what further evidence is needed and who should provide it, how much time the final hearing needs or whether the appeal should be 'struck out' because of a failure to comply with a direction;
- deciding the form of any hearing (eg, the order in which parties speak or give evidence and who questions the appellant), and how to manage the hearing if one parent is worried about intimidation by the other – eg, warning all parties in advance about behaviour, or organising the hearing so that the parties are not in the same room at the same time;[45]
- postponing or adjourning a hearing – eg, to enable further evidence to be produced;
- requiring a party to produce a 'bundle' (an indexed set of documents relating to the appeal) for a hearing, although the tribunal must take into account the resources of the parties when issuing a direction;
- requiring witnesses to attend a hearing, answer questions or produce documents;
- 'staying' (or, in Scotland, 'sisting') proceedings, allowing the tribunal to put the case on hold – eg, pending the outcome of another appeal in which it is expected that relevant legal issues will be decided;
- transferring proceedings to another court or tribunal – eg, if parentage is being disputed;
- suspending the effect of its decision pending an application for permission to appeal.

A direction can be given at any time, either on the initiative of the tribunal or following an application by a party to the appeal.[46] Applications for directions may be made orally (at a hearing) or in writing, and must include the reasons for seeking them. Unless it considers there is a good reason not to do so, the tribunal must send written notice of any directions to every party and to anyone else affected.

Any party unhappy with a direction can apply to have it amended, suspended or sets aside.

Failure to comply with a direction may result in the appeal being 'struck out' (see p221) or the transgressing party being barred from taking part in any hearing (see p222).

It may be possible to appeal to the Upper Tribunal about the content of a particular direction – eg, to exclude or to include certain evidence.[47]

Evidence

The tribunal can give directions about:[48]

- the issues on which it requires evidence or submissions;
- the nature of the evidence or submissions required, and how and when they are to be provided;
- the requirement for, or permission to provide, expert evidence;
- any limit on the number of witnesses upon whose evidence a party may rely.

The tribunal can exclude evidence if:

- it was not provided within a time limit set in a direction or practice direction;
- it does not comply with a direction or a practice direction in some other way;
- it would be unfair to admit it.

Harmful evidence

If you are a party to the appeal (ie, a person with care or non-resident parent, or, in Scotland, a child applicant) and have told the Child Maintenance Service (CMS) or tribunal that you would like your address, or the address of a child, to be kept confidential, the tribunal and the CMS must ensure that it (or information that could be used to identify it) is not revealed to other parties.[49] The tribunal can also order that documents or information should not be disclosed, or that any matter which could allow the public to identify the people involved should not be disclosed.[50]

The tribunal can also direct that a particular person is not to receive a document or information if this would be likely to cause them, or another person, serious harm. The tribunal must be satisfied, having regard to the interests of justice, that it is proportionate to give such a direction.[51]

You can ask the tribunal to direct that a particular document or piece of information that you must provide be withheld from another party, although you must send a copy of it to the tribunal explaining why.[52]

The tribunal may, however, disclose the document or information to the party's *representative* if it is satisfied that they will not disclose the document to another person without the consent of the tribunal and that such disclosure is in the interests of justice.[53] If any evidence is withheld, the tribunal must still ensure that there is a fair hearing and that each party has sufficient information to conduct the case. Evidence should not be withheld from the tribunal itself.[54]

Witnesses

The tribunal can summon (in Scotland, 'cite') witnesses and order other documents to be produced.[55] The tribunal may require someone to attend as a witness at a hearing, to answer any questions and to provide documents related to the proceedings.

The tribunal must give notice of the hearing to such a witness – either 14 days' or such shorter period as it may direct. If the person summoned is not a party to the proceedings, the tribunal must make provision for their expenses to be paid.[56]

Note: the tribunal cannot summon a child if this would be detrimental to their welfare. The tribunal must consider how to assist any children under 18, or any vulnerable (eg, people aged 18 or over who are mentally or physically disabled) or sensitive witnesses, to give evidence (including, for example, by telephone or video link).[57] A Practice Direction applicable to both the First-tier Tribunal and Upper Tribunal defines child, vulnerable adult and sensitive witnesses. It stipulates that:[58]

- attendance of such a witness is only required where their evidence is necessary to enable a fair hearing and their welfare would not be prejudiced by their attendance; *and*
- the tribunal, in determining the necessity of attendance of such a witness, should have regard to all the available evidence and representations; *and*
- the tribunal may invite submissions from 'interested persons' in determining whether the welfare of such a potential witness would be prejudiced; *and*
- the tribunal *may* decline to permit evidence from, or to issue a witness summons to, such an individual, if satisfied that their evidence is not necessary for a fair hearing, and *must* decline to do so where their welfare would be prejudiced by their giving evidence.

The tribunal must consider how to assist such individuals in giving evidence. This includes allowing them to give evidence by telephone, video link or other means, or appointing someone with special expertise to help the person give evidence.[59]

If you are a child, vulnerable adult or sensitive witness, and you need special arrangements to be made, you or your representative should write to the tribunal as soon as possible in advance of the hearing.[60] The tribunal should make a note in its record of proceedings that it has considered how to assist you.

Costs

Neither the First-tier Tribunal nor the Upper Tribunal can award costs, except in judicial review proceedings in the Upper Tribunal (see p233).[61]

Striking out an appeal

In certain circumstances, the tribunal can dismiss an appeal, or part of an appeal, without considering it. This is known as '**striking out**' an appeal.

The tribunal *must* strike out an appeal, or part of an appeal, if:

- the person who appealed has failed to comply with a direction which stated that the appeal, or that part of the appeal, *would* be struck out for failure to comply;[62] *or*
- it does not have jurisdiction to decide the appeal (or that part of it) and has not transferred it to another tribunal or court.[63]

The tribunal *may* strike out an appeal, or part of an appeal, if:

- the person who appealed has failed to comply with a direction which stated that the appeal, or that part of the appeal, *could* be struck out for failure to comply; *or*
- that person has failed to co-operate with the tribunal to such an extent that the tribunal cannot deal with the proceedings fairly and justly;[64] *or*
- it considers that the appeal (or the particular part of the appeal) has no reasonable prospects of success.[65]

The tribunal must consider whether it would be fair and just to strike out the appeal.

An appeal should only be struck out for failure to comply with a direction in exceptional cases, and as a last resort.[66] Even then, the appellant can apply for the appeal to be reinstated.[67] This should be done within one month of the tribunal sending the notice of the strike out.[68] This one-month time limit can be extended if the tribunal considers it fair and just so to do.[69] If an application to reinstate an appeal is rejected, a further application can be made upon provision of further evidence or if circumstances have changed.[70]

It is not possible for an appeal, or part of it, to be reinstated if it is struck out for any other reason. However, before striking out an appeal, the tribunal must invite the appellant to make representations.[71]

The tribunal must give a written notice of its decision to strike out an appeal, or part of an appeal, and should explain why it is doing so.[72] A party to the appeal can ask for a written statement of reasons for the decision and can seek permission to appeal to the Upper Tribunal against a striking-out decision by the First-tier Tribunal.[73]

Note: if the other party or the CMS (ie, any 'respondent') fails to comply with a direction, they can be **'barred'** from taking any further part in the proceedings.[74] When the tribunal 'bars' a respondent, it need not consider any response or other submission made by that respondent. A barred respondent can apply to be reinstated.

Sending and receiving documents

If there is a time limit for the provision of a document, this starts to run from when the tribunal sends the request. The time limit is met when the tribunal receives the response. The tribunal can extend (or shorten) any time limit, and has powers to deal with any failure to comply with rules and directions (see p217).[75]

See p214 for details of how time limits are calculated.

Documents should be sent to the tribunal at its specified address by hand, by email or by post. The tribunal may give directions permitting documents to be sent by other methods.[76]

If an email address or other method has been provided for the receipt of documents electronically, delivery must be accepted by that method unless an explicit statement that this is not acceptable has been made.[77]

If a document is sent electronically, the recipient can request a hard copy and the sender must supply it. Such a request should be made as soon as reasonably practicable after the receipt of the electronic document.[78]

A party should assume that the address provided by another party remains valid unless a written notice to the contrary has been received.[79]

Representatives

A party is entitled to appoint a representative (whether legally qualified or not) to represent them in the proceedings. Once appointed, a representative can do anything permitted or required to be done by that party except the signing of a witness statement.[80]

Upon receipt of the notice of the appointment of a representative, the tribunal must provide them with any documents required to be sent to that party and need not send the documents to the party.[81] Any other party to the appeal must also be notified of the appointment and must send any documents required to the representative.

Even if a party has not appointed a representative, that party can still be accompanied at the hearing. The companion may act as a representative or otherwise assist in presenting the case at the hearing, provided the tribunal agrees.[82] The Upper Tribunal has reminded not-for-profit organisations that there is a difference between appearing as a representative and as a witness: a representative who also wishes to appear as a witness should flag this up so that the tribunal keeps an accurate note of anything said by the representative that is intended to be in evidence.[83]

Withdrawing an appeal

An appeal may be withdrawn, in full or in part, by way of written request to the tribunal before the hearing, or orally at the hearing itself.[84]

The First-tier Tribunal's consent is not required for an appeal to be withdrawn before the hearing, unless it has already given a direction that withdrawal can only be with its consent.[85] An oral notice given at a hearing to withdraw an application will only take effect with the consent of the tribunal.[86]

In the Upper Tribunal, consent is always needed to withdraw an appeal (even if the request is made in writing in advance), unless the case is still at the stage of awaiting permission to appeal.[87]

Once an appeal has been withdrawn, it may be reinstated if a request is made in writing within one month of the notice of withdrawal being received by the tribunal, or within one month of the date of the hearing at which the appeal was withdrawn. Other parties to the appeal are also entitled to request that it be reinstated.

When an appeal is withdrawn, the tribunal must notify the other parties.

Note: an appellant may only withdraw once, and apply to reinstate once. Similarly, a respondent may only apply to reinstate an appeal once. Therefore, if an appeal is withdrawn and subsequently reinstated, it cannot be withdrawn again.[88]

4. Preparing a case

The First-tier Tribunal may be the first chance for an independent evaluation of the decision being appealed. It may also be the last chance because its decision can only be appealed further to the Upper Tribunal on a point of law. Therefore, each party (ie, the person with care (PWC) and non-resident parent (NRP), and, in Scotland, a child applicant) should make sure that the First-tier Tribunal knows the facts and arguments about the case. You may wish to attend the hearing (see p226) to put forward your views and evidence, even if you are not the person who appealed. You should also consider getting advice and asking an adviser to assist in preparing the case and to represent (see p223) you at the hearing.

Considering the facts and law

- Read the response from the Child Maintenance Service (CMS) together with any other documents attached to see whether it now accepts some of the arguments it previously rejected or ignored. Just because the CMS accepts part of a person's case does not mean that the tribunal will, especially if the other party disputes it.
- Check the law using this *Handbook, Child Support: the legislation* (see Appendix 4) and other sources. If the CMS quotes a decision of the Upper Tribunal (or of the previous commissioners), consider getting a copy.[89] HM Courts and Tribunals Service (HMCTS) does not have copies of unreported decisions (those considered less legally significant), so any party, including the CMS, relying upon an unreported decision should provide copies to the other parties and to the tribunal, preferably by sending a copy to the tribunal clerk in advance of the hearing. A party (including the CMS) may cite the CMS's internal procedural guidance, but it is important to remember that this guidance is not legally binding.

- Check the documents attached to the response. If anything relevant is missing, write to the tribunal asking it to direct the CMS to provide it.

The CMS must provide a response to an appeal within 42 days (see p215). If the CMS delays producing its response, you can write to the tribunal, asking that your appeal be heard. This may mean that the tribunal does not have all the evidence the CMS has. However, you (or the other party) can ask the tribunal to direct the CMS (see p218) to provide copies of all the papers, explaining why these are needed.

Further evidence

- Consider whether you have (or can get) any further relevant written evidence. This can be sent to the First-tier Tribunal at any stage, but it is best to do this soon after the response is sent out, so papers can be copied to the other parties. If evidence or unreported caselaw decisions are produced at the hearing or sent in shortly before, this may cause a postponement or an adjournment.
- Check how best to explain the facts and law at the hearing. For example, telling the tribunal 'I look after the child from Friday night to Monday night' may be the best evidence of those facts.
- Decide whether to call any witnesses at the hearing (see p221).

Information relating to court proceedings concerning children heard in private or financial remedy proceedings (ie, dealing with money and property) can be disclosed to the tribunal by any party without permission being sought, provided the court does not direct otherwise.[90] This means that one parent can supply information about the finances of the other parent which was disclosed in the course of matrimonial finance or Schedule 1 CA 1989 (financial remedy) proceedings.

Obtaining information and evidence

A request may be made to the First-tier Tribunal for provision of further information or documents by another party or the CMS. It is best to send a prepared list to HMCTS, which is as specific as possible and gives reasons for the disclosure sought. For example, if a PWC believes that a NRP has undisclosed income, they could ask for bank statements for a certain period. A person who is not a party (eg, an employer) cannot be directed to provide evidence, but can be ordered to attend as a witness and to produce documents (see p221). This should be done before the full hearing so that all the parties may consider that evidence.

The tribunal may decide that a failure to comply, without good explanation, indicates that a person has something to hide and that person may not therefore be believed.[91] If that individual is the appellant, the appeal may be 'struck out' (see p221).

5. Hearings

The First-tier Tribunal must hold an oral hearing before making a final decision in an appeal unless:[92]

- it is 'striking out' the proceedings (see p221); *or*
- it considers that it can decide the matter fairly and justly without one, and none of the parties object;[93] *or*
- it is deciding whether to accept an application for permission to appeal, set aside a decision or correct a decision; *or*
- it is making a consent order (see p230).

An oral hearing includes one conducted by video link, telephone or other instant two-way communication.[94]

The Upper Tribunal may decide any case without a hearing, but must consider a party's views when deciding whether to hold a hearing.[95]

If there is no hearing, the tribunal makes its decision by considering what has been said on the appeal form, any other evidence provided by the parties, and the response from the Child Maintenance Service (CMS). This is known as a 'paper hearing'.

Hearings during the coronavirus pandemic

Temporary rules relating to disruption due to the coronavirus pandemic gave tribunals more flexibility in relation to hearings. These expired on 25 March 2022. The First-tier Tribunal and Upper Tribunal were able to direct that all or part of a hearing be conducted remotely by live video or audio link.[96] The arrangements had to allow each person taking part in the hearing to be able to see or hear all the other people taking part. The tribunal was able to direct that all or part of the hearing be broadcast to designated premises in such a way as to be public, and that the hearing be recorded. If it was not practicable for a court or tribunal venue to be accessed by anyone other than those directly involved in the hearing, the tribunal was also able to direct that all or part of the hearing was to be private. If held in private, the tribunal had to direct that it was recorded.[97] Tribunals were also empowered to decide an appeal without a hearing if the matter was urgent, if it was not practicable to hold a hearing (including a live video or audio hearing) and it was in the interests of justice to decide the appeal without a hearing. If the parties in a First-tier Tribunal case had not already consented to the appeal being decided without a hearing, the tribunal judge could decide whether doing so would be appropriate. A tribunal considering it could decide the appeal without a hearing, would send a provisional decision to the parties and ask whether they consented to a final decision being made in those terms. If a party did not agree and instead sought a hearing, that was likely to take place remotely where arrangements could be made.[98]

Notice

If an oral hearing is to be held, the tribunal must give reasonable notice of the time and place, and of any changes to the arrangements.[99] This must be at least 14 days, although shorter notice can be given with the parties' consent or in urgent or exceptional circumstances (if shorter notice is given, it must still be reasonable).[100] Where the tribunal shortens the notice period or gives late notice of a change of time, it must ensure that a party who requested a supporter (eg, a 'McKenzie friend' rather than a representative) at the hearing is able to rearrange this.[101] A supporter may provide moral support, help with communication or help the party by making suggestions.

Papers, including evidence sent to the tribunal, should be sent to all the parties in good time before the hearing.[102]

Attending a hearing

Generally, all hearings must be held in public and each party has a right to attend. However, the tribunal may direct that all, or part, of a hearing is to be held in private and may determine who is allowed to attend.

Even in a public hearing, the tribunal may exclude from all or part of it:[103]

- anyone whose conduct is disrupting, or is likely to disrupt, the hearing; *and*
- anyone whose presence is likely to prevent another person from giving evidence or making submissions freely; *and*
- anyone who should be excluded in order to prevent them hearing information that is likely to cause harm; *and*
- anyone whose attendance would defeat the purpose of the hearing; *and*
- a witness in the proceedings (until they are to give evidence).

If a party fails to attend a hearing and the tribunal is satisfied that they have been notified or that reasonable steps to notify them have been taken, it may proceed with the hearing if it is in the interests of justice.[104] If a party arrives late, after the tribunal has decided to proceed in their absence, the tribunal should still consider whether to allow them to participate or whether to adjourn the hearing to allow them the opportunity to attend.[105]

If you choose not to attend, you cannot then claim that the tribunal has acted unfairly if it decides the case on evidence given at the hearing that you have not had a chance to contest.[106]

Composition of the tribunal

When the First-tier Tribunal deals with a case involving a child support decision, it usually comprises a single member – a 'tribunal judge'.[107] The judge is legally qualified.[108] If the appeal raises difficult issues about financial accounts, the First-tier Tribunal can include a financially qualified member (a 'tribunal member') – ie, a chartered or certified accountant.[109] If there is more than one member, the judge is the 'presiding member', who regulates the proceedings and who has the casting vote.[110]

The Upper Tribunal almost always comprises a single judge, who is legally qualified. If the case is particularly difficult or if there is conflicting caselaw, there may be a panel of two or three judges.[111]

If an appeal is meant to be heard by a tribunal of two or more members but some of them are absent, the hearing can still go ahead, but only if all the parties and the CMS agree.[112]

The venue

There should normally be separate waiting rooms available at the hearing venue for the non-resident parent, person with care and the CMS presenting officer. If you are worried about this, check with HM Courts and Tribunals Service (HMCTS) whether there are separate waiting areas available before the hearing and, if not, explain any problems this may cause. If the other party or witness could become violent, tell the tribunal clerk as soon as possible and ask what steps will be taken.

The hearing is usually held in the appellant's area. Expenses, including travel expenses, subsistence and some compensation for loss of earnings, can be claimed by those who attend as a party, witness or unpaid representative. The tribunal clerk will provide a claim form. Keep any receipts. In very exceptional circumstances, HMCTS will pay travelling expenses in advance of the hearing. If you are unable to use public transport (eg, because of a disability), HMCTS can authorise payment of a taxi fare, but only if this is agreed in advance.[113]

If it is difficult for you to attend the hearing (eg, because of disability), inform the tribunal clerk. An alternative venue may be possible, but convenience to the other parties to the appeal is also considered. If you are unable to attend a hearing at a venue, in rare cases a hearing may be arranged in your home. You may also be able to arrange to participate via telephone or video link. Contact the tribunal to see whether this is possible.

Conduct of the hearing

The First-tier Tribunal attempts to be informal. The judge and any other member usually sit on one side of a table. The tribunal clerk (who does not take any part in making the decision) shows the parties into the room. The parties usually sit on the other side of the table from the tribunal. The presenting officer (an official representing the CMS) usually sits between the parties. The judge introduces everyone and explains the tribunal's role.

Hearings can take an hour or longer. Each party can address the tribunal, give evidence, call witnesses and put questions to any other party, the presenting officer and witnesses. The order in which the parties present their cases is up to the judge. The CMS is there to explain the decision, not to argue for the CMS. The presenting officer has a role, for example, to inform the tribunal about CMS procedures. It is rare for the presenting officer to call any witnesses. The tribunal may require any witness, including a party, to take an oath or affirmation.[114]

Ask the judge for clarification if you are unclear about what is happening or about anything that has been said.

If you need an interpreter, the tribunal will arrange this if you request it in good time.

The tribunal can adjourn a hearing at any point – eg, if more documents are needed. It should adjourn a hearing if, for example, one party is unable to attend and their evidence could play an important part in its reaching a decision.[115] If evidence has been taken, a new panel hearing the case must be made up of either exactly the same, or entirely different, members.

6. Decisions of the First-tier Tribunal

After the hearing, the First-tier Tribunal considers the case and makes its decision. If the tribunal reaches a different conclusion from that of the Child Maintenance Service (CMS), it allows the appeal. **Note:** it may make a decision that is less advantageous to the person appealing.[116]

If the appeal is allowed, the decision of the tribunal replaces that of the CMS. If the appeal is dismissed, the decision of the CMS remains in force.

In making its decision, the tribunal looks afresh at the situation on the date of the CMS decision that is being appealed.[117] It cannot take into account any change of circumstances that has occurred after the date of the decision, although it can take account of evidence that is relevant to the period up to the date of the decision, but which only became available later.[118] If it decides to allow the appeal because the decision was wrong on the facts at the time it was made, it cannot then direct how the CMS should deal with a later change of circumstances.

The whole appeal process can take some time, so if circumstances change while waiting for an appeal to be decided, a person with care or non-resident parent (or child applicant in Scotland) may also wish to make a new child support application or request a supersession (see p204) and then challenge that decision if necessary.

The tribunal can consider any evidence and arguments, including those rejected or overlooked by the CMS and those which have not been used before.[119] The tribunal does not have to consider any issue not raised in the appeal.[120] However, it is 'inquisitorial', which means that it can consider legal arguments and factual questions on its own initiative, if appropriate, but should give its reasons for doing so.[121] The tribunal must decide what it believes are the relevant facts by evaluating all the relevant available evidence.[122] The tribunal can draw conclusions from the failure of a party to provide evidence.[123]

The tribunal can make a provisional decision, which will become final in specified circumstances. This may be done, for example, if it wants to give one last chance to a party to provide certain information within a specified time. The time limit for any further appeal runs from the date of the final decision.[124]

Decision notices

Usually, the parties are invited to wait outside the hearing room and then asked back in to be told the decision. The First-tier Tribunal must also give a decision notice to the parties (unless it decides to withhold harmful information) as soon as reasonably practicable, stating:[125]

- its decision; *and*
- any right to apply for reasons for the decision; *and*
- any right of appeal against the decision, together with information about the time and manner in which such an appeal must be made.

The tribunal can decide to issue a full statement of the reasons for its decision, either verbally at the hearing or in writing to each party.[126] If it does not do this, you can apply for a written statement of reasons, provided this application is received by the tribunal within a month of the decision notice being given or sent to the parties.[127]

Unless the decision was a consent order (see below), the tribunal must send the statement of reasons within one month of receiving the application, or as soon as reasonably practicable after that.[128]

Record of proceedings

The presiding member of the First-tier Tribunal must keep a record of proceedings. This should include any evidence taken, submissions made and any procedural issues – eg, if a party asked for an adjournment.[129]

The record must be kept by HMCTS for at least six months from whichever is the later of:[130]

- the date of the decision; *or*
- the date the reasons for the decision were given; *or*
- the date the decision was corrected; *or*
- the date a refusal to set aside was made; *or*
- the date of the determination of an application for permission to appeal (unless the documents are sent to the Upper Tribunal before the six months expire).

You can request a copy of the record of proceedings within this six-month period and it must be provided.

Consent orders

If all the parties agree, they can request that the tribunal make an order disposing of (ie, cancelling) the proceedings with their consent. It only does so if it considers that it is appropriate.[131] The tribunal may simply make a decision on the appeal in the usual way. Dealing with an appeal by a consent order is only appropriate if it is clear that all parties have fully understood its implications.[132]

If a consent order is made, there does not have to be a hearing and no reasons for the order need to be given. Before agreeing to request a consent order, get independent advice.

7. Changing a First-tier Tribunal decision

If you are a party to the appeal (ie, a person with care or non-resident parent or, in Scotland, a child applicant), you or the Child Maintenance Service (CMS) can apply to have the First-tier Tribunal's decision changed. A First-tier Tribunal can:

- correct an accidental error (see below);
- 'set aside' the decision (see below);
- review the decision (see p232);
- allow an appeal to the Upper Tribunal (see p232).

An application for any of the above can be treated by the tribunal as an application for any of the others.

Note: this list does not include the possibility of pursuing action for judicial review of non-appealable decisions.

Correcting an error

The First-tier Tribunal can, at any time, correct a clerical mistake or accidental slip or omission in a decision, direction or any document it produces (but not the decision itself) by sending a notice of the amended decision or direction to all parties.[133]

Setting aside the decision

A decision, or part of a decision, can be 'set aside' (ie, cancelled) by the First-tier Tribunal if it considers it to be in the interests of justice to do so. It can do this if:[134]

- a document relating to the proceedings was not sent to or received by the tribunal, a party or representative at an appropriate time; *or*
- a party or representative was not present at the hearing;[135] *or*
- there has been some other procedural irregularity.

An application for a set-aside must be received within one month of being sent the decision by the tribunal.

The First-tier Tribunal is not empowered to set aside a decision of its own volition – ie, without an application being made.[136]

If the decision is set aside, the appeal is heard again, usually by a differently constituted tribunal, and a new decision is made. You should be given the opportunity to decide whether to request an oral hearing, even if the appeal was previously decided on the papers.[137]

If an application for permission to appeal has been made to the First-tier Tribunal and all the parties (including the CMS) argue that the decision is an error of law, it will be set aside and referred to a differently constituted First-tier Tribunal to determine.[138]

Note: it is impossible to appeal against a decision that has been set aside, because the decision ceases to exist.[139]

Reviewing a decision

The First-tier Tribunal can 'review' its decision.[140] It must consider whether to do so[141] before considering whether to grant permission to appeal to the Upper Tribunal and so, in practice, every application for permission to appeal is effectively an application for a review.

The tribunal can only review a decision if an application for permission to appeal has been made and it considers that there is an error of law.[142]

If the tribunal considers that it is appropriate to amend the reasons for its decision, you should be given an opportunity to make suitable representations. The notice sent to you and the other parties should identify the error of law and the course of action the tribunal proposes to take.[143]

Note: a decision that has been reviewed can still be appealed to the Upper Tribunal. The First-tier Tribunal must notify the parties of the outcome of any review and of any right of appeal against it.[144]

8. Appealing to the Upper Tribunal

Any party, including the Child Maintenance Service (CMS), can appeal to the Upper Tribunal against a final decision of the First-tier Tribunal. An appeal will only succeed if there is an error of law in the First-tier Tribunal's decision. See p205 and CPAG's *Welfare Benefits and Tax Credits Handbook* for information about when a decision contains an error of law. The tribunal's statement of reasons should include enough detail to allow all the parties to understand how the main issues in the case were decided.[145]

The Upper Tribunal can give the decision it thinks the First-tier Tribunal should have given. Alternatively (particularly if it thinks the First-tier Tribunal did not consider all the relevant facts or evidence properly), it may refer the case back to the First-tier Tribunal for a new decision to be made. If a case is referred back, the First-tier Tribunal must apply the law in the way that the Upper Tribunal has instructed.

Before an appeal can be dealt with by the Upper Tribunal, you must apply for permission to appeal from the First-tier Tribunal. If this is refused, you can apply for permission directly to the Upper Tribunal. Permission should only be granted if it is arguable that there is an error of law in the First-tier Tribunal decision.

Note: a decision of the First-tier Tribunal which is a procedural decision or ruling (against which there is normally no right of appeal) can be challenged by judicial review. The case is normally heard by the Upper Tribunal. See CPAG's *Welfare Benefits and Tax Credits Handbook* for details.

Applying to the First-tier Tribunal for permission to appeal

You must first apply to the First-tier Tribunal for permission to appeal to the Upper Tribunal. An application must be in writing and be received by the tribunal within one month of being sent the following, whichever is the latest:[146]

- a written statement of reasons for the decision; *or*
- following a review, a notice that the reasons for the decision were amended or the decision corrected; *or*
- a notice that an application for the decision to be set aside made within the time limit was refused.

The application must state:[147]

- the decision of the First-tier Tribunal to which it relates; *and*
- the alleged errors of law in the decision; *and*
- the result you are seeking.

If you apply late, you must explain why and include a request for an extension of time.[148] The First-tier Tribunal can extend the time limit, but there is no guarantee that you will be given longer, so you should apply within the time limit wherever possible. It is not open to the tribunal administration to reject an application that is late or lacks a statement of reasons: that is a decision for the tribunal.[149]

Usually, it is necessary to have obtained the full statement of reasons for a decision before seeking permission to appeal. If you have not requested a statement of reasons, the First-tier Tribunal must treat the application as an application for a statement of reasons (see p230), rather than as an application for permission to appeal.[150] If reasons are issued, you must then make a new application for permission to appeal. If a request for a statement of reasons has been refused because it was made late, the First-tier Tribunal can only grant permission to appeal if it is in the interests of justice to do so.[151]

When considering an application, the First-tier Tribunal must consider whether to review its decision.[152] If it has not changed the decision (or part of it) on review, it must consider whether to grant permission to appeal in respect of its decision, or the unchanged part of it.

The First-tier Tribunal must send a record of its decision on the application for permission to appeal to the parties.[153] If permission is refused, the notice must include the reasons for this. It must also include notice of the right to apply directly to the Upper Tribunal for permission to appeal, and details of how to do so.[154]

The First-tier Tribunal may grant permission to appeal against part of a decision. If this is the case, you may wish to file that appeal with the Upper Tribunal, and also to seek permission directly from the Upper Tribunal to appeal about the parts of the decision for which permission has not been granted.

Applying to the Upper Tribunal for permission to appeal

If permission to appeal has been refused (in whole or in part), or an application has not been admitted, by the First-tier Tribunal, you may apply to the Upper Tribunal for permission.[155]

The application to the Upper Tribunal must be made in writing and within one month of being sent the refusal of permission.[156] If made late, the application must include an explanation for why it is late. The Upper Tribunal can extend the time limit, but there is no guarantee that you will be given longer, so you should apply within the time limit wherever possible.[157] If the earlier application for a written statement of reasons to the First-tier Tribunal or the application for permission to appeal to the First-tier Tribunal was made late, you must give an explanation. It can only be considered if the Upper Tribunal considers it in the interests of justice to do so.[158]

The application must include details of:[159]

- your name and address and any representative; *and*
- an address for sending or delivering documents; *and*
- details (including a full reference) of the decision challenged; *and*
- the grounds for the appeal; *and*
- whether you want a hearing of the application.

The application must include copies of:[160]

- the written record of the decision challenged; *and*
- the written statement of reasons for the decision (if it exists); *and*
- the First-tier Tribunal's notice refusing permission to appeal or refusing to admit the application.

Using Form UT1, *Application for Permission to Appeal to an Upper Tribunal Judge and Notice of Appeal,* should ensure that your application is correctly made.[161]

The Upper Tribunal must send you (but not the other parties) its reasons for refusing an application.[162] There is no right of appeal against a decision of the Upper Tribunal to refuse permission to appeal.[163] Your only legal remedy is to seek judicial review (see p237).

The Upper Tribunal must send notice of permission to appeal to all the parties.[164] If this happens, generally the application for permission is treated as the notice of appeal. The Upper Tribunal sends a copy of this to all the parties and explains that it is treating the application for permission as the actual appeal.[165] If the parties agree, the Upper Tribunal can then determine the appeal without the need for any further response from them.[166]

Notice of appeal

If the First-tier Tribunal grants you permission to appeal, you should send a notice of appeal to the Upper Tribunal.[167] You are sent Form UT1 on which to do this.

If you have received permission to appeal directly from the Upper Tribunal, that is usually treated as the notice of appeal, unless the Upper Tribunal directs otherwise.[168]

The notice of appeal must be received by the Upper Tribunal within one month of your being sent the notice of permission to appeal by the First-tier Tribunal.[169]

The same information and documents must be included with the notice of appeal as for an application for permission to appeal.[170]

Late notices of appeal must include a request for an extension of time and the reasons why the notice was not provided in time. The Upper Tribunal can extend the time limit, but there is no guarantee that you will be given longer, so you should send the notice of appeal within the time limit wherever possible.[171]

The Upper Tribunal must send a copy of the notice of appeal and accompanying documents to each party and to the CMS.[172]

Responses and replies

Any other party can respond to the appeal, but does not have to unless:[173]

- directed to by the Upper Tribunal; *or*
- they wish the Upper Tribunal to uphold the decision for reasons other than those given by the tribunal; *or*
- they rely on any grounds on which they were unsuccessful in the proceedings which are the subject of the appeal.

In the case of the second and third bullet points above, if the respondent needs any permission, including permission to appeal, the response must include an application to the Upper Tribunal for such permission.[174] A response must be in writing and received by the Upper Tribunal within one month of the respondent's being sent the notice of appeal (or the notice granting permission to appeal, if this is treated as the notice of appeal). A late response must request an extension of the time limit and explain why it is late.[175]

The response must state:[176]

- the name and address of the respondent and any representative; *and*
- an address for sending or delivering documents; *and*
- whether the respondent opposes the appeal; *and*
- the grounds on which the respondent intends to rely in the appeal; *and*
- whether the respondent wants a hearing.

The Upper Tribunal must provide a copy of the response to the appellant and the other parties.[177]

The person who appealed may then reply to the response, but does not have to unless directed to by the Upper Tribunal. The reply must be received within one month of your being sent the response and is then copied to the other parties by the Upper Tribunal.[178]

Fresh evidence on appeal

The Upper Tribunal has power to permit or require a party or another person to provide information, documents, evidence or submissions to the Upper Tribunal or a party.[179] Further, the Upper Tribunal may admit evidence whether or not the evidence would be admissible in a civil trial in the UK and whether or not the evidence was available to a previous decision maker.[180]

There are conflicting Upper Tribunal authorities on the admission of fresh evidence on appeal. The civil test (in the courts, as opposed to the Upper Tribunal) is set out in the well-known judgment of Denning LJ in *Ladd v Marshall*.[181] See *SM v SSWP (II)* [2020] UKUT 287 (AAC) and *PR v SSWP (PIP)* [2021] UKUT 35 (AAC). In light of the steer given by the Upper Tribunal (Tribunal Procedure) Rules, it would seem to the authors of this book that *SM v SSWP* is the preferable analysis.

Decisions of the Upper Tribunal

The Upper Tribunal's decision may replace the decision of the First-tier Tribunal, or it can direct that the case be reconsidered by a new First-tier Tribunal.

The Upper Tribunal may announce its final decision verbally at a hearing (although holding an oral hearing is far less common than at the First-tier Tribunal (see p226) and announcing the decision verbally after a hearing is also less common). The Upper Tribunal must then (unless it decides to withhold harmful information) provide the parties with a notice stating its decision and details of any further rights of review and appeal. The parties are not normally referred to by name in the decision. The Upper Tribunal must always give reasons for its decision, unless it was made with the consent of the parties or the parties have consented to a decision being given without reasons.[182]

If the proceedings are recorded, this should be kept for six months. You can apply for a transcript, but will have to pay for it unless you have challenged or intend to challenge the decision, the transcript is necessary in order to bring that challenge, and the Upper Tribunal is satisfied that you cannot afford to pay.

Challenging an Upper Tribunal decision

Note: you should get legal advice if you are considering whether to challenge an Upper Tribunal decision.

Upper Tribunal decisions can be changed by:

- correcting an accidental error (see p231);[183] *or*

- 'setting aside' the decision (see p231);[184] *or*
- appealing to the Court of Appeal (in Scotland, the Court of Session). Permission is needed for this, and the appeal must be on the grounds that the Upper Tribunal made an error of law. An application for permission must first be made to the Upper Tribunal.[185] This is similar to the procedure for applying for permission from the First-tier Tribunal, except that the time limit is three months. The Upper Tribunal must consider a review before deciding whether to grant permission. If the Upper Tribunal refuses permission, the request can be made directly to the Court of Appeal/Court of Session. The Upper Tribunal's refusal decision should include a statement of reasons, details of the relevant court and the time limit for applying.[186] Permission can only be granted if the Upper Tribunal or court considers the appeal would raise an important point of principle or practice, or there is some other compelling reason to grant it;[187] *or*
- reviewing the decision (see p232). The procedure is as for the First-tier Tribunal, except that the Upper Tribunal can only review the decision if it overlooked a legislative decision or binding legal authority which could have affected it or, since giving its decision, a court has made a decision that could have affected it.[188]

The Upper Tribunal may treat an application for a decision to be corrected, set aside or reviewed, or an application for permission to appeal against a decision, as an application for any one of these things.[189]

A decision of the Upper Tribunal that cannot be appealed (eg, a refusal to grant leave to appeal from the First-tier Tribunal to the Upper Tribunal) can be challenged by applying for judicial review (see p198) to the High Court (in England and Wales) or the Court of Session (in Scotland). This can only be done if the case would raise some important point of principle or practice, or if there is some other compelling reason.[190]

For further details about challenging Upper Tribunal decisions, see CPAG's *Welfare Benefits and Tax Credits Handbook.*

9. **Test case rules**

Special rules apply if a court or Upper Tribunal decision on a 'test case' is pending, or an Upper Tribunal or court decision on a test case has been made. A 'test case' is one in which a person is challenging the Child Maintenance Service's (CMS's) interpretation of the law in a way that affects other cases more generally, even if it is the CMS's own appeal and even if the person does not consider the case to be a test case.

These rules apply to child support calculation decisions, revision and supersession decisions, and appeals to the First-tier or Upper Tribunal.

If there is a test case pending

If an appeal in what could be a test case is still pending before the Upper Tribunal or a court, the CMS can:[191]

- postpone making a decision on an application, revision or supersession in any other case which might be affected by the decision in that appeal until the test case appeal has been decided; *or*
- make a decision as if the test case had already been decided in a way that would result in the lowest possible amount of child support being payable in a case that might be affected by the decision. This only applies if there is no calculation in force in the case that might be affected by the test case decision.[192]

An appeal is 'pending' before a court if:[193]

- an appeal (including an application for judicial review) about child support has been made to the High Court, Court of Appeal, Court of Session or Supreme Court, but has not been determined;
- an application for permission to make such an appeal (or judicial review) has been made, but has not been determined;
- the CMS has certified in writing that it is considering making such an appeal or application and the time for appealing or applying has not expired, and the CMS considers that the appeal might result in the non-resident parent having no, or lesser, liability for child support.[194]

If the CMS does not make an application or appeal in time on the test case, it can no longer postpone making a decision on other cases.

A decision to suspend or make a decision on the assumption that the CMS will win the test case is a discretionary one. The CMS must therefore take into account the welfare of any child likely to be affected by the decision when making it.[195]

How a pending test case affects similar cases

If a test case pending before a court may affect a similar case awaiting a decision from the First-tier Tribunal or Upper Tribunal, or there is a possibility that the CMS may appeal, the CMS may:[196]

- direct the tribunal to refer the similar case to the CMS. The CMS makes no decision until the test case is decided. It then revises the CMS decision under appeal or supersedes the tribunal decision under appeal; *or*
- direct the tribunal to deal with the case itself. The tribunal must then either:
  - postpone its decision until the test case is decided; *or*
  - decide the appeal as if the test case appeal has already been decided against the person who appealed in the similar case. It should only do this if it considers that it is in the appellant's interests. If the test case is later decided in that person's favour, the CMS supersedes the tribunal decision in the similar case.

Test case decisions

If a decision of the Upper Tribunal or court interprets child support law in the same way as the CMS, the CMS must usually apply that interpretation in the period before the decision was given. This usually requires the CMS to supersede all decisions which are affected.

However, if the Upper Tribunal/court rejects the CMS's interpretation of the law, that test case decision only has effect from the date it is made.[197] For the period before that date, the CMS (and either tribunal) assumes that it was right in its interpretation of the law when making the original decision which led to the appeal.[198]

This rule does not apply to:

- an application for child support made on or before 1 June 1999;[199] *or*
- a revision or supersession of any decision made on or before 1 June 1999;[200] *or*
- a decision in a case where the CMS had suspended a decision under the rules on pending test cases (see p238);[201] *or*
- a revision or supersession decision in a case where the CMS had required the First-tier or Upper Tribunal to refer the case to the CMS, or deal with it on the assumption that the test case had already been decided against the appellant.[202]

Notes

1. **Considering an appeal**

1 s20(4)(c) CSA 1991; reg 14A(4) CSMC Regs
2 s20 CSA 1991
3 Reg 12(1) CS(MPA) Regs
4 *TB v SSWP and others (CSM)* [2019] UKUT 79 (AAC)
5 *TR v SSWP and PR (CSM)* [2020] UKUT 339 (AAC)
6 **EW** Arts 3 and 4 CSA(JC)O
S Arts 2, 3 and 4 CSA(JC)(S)O
7 r5(3)(k) TP(FT) Rules

2. **Appealing to the First-tier Tribunal**

8 s20(3) CSA 1991; regs 24-26 CSMC Regs
9 gov.uk/government/collections/social-security-and-child-support-forms
10 r22(3) TP(FT) Rules
11 r22(4) TP(FT) Rules
12 *MM v SSWP (PIP)* [2016] UKUT 36 (AAC)
13 r22(2)(d) and Sch 1 TP(FT) Rules
14 R(IB) 4/02
15 r12 TP(FT) Rules. The same rules about calculating time apply to the Upper Tribunal: r12 TP(UT) Rules.
16 Reg 7(2) CSMC Regs as amended by reg 24 CS(ARECI) Regs
17 Statement from the President of the Upper Tribunal Administrative Appeals Chamber, *Contingency Arrangements*, 20 March 2020
18 r22(8) TP(FT) Rules
19 r22(8) TP(FT) Rules
20 *KK v Sheffield City Council (CTB)* [2015] UKUT 367 (AAC); *PM v SSD (AFCS)* [2015] UKUT 647 (AAC); *PH and SM v SSWP (DLA) (JSA)* [2018] UKUT 404 (AAC)

21 Sch 1 para 2 CSMC Regs revoked by the Social Security, Child Support, Vaccine Damage and Other Payments (Decisions and Appeals) (Amendment) Regulations 2013 No.2380 from 28 October 2013, subject to transitional and savings provisions.
22 rr2(1), (2) and (3)(a) and 5(3)(a) TP(FT) Rules; *Information Commissioner v PS* [2011] UKUT 94 (AAC); *CD v First-tier Tribunal (CICA)* [2010] UKUT 181 (AAC), reported as [2011] AACR 1
23 r22(6) TP(FT) Rules
24 *LS v LB Lambeth (HB)* [2010] UKUT 461 (AAC)
25 r22(7) TP(FT) Rules
26 r33 and Sch 1(1) CSMC Regs
27 r24(1)(b)(ii) TP(FT) Rules
28 r24(2)(a)-(d) TP(FT) Rules
29 r24(2)(e) TP(FT) Rules
30 r24(3) TP(FT) Rules
31 r24(4) TP(FT) Rules
32 *TR v SSWP and PW(CSM)* [2013] UKUT 80 (AAC)
33 r24(6) and (7) TP(FT) Rules
34 r19(2) and (3) TP(FT) Rules

3. **Tribunal procedures**
35 R(IS) 11/99; *KB v SSWP (DLA)* [2011] UKUT 388 (AAC)
36 r7 TP(FT) Rules; r7 TP(UT) Rules
37 s25 TCEA 2007; r7(3) TP(FT) Rules; r7(3) and (4) TP(UT) Rules
38 Courts and Tribunals Judiciary Practice Statement, *Authorising Tribunal Caseworkers First-tier Tribunal (Social Entitlement Chamber) to Carry Out Functions of a Judicial Nature*, 16 July 2018
39 r4 TP(FT) Rules; Courts and Tribunals Judiciary Practice Statement, *Authorising Legal Officers to Carry Out Functions of a Judicial Nature,* 26 July 2022; Courts and Tribunals Judiciary Practice Statement, *Delegation of Functions to Registrars First-tier Tribunal (Social Entitlement Chamber),* 1 December 2016
40 r2 TP(FT) Rules; r2 TP(UT) Rules
41 r2(3) TP(FT) Rules; r2(3) TP(UT) Rules
42 r2(2) TP(FT) Rules; r2(2) TP(UT) Rules
43 *MS v SSWP* [2009] UKUT 211 (AAC)
44 r2(4) TP(FT) Rules; r2(4) TP(UT) Rules
45 *WA v SSWP and P (CSM)* [2016] UKUT 86 (AAC)
46 r6(1) TP(FT) Rules; r6(1) TP(UT) Rules
47 *LM v London Borough of Lewisham* [2009] UKUT 204 (AAC)
48 r15 TP(FT) Rules; r15 TP(UT) Rules
49 r19(4) TP(FT) Rules; r19(2) and (4) TP(UT) Rules
50 r14(1) TP(FT) Rules; r14(1) TP(UT) Rules
51 r14(2) TP(FT) Rules; r14(2) TP(UT) Rules
52 r14(3) TP(FT) Rules; r14(3) TP(UT) Rules
53 r14(5) and (6) TP(FT) Rules; r14(5) and (6) TP(UT) Rules
54 R(CS) 3/06
55 r16 TP(FT) Rules; r16 TP(UT) Rules
56 r16(2) TP(FT) Rules; r16(2) TP (UT) Rules
57 Tribunals Judiciary Practice Direction, *First-tier and Upper Tribunal: child, vulnerable adult and sensitive witnesses,* 30 October 2008; *SW v SSWP (DLA)* [2015] UKUT 319 (AAC); *LO'L v SSWP (ESA)* [2016] UKUT 10 (AAC), reported as [2016] AACR 31
58 Tribunals Judiciary Practice Direction, *First-tier and Upper Tribunal: child, vulnerable adult and sensitive witnesses,* 30 October 2008
59 *RT v SSWP (PIP)* [2019] UKUT 207, reported as [2020] AACR 4, paras 83, 84 and 92-94; *R(NL) v FTT and CICA* [2021] UKUT 158 (AAC); *AA and BA v A LA (SEN)* [2021] UKUT 54 (AAC); *JE v SSWP (PIP)* [2020] UKUT 17
60 *RT v SSWP (PIP)* [2019] UKUT 207 (AAC)
61 r10 TP(FT) Rules; r10 TP(UT) Rules
62 r8(1) TP(FT) Rules; r8(1) TP(UT) Rules
63 r8(2) TP(FT) Rules; r8(2) TP(UT) Rules
64 r8(3)(b) TP(FT) Rules; r8(3)(b) TP(UT) Rules
65 r8(3)(c) TP(FT) Rules; r8(3)(c) TP(UT) Rules
66 *DTM v Kettering Borough Council (CTB)* [2013] UKUT 625 (AAC)
67 r8(5) TP(FT) Rules; r8(5) TP(UT) Rules
68 r8(6) TP(FT) Rules; r8(6) TP(UT) Rules
69 rr2(1) and (3)(a) and 5(3)(a) TP(FT) Rules; rr2(1), 3(a) and 5(3)(a) TP(UT) Rules
70 *R (BD) v First-tier Tribunal (CIC)* [2013] UKUT 332 (AAC)
71 r8(4) TP(FT) Rules; r8(4) TP(UT) Rules
72 *RN v SSWP (RP)* [2013] UKUT 461 (AAC)
73 *Synergy Child Services Ltd v Ofsted* [2009] UKUT 125 (AAC); *LS v London Borough of Lambeth (HB)* [2010] UKUT 461 (AAC), reported as [2011] AACR 27
74 r8(7) and (8) TP(FT) Rules; r8(7) and (8) TP(UT) Rules
75 rr5(3)(a) and 7 TP(FT) Rules; rr5(3)(a) and 7 TP(UT) Rules
76 r13(1) TP(FT) Rules; r13(1) TP(UT) Rules
77 r13(2) and (3) TP(FT) Rules; r13(2) and (3) TP(UT) Rules
78 r13(4) TP(FT) Rules; r13(4) TP(UT) Rules

79 r13(5) TP(FT) Rules; r13(5) TP(UT) Rules
80 r11(5) TP(FT) Rules; r11(3) TP(UT) Rules
81 r11(6) TP(FT) Rules; r11(4) TP(UT) Rules
82 r11(7) and (8) TP(FT) Rules; r11(5) and (6) TP(UT) Rules
83 *JE v SSWP (PIP)* [2020] UKUT (17) AAC, para 19
84 r17 TP(FT) Rules; r17 TP(UT) Rules
85 *WM v SSWP (DLA)* [2015] UKUT 642 (AAC)
86 r17(1)(b), (2) and (3)(c) TP(FT) Rules
87 r17(1) and (2) TP(UT) Rules
88 *FI v (1) SSWP (2) MC (CSM)* [2020] UKUT 173 (AAC)

4. **Preparing a case**

89 Upper Tribunal decisions are at gov.uk/administrative-appeals-tribunal-decisions - select 'Child Support' and/or 'Tribunal Procedure and Practice' (depending on your case)
90 rr12.73 and 9.46 and practice directions 9B and 12G Family Procedure Rules 2010; *MC v SSWP and TM (CSM)* [2020] UKUT 157 (AAC)
91 CCS/3757/2004

5. **Hearings**

92 r27 TP(FT) Rules; *LM v SSWP (ESA)* [2020] UKUT 41 (AAC)
93 *MM v SSWP (ESA)* [2011] UKUT 334 (AAC); *JP v SSWP (IB)* [2011] UKUT 459 (AAC)
94 r1(3) TP(FT) Rules; r1(3) TP(UT) Rules
95 r34 TP(UT) Rules
96 ss29ZA-ZD TCEA 2007, as inserted by s55 and Sch 25 para 2 Coronavirus Act 2020 until the expiry of the 2020 Act (25 March 2022)
97 rr5A, 30(3A) and 30A TP(FT) Rules and rr5A, 37(2ZA) and 37A TP(UT) Rules, as inserted by rr4 and 5 of the Tribunal Procedure (Coronavirus) (Amendment) Rules 2020 No.416 from 10 April 2020 until the expiry of the 2020 Act (25 March 2022)
98 Tribunal Judiciary Pilot Practice Direction, *Contingency Arrangements in the First-tier Tribunal and the Upper Tribunal*, 19 March 2020
99 r29(1) TP(FT) Rules; r36(1) TP(UT) Rules
100 r29(2) TP(FT) Rules; r36(2)(b) TP(UT) Rules. The only other exception to this is when the Upper Tribunal is conducting a hearing of an application for permission to bring judicial review, in which at least two working days' notice must be given. Such proceedings are outside the scope of this *Handbook*.
101 *MB v SSWP (PIP)* [2020] UKUT 296 (AAC), paras 12 and 13
102 CCS/1925/2002
103 r30 TP(FT) Rules; r37 TP(UT) Rules
104 r31 TP(FT) Rules; r38 TP(UT) Rules
105 *AK v HMRC (TC)* [2016] UKUT 98 (AAC)
106 CCS/1689/2007; CCS/2901/2001; CCS/2676/2001
107 Art 2 FT&UT(CT)O; Tribunals Judiciary Practice Statement, *Composition of Tribunals in Social Security and Child Support Cases in the Social Entitlement Chamber on or after 1 August 2013*, July 2013, para 6
108 Sch 2 para 1(2) TCEA 2007
109 Tribunals Judiciary Practice Statement, *Composition of Tribunals in Social Security and Child Support Cases in the Social Entitlement Chamber on or after 1 August 2013*, July 2013, para 7
110 Tribunals Judiciary Practice Statement, *Composition of Tribunals in Social Security and Child Support Cases in the Social Entitlement Chamber on or after 1 August 2013*, July 2013, para 12; Art 8 FT&UT(CT)O
111 Tribunals Judiciary Practice Statement, *Composition of Tribunals in Relation to Matters that Fall to be Decided by the Administrative Appeals Chamber of the Upper Tribunal on or after 26 March 2014*, March 2014, para 3a; arts 3 and 4 FT&UT(CT)O
112 Sch 4 para 15(6) TCEA 2007; *PF v SSWP (ESA)* [2015] UKUT 553 (AAC)
113 Form SSCS2A, January 2022, pp19-20
114 r15(3) TP(FT) Rules; r15(3) TP(UT) Rules
115 *DC v SSWP (ESA)* [2015] UKUT 150 (AAC)

6. **Decisions of the First-tier Tribunal**

116 R(IB) 2/04
117 s20(7) CSA 1991
118 s20(7)(b) CSA 1991; R(CS) 1/03; *MT v SSWP and MB (CSM)* [2015] UKUT 492 (AAC)
119 CCS/16351/1996; *MB v CMEC* [2009] UKUT 29 (AAC), para 16
120 s20(7)(a) CSA 1991

121 R(IB) 2/04; *A P-H v SSWP (DLA)* [2010] UKUT 183 (AAC); *JW v SSWP & MC & JC (CSM)* [2013] UKUT 407 (AAC), reported as [2014] AACR 8; *JR v SSWP and TR (CSM)* [2015] UKUT 582 (AAC); *ET v SSWP (PIP)* [2017] UKUT 478 (AAC)
122 CCS/2861/2001, paras 7 and 11
123 CCS/3757/2004, paras 19-29
124 *AB v CMEC (CSM)* [2010] UKUT 385 (AAC), paras 11 and 12
125 r33 TP(FT) Rules
126 r34(2)(b) TP(FT) Rules
127 r34(3) and (4) TP(FT) Rules
128 r34(5) TP(FT) Rules
129 Tribunals Judiciary Practice Statement, *Record of Proceedings in Social Security and Child Support Cases in the Social Entitlement Chamber on or after 3 November 2008*, November 2008
130 *DT v SSWP* [2015] UKUT 509 (AAC)
131 r32 TP(FT) Rules; r39 TP(UT) Rules; *AW v SSWP and AL (CSM)* [2017] UKUT 235 (AAC)
132 *MM v SSWP and IJ (CSM)* [2015] UKUT 590 (AAC), paras 2, 17 and 19

7. **Changing a First-tier Tribunal decision**
133 r36 TP(FT) Rules; s9 TCEA 2007; *AS v SSWP (ESA)* [2011] UKUT 159 (AAC); *CG v SSWP (DLA)* [2011] UKUT 453 (AAC)
134 r37 TP(FT) Rules
135 See, for example, *SB v SSWP* [2020] UKUT 198 (AAC), paras 6-9
136 *MA v SSWP (PIP)* [2020] UKUT 172 (AAC), paras at 20 and 27, affirming *RR v SSWP (ESA)* [2017] UKUT 403 (AAC), paras 5 and 12
137 CIB/4193/2003, paras 5 and 6
138 s23A CSA 1991
139 *HMRC v RS (CTC)* [2021] UKUT 310 (AAC), paras 54-55
140 Introduced by s9 TCEA 2007; see also r40 TP(FT) Rules
141 r39 TP(FT) Rules
142 r40(2) TP(FT) Rules
143 *JS v SSWP (DLA)* [2013] UKUT 100 (AAC), reported as [2013] AACR 30
144 r40(3) TP(FT) Rules

8. **Appealing to the Upper Tribunal**
145 *MW v SSWP (II)* [2011] UKUT 465 (AAC), para 6
146 r38(2) and (3) TP(FT) Rules
147 r38(6) TP(FT) Rules
148 r38(5) TP(FT) Rules
149 TP(FT) Rules – especially ss5, 38(5)(b) and 38(7)(c) and *SB v SSWP* [2020] UKUT 198 (AAC), para 13 (albeit *obiter dicta*)
150 r38(7) TP(FT) Rules
151 r38(7)(c) TP(FT) Rules
152 r39(1) TP(FT) Rules
153 r39(3) TP(FT) Rules
154 r39(4) TP(FT) Rules
155 r21(2) TP(UT) Rules
156 r21(3)(b) TP(UT) Rules
157 r21(6) TP(UT) Rules
158 r21(7) TP(UT) Rules
159 r21(4) TP(UT) Rules
160 r21(5) TP(UT) Rules
161 Form UT1 is available from gov.uk/government/collections/administrative-appeals-chamber-upper-tribunal-forms
162 r22(1) TP(UT) Rules
163 *R (Cart) v Upper Tribunal and R (MR (Pakistan)) v Upper Tribunal and SSHD* [2011] UKSC 28, reported as [2011] AACR 38
164 r22(2)(a) TP(UT) Rules
165 r22(2)(b) TP(UT) Rules
166 r22(2)(c) TP(UT) Rules
167 r23(2) TP(UT) Rules
168 r23(1) TP(UT) Rules
169 r23(2) TP(UT) Rules
170 r23(3) and (4) TP(UT) Rules
171 r23(5) TP(UT) Rules
172 r23(6) TP(UT) Rules
173 r24(1A) and (1B)(a) and (b) TP(UT) Rules
174 r24(1C) TP(UT) Rules
175 r24(2) and (4) TP(UT) Rules
176 r24(3) TP(UT) Rules
177 r24(5) TP(UT) Rules
178 r25 TP(UT) Rules
179 r5(3)(d) UT(TP) Rules
180 r15(2)(a) UT(TP) Rules
181 [1954] 1 WLR 1489 at 1491, per Denning LJ
182 r40 TP(UT) Rules
183 r42 TP(UT) Rules
184 r43 TP(UT) Rules
185 s13 TCEA 2007; rr44 and 45 TP(UT) Rules
186 r45(4) TP(UT) Rules
187 s13(6) and (6A) TCEA 2007; AUTCAO; Sch 2 r41.57 Act of Sederunt (Rules of the Court of Session 1994) 1994 No.1443 (S.69)
188 rr45 and 46 TP(UT) Rules
189 r48 TP(UT) Rules

190 *Eba v Advocate General for Scotland* [2011] UKSC 29; *R (Cart) v Upper Tribunal and R (MR (Pakistan)) v Upper Tribunal and SSHD* [2011] UKSC 28, reported as [2011] AACR 38

9. **Test case rules**
191 s28ZA(1) and (2) CSA 1991
192 Reg 28(1) CSMC Regs
193 s28ZA(4) and (5) CSA 1991
194 s28ZA(4)(c) CSA 1991; reg 28(2) CSMC Regs
195 s2 CSA 1991
196 s28ZB CSA 1991
197 s28ZC(1) and (3) CSA 1991; regs 30 and 32 CSMC Regs
198 s28ZC(1) and (3) CSA 1991
199 s28ZC(1)(b)(i) CSA 1991
200 s28ZC(1)(b)(ii) and (iii) CSA 1991
201 s28ZC(2)(a) CSA 1991
202 s28ZC(2)(b) CSA 1991

Chapter 11

Complaints

This chapter covers:

1. Grounds for a complaint

If you disagree with a decision about child support, you can usually challenge it by applying for a revision, mandatory reconsideration or, if necessary, by lodging an appeal (see Chapters 9 and 10).

A complaint is a separate process from a revision, mandatory reconsideration or an appeal. You can complain about any aspect of the administration of the statutory child support scheme – eg, a delay in dealing with your case, poor administration, the behaviour of staff, incorrect information or advice provided by officials or the way in which a particular policy or practice has affected you. However, a complaint may not lead to a decision being changed.

In some cases, it may be appropriate both to challenge a decision and to make a complaint – eg, if you think that child support has been wrongly calculated and you want to challenge the decision, but you also wish to complain about a delay in making the calculation or about some other aspect of the way your case has been handled or you have been treated. If you intend to challenge the decision, it is important to request a revision or mandatory reconsideration within your complaint.

A complaint may be appropriate if there is no right to appeal the decision in question (see p198). In this situation, judicial review may also be possible (instead of, or as well as, making a complaint). Get legal advice if you are considering judicial review (see also p198).

It may be appropriate to seek a compensation payment for any loss related to a complaint (see below).

The Parliamentary and Health Service Ombudsman (see p250) has a website (ombudsman.org.uk/making-complaint) to support and to assist people in complaining about government departments and agencies.

Who the complaint is about

It is important to be clear which organisation has caused the problem. In most cases, this will be the Child Maintenance Service (see p246). Problems concerning the deduction of payments from benefits may be caused by Jobcentre Plus, and complaints about any of its functions should be made to the Department for Work and Pensions (see p248). If there is a delay or poor administration of an appeal by HM Courts and Tribunals Service (HMCTS), or you are unhappy about the way you were treated by a tribunal judge or member (ie, not that you simply disagree with the decision of the tribunal), the complaint should be made to HMCTS. For information about making complaints to HMCTS, see CPAG's *Welfare Benefits and Tax Credits Handbook*.

2. Compensation payments

If you have not received prompt, courteous and efficient service, or you have lost out because of an error, delay or poor standard of service by the Child Maintenance Service (CMS) or by Jobcentre Plus, it may be appropriate to request compensation or a consolatory payment when making a complaint. *Ex gratia* payments can be made if someone has experienced a financial loss or significant delay, or has been caused severe distress or inconvenience.

A Department for Work and Pensions guide explains the rules on whether financial compensation should be paid and, if so, how much is appropriate. It is available on gov.uk[1] or upon request from the CMS and Jobcentre Plus.

There is no legal right to these payments, but it can sometimes be useful to make it clear that financial compensation would help to resolve the complaint. The CMS cannot be sued for negligence.[2]

Compensation payments may be appropriate if there has been:

- significant delay – eg, in making calculations or reviewing liability; *or*
- delays or errors in enforcement; *or*
- delays in passing child support payments to the person with care; *or*
- wrong identification of a non-resident parent); *or*
- financial loss because of CMS or Jobcentre Plus error – eg, in bank, postal or telephone charges; *or*
- other examples of gross inconvenience, embarrassment, breach of confidentiality or severe distress.

The CMS should automatically consider whether a compensation payment should be made in appropriate cases, but you should still contact the CMS and request a reconsideration if you are unhappy with the way your case has been administered. You should consider asking for a payment equal to any money you may have lost plus any additional expenses you have incurred, and an amount to compensate you for any hardship or distress.

If you are not offered compensation, or you are not offered as much as you consider appropriate, you could consider taking the complaint further – ie, by asking the CMS to review its decision and then, if you are still unsatisfied, by complaining to the Independent Case Examiner (see p248) or the Ombudsman (see p250).

Consolatory payments

Consolatory payments are payments that may be made if action by the CMS or Jobcentre Plus has caused serious inconvenience because the same mistakes were made more than once, or the mistakes caused severe embarrassment or humiliation. They are smaller than compensation payments. Evidence of your (or a family member's) health being affected as a result may also be considered if it can be shown to be a direct result of errors made by the CMS or by Jobcentre Plus. Consolatory payments are made in recognition of the effect of an error on someone's life and therefore it is possible to claim them even if there is no financial loss.

Many people experience inconvenience and frustration when using the CMS and Jobcentre Plus, but that alone is not enough to secure a consolatory payment.

Separate decisions are made on whether to award compensation or a consolatory payment, based on the facts of each case. In some cases, both may be paid. The *Financial Redress for Maladministration* guide covers both compensation and consolatory payments.[3]

3. Complaining about the Child Maintenance Service

Most complaints involving child support are made to the Child Maintenance Service (CMS). Complaints are likely to be about:

- standards of service, including delays, staff communications, poor administration and lost papers; *or*
- how discretionary decisions are made – eg, failure to follow guidance, following it too strictly or failing to take into account all the relevant circumstances. It may be appropriate to get advice on whether judicial review is also possible if you think a discretionary decision is unreasonable or unfair.

It is advisable to make your complaint in writing, which can be posted to the CMS or can be submitted through the online service by using the 'Upload a Document' facility. You can also telephone the CMS, but it is advisable to follow up your complaint in writing. An acknowledgement will be issued, informing you that a response will follow within seven days. The impact of the coronavirus pandemic has affected timescales for complaint responses, so it may take much longer before your receive any reply. Seeking the help of your local MP (see p249), at the early stages of your complaint can often encourage CMS to respond more quickly.

Records of all communications should be kept until the complaint has been fully investigated and resolved and in case you need to refer to it in the future. A complaint made by letter should be clearly headed 'Complaint' – see Appendix 1 for the CMS address.

If the CMS officer or manager cannot resolve the complaint, it can be taken further by contacting the complaints resolution team at the CMS address. Contact details should be given in any letters sent. The CMS calls this 'complaints stage 1'.

If there has been an unreasonable delay or you are still not satisfied with the outcome after the complaints resolution team has looked at your complaint, you may ask for a review. The CMS calls this review 'complaints stage 2'. Contact details for requesting a review should be given in the letter from the complaints resolution team.

More information about the complaints procedure is available at gov.uk/child-maintenance-service/complaints-and-appeals.

If you are not satisfied that the complaint has been resolved, you can contact the Independent Case Examiner. You can only escalate your complaint to the ICE if you have exhausted the CMS internal complaints process.

The final option is to complain, via your MP, to the Parliamentary and Health Service Ombudsman (see p250).

Standards of service

When considering whether, or at what point, to make a complaint, it may be useful to be aware of the standards of service that the CMS says it will meet.

The CMS no longer publishes detailed information about its service standards. However, standards that should be expected include for the CMS to:

- start gathering information from the non-resident parent (NRP) within four weeks of a child support application, if it has contact details;
- make an accurate decision on an application within 12 weeks (but in some cases, a decision may take up to 26 weeks);
- make payments to the person with care within a week of receiving the money from the NRP, if the collection service is being used;
- take action to use a deduction from earnings order, where appropriate, within four months of a NRP's first being informed of their liability;
- answer telephone calls within one minute;

- respond to letters, and either resolve complaints or agree on the next course of action, within three weeks of receiving them.

4. Complaining about Jobcentre Plus

Other parts of the Department for Work and Pensions (DWP) have a similar complaints procedures to the Child Maintenance Service (CMS). If you are a non-resident parent, you may want to complain about the way in which child support payments have (or have not) been deducted from your benefits. If you disagree with the rate of child support you should be paying (and therefore with the deduction being made from any benefits), you should challenge the decision of the CMS, as opposed to making a complaint to Jobcentre Plus. A complaint to Jobcentre Plus can be made if it is about the administration of the deductions. Jobcentre Plus can, if appropriate, make compensatory payments.

See CPAG's *Welfare Benefits and Tax Credits Handbook* for more information about how to complain about any part of the DWP.

If you have gone through every stage of the DWP complaints procedure and you are still not satisfied, you can complain to the Independent Case Examiner (see below) or, via your MP, to the Parliamentary and Health Service Ombudsman (see p250).

Remember that some decisions about benefits can be challenged. It may be necessary to do this as well as, or instead of, complaining.

5. Complaining to the Independent Case Examiner

The Independent Case Examiner's (ICE's) office can help resolve situations where people believe that certain government agencies have not dealt with them fairly or resolved complaints to their satisfaction. ICE is an independent referee, completely separate from the Child Maintenance Service (CMS), Jobcentre Plus or any other government department.

A complaint can only go to ICE after the CMS's (or other agency's) complaints procedure has been used and a final response received – ie, a decision on a review of the complaint (ie, a stage 2 complaint), which advises that the complaint can be made to ICE. The complaint to ICE must be made within six months of the final response. ICE cannot look at complaints made after this date.

ICE cannot consider a complaint which is being investigated, or which has been investigated, by the Parliamentary and Health Service Ombudsman (see p250). There may be a choice of complaining directly to the Ombudsman via an MP, but the Ombudsman's office usually encourages people to use ICE first.

Complaints may be made in writing (see Appendix 1 for the address) or by telephone on 0800 414 8529. Contact details are on the ICE website.[4] Include all the relevant facts and details of the complaint and any responses you have received so far, including details of the particular office being complained about (if possible), and whether the complaint is about the CMS or Jobcentre Plus. ICE can give further advice on making a complaint, or on the appointment of a representative to act on your behalf, if required.

ICE first investigates and decides whether or not it can accept the complaint. It aims to decide this within two weeks. If ICE accepts the complaint, it attempts to settle it by suggesting ways in which you could come to an agreement with the CMS or with Jobcentre Plus. It aims to resolve complaints this way within eight weeks of accepting them.

In 2020/21, ICE fully or partially upheld 78 per cent of the complaints relating to child support that it investigated.[5] If it makes a recommendation of action to the CMS or Jobcentre Plus, that is almost always followed. Common issues raised in complaints to ICE include failure of the CMS to pursue enforcement action and problems with payment plans.

If you are unhappy with the way that ICE has dealt with a complaint, you can use ICE's own complaints process. Details of ICE's standards of service are available on its website. If you remain unhappy, you can ask your MP to consider referring the case to the Parliamentary and Health Service Ombudsman.

6. **Using your MP**

It may be appropriate to consult your MP at any stage of the complaints process. An MP may be able to provide advocacy or other support to get the matter resolved more quickly. However, consulting an MP is particularly important if you have been through the complaints process of the Child Maintenance Service or Jobcentre Plus without a satisfactory resolution, and even more so if you have used the Independent Case Examiner but still want to take matters further.

An MP may be able to advise on whether taking the complaint further is worthwhile. It may be that you are unhappy about an aspect of child support law, in which case a complaint is not appropriate. Whether the issue concerns law or procedure, an MP may be willing to take matters further to try to get legislation changed or practice improved. An MP may also refer the complaint to the Parliamentary and Health Service Ombudsman (see p250).

To find out how to contact your MP, see members.parliament.uk/constituencies, call the House of Commons Enquiry Service on 0800 112 4272 (freephone) or 020 7219 4272, or email hcenquiries@parliament.uk. Most MPs have local surgeries where they meet constituents.

7. Complaining to the Ombudsman

The Parliamentary and Health Service Ombudsman investigates complaints about a range of government departments and other public bodies.

Before using the Ombudsman, the organisation should have a full opportunity to respond to your complaint and put things right. For complaints about the Child Maintenance Service and Jobcentre Plus, the Independent Case Examiner (ICE) (see p248) can also be used. This does not need a referral from an MP, and the Ombudsman's office encourages people to use the ICE first.

The first stage of using the Ombudsman is to download a complaints form from the Ombudsman website and send the complaint to your MP, asking them to consider the complaint, sign the form and send it to the Ombudsman. Normally, the Ombudsman does not investigate if the complaint is passed to an MP more than 12 months after the complainant became aware that they had a good reason to complain – ie, that there was a need to take the complaint further.

If the complaint is investigated, the MP is sent a full report. The Ombudsman may recommend an apology and possibly compensation. Ombudsman reports can also lead to changed practices and procedures in the agencies under investigation.

More information about the Ombudsman is available at ombudsman.org.uk or from the helpline on 0345 015 4033.

Notes

2. **Compensation payments**
   1 *Financial Redress for Maladministration: staff guide*, November 2020, available at gov.uk/government/publications/compensation-for-poor-service-a-guide-for-dwp-staff
   2 *Rowley and others v SSWP* [2007] EWCA Civ 598
   3 *Financial Redress for Maladministration: staff guide*, November 2020, available at gov.uk/government/publications/compensation-for-poor-service-a-guide-for-dwp-staff

5. **Complaining to the Independent Case Examiner**
   4 gov.uk/government/organisations/independent-case-examiner
   5 Independent Case Examiner for the DWP, *Annual Report, 1 April 2020 – 31 March 2021*, 21 October 2021

Appendix 1

Useful addresses

Department for Work and Pensions

gov.uk/government/organisations/
department-for-work-pensions

Child Maintenance Service

Child Maintenance Service 21
Mail Handling Site A
Wolverhampton WV98 2BU
National enquiry line:
0800 171 2345
Welsh language: 0800 232 1979
Mon to Fri 8.30am to 4pm
Webchat: Mon to Fri 8am to 7.30pm,
Sat 9am to 1pm
gov.uk/child-maintenance

Northern Ireland Child Maintenance Service

Child Maintenance Service 24
Mail Handling Site A
Wolverhampton WV98 2BY
Tel: 0800 232 1956
Relay UK (if you cannot hear or speak on the phone):
18001 then 0800 232 1956
Mon to Fri 8am to 3.30pm
belfast.2012inbound@dfcni.gov.uk
nidirect.gov.uk/contacts/
child-maintenance-service

Child Maintenance Choices

(Northern Ireland)
Tel: 0800 028 7439
Relay UK (if you cannot hear or speak on the phone):
18001 then 0800 028 7439
Mon to Fri 9am to 5pm
nidirect.gov.uk/contacts/
child-maintenance-choices

HM Courts and Tribunals Service

Appeals should be sent to:

England and Wales

HMCTS Benefits Appeals
PO Box 12626
Harlow CM20 9QF
General enquiries: 0300 123 1142
contactsscs@justice.gov.uk
Welsh language: 0300 303 5170

Scotland

HMCTS SSCS Appeal Centre
PO Box 13150
Harlow CM20 9TT

General enquiries: 0300 790 6234
sscsa-glasgow@justice.gov.uk
Information about your nearest tribunal venue can be found at:
courttribunalfinder.service.gov.uk

Upper Tribunal (Adminstrative Appeals Chamber)

gov.uk/courts-tribunals/upper-tribunal-administrative-appeals-chamber

England and Wales

5th Floor
7 Rolls Buildings
Fetter Lane
London
EC4A 1NL
Tel: 020 7071 5662
Relay UK (if you cannot hear or speak on the phone):
18001 then 020 7071 5662
adminappeals@justice.gov.uk

Scotland

George House
126 George Street
Edinburgh
EH2 4HH
Tel: 0131 271 4310
UTAACmailbox@justice.gov.uk

Northern Ireland

Tribunal Hearing Centre
2nd Floor
Royal Courts of Justice
Chichester Street
Belfast
BT1 3JF
Tel: 028 9072 4883
tribunalsunit@courtsni.gov.uk
justice-ni.gov.uk/topics/courts-and-tribunals

Independent Case Examiner

PO Box 209
Bootle L20 7WA
Tel: 0800 414 8529
Relay UK (if you cannot hear or speak on the phone):
18001 then 0800 414 8529
ice@dwp.gov.uk
gov.uk/government/organisations/independent-case-examiner

The Parliamentary and Health Service Ombudsman

Citygate
Mosley Street
Manchester M2 3HQ
Tel: 0345 015 4033
Text 'call back' service:
07624 813 005 (text 'call back' and your name and mobile number)
ombudsman.org.uk

Appendix 2

Statutes

A man is assumed to be the father of a child for child support purposes (see p41) if he is found to be the father by a court in England or Wales in proceedings under one of the following statutes.

s42 National Assistance Act 1948
Affiliation Proceedings Act 1957
s6 Family Law Reform Act 1969
Guardianship of Minors Act 1971
Children Act 1975
Child Care Act 1980
s26 Social Security Act 1986
s4 Family Law Reform Act 1987
Children Act 1989
s105 Social Security Administration Act 1992

A maintenance order only prevents an application to the Child Maintenance Service under section 4 or 7 of the Child Support Act 1991 (see p19) if it was made in proceedings under one of the following statutes (this applies even if it was made under a statute that is now repealed).

Conjugal Rights (Scotland) Amendment Act 1861
Court of Session Act 1868
Sheriff Courts (Scotland) Act 1907
Guardianship of Infants Act 1925
Illegitimate Children (Scotland) Act 1930
Children and Young Persons (Scotland) Act 1932
Children and Young Persons (Scotland) Act 1937
Custody of Children (Scotland) Act 1939
National Assistance Act 1948

Affiliation Orders Act 1952
Affiliation Proceedings Act 1957
Matrimonial Proceedings (Children) Act 1958
Guardianship of Minors Act 1971
Part II Matrimonial Causes Act 1973
Guardianship Act 1973
Children Act 1975
Supplementary Benefits Act 1976
Domestic Proceedings and Magistrates' Courts Act 1978
Part III Matrimonial and Family Proceedings Act 1984
Family Law (Scotland) Act 1985
Social Security Act 1986
Schedule 1 Children Act 1989
Social Security Administration Act 1992
Schedule 5, 6 or 7 Civil Partnership Act 2004

The court order usually states the legal provisions under which it was made.

Appendix 3

Information and advice

It may be easier to get a positive response from the Child Maintenance Service if you have obtained advice about your rights or have an adviser assisting you.

Unfortunately, CPAG is unable to deal with enquiries, either from advisers or members of the public, on child support issues.

The following may be able to help.

- Citizens Advice and other local advice centres provide information, and may be able to represent you. You can find your nearest office at citizensadvice.org.uk.
- Law centres can help with advice and representation, but may not cover child support problems and may limit their help to people who live and work in certain areas. You can find your nearest law centre at lawcentres.org.uk.
- Child maintenance specialists may be able to provide advice. These include NACSA, 193 Wolverhampton Street, Dudley, West Midlands DY1 1DU (nacsa.co.uk). For general enquiries, you can telephone (01384 572 525) or email (admin@nacsa.co.uk).
- Solicitors can give free legal advice to people on low incomes under the 'legal help' scheme (advice and assistance scheme in Scotland). This does not cover the cost of representation at an appeal hearing, but it can cover the cost of preparing written submissions and obtaining evidence such as medical reports. However, solicitors do not always have a good working knowledge of the child support rules and you may need to shop around until you find one who does.
- Some barristers are available directly to the general public under the Bar Council's Direct Public Access scheme (see barcouncil.org.uk/bar-council-services/for-the-public/direct-access-portal.html) and a minority have expertise in child maintenance disputes. Further, some barristers carry out pro-bono work, and Advocate (weareadvocate.org.uk) may be able to assist you in finding an appropriate barrister to advise you, or to represent you at a tribunal.
- find-legal-advice.justice.gov.uk can be used to find high-quality legal advisers in England and Wales, including advice agencies and solicitors.
- Local authority welfare rights workers provide an advice and representation service for benefit claimants in many areas.

- Lone-parent organisations may offer help and advice about child support, or it may help to talk to other parents about their experiences. For details of your local group and for helpline advice, contact Gingerbread (helpline: 0808 802 0925; gingerbread.org.uk) or One Parent Families Scotland (helpline: 0808 801 0323; opfs.org.uk).
- Many trade unions provide advice to members on child support.

Representation at appeals

Some parents may find it difficult to obtain representation at appeal hearings. Although many parents, especially with the help of Chapter 10, will be able to present their own case, it can be invaluable to obtain objective independent advice which draws on the legislation. An advice centre which has a copy of the legislation (see Appendix 4) and experience of representing at tribunals in other sorts of cases (eg, social security) may be able to provide a representative for a child support appeal. It is possible to instruct a barrister directly (see p255), or via Advocate (if you meet its criteria for pro bono assistance), or a child maintenance specialist.

Appendix 4

Useful publications

1. Caselaw and legislation

All the legislation listed in Appendix 5 can be found at legislation.gov.uk. Most is updated. It is sometimes useful to consult the online legal databases at a specialist law library in order to ascertain definitively whether a particular statute or statutory instrument is in force, and whether there have been recent amendments to any legislation. If you are unsure about the law, it is important that you seek appropriate legal advice, either from a qualified lawyer or support service that specialises in child maintenance.

Child Support: the legislation
E Jacobs (CPAG)
Legislation with detailed commentary.

Sweet and Maxwell's social security legislation with commentary:
Volume I: Non-Means-Tested Benefits and Employment and Support Allowance
Volume II: Universal Credit, State Pension Credit and the Social Fund
Volume III: Administration, Adjudication and the European Dimension
Volume IV: HMRC-administered Social Security Benefits and Scotland

CPAG's Housing Benefit and Council Tax Reduction Legislation.
Legislation with commentary.

2. Department for Work and Pensions publications

Many leaflets and factsheets explaining the statutory child support schemes are available through gov.uk/making-child-maintenance-arrangement.

Leaflets and most other Child Maintenance Service publications can also be obtained from the national enquiry line: 0800 171 2345.

Bulk copies of leaflets can be ordered by advice agencies. An order form is available at gov.uk/government/publications/dwp-leaflets-order-form.

Leaflets cover a wide range of subjects, including:

- how to apply;
- how child support is worked out and paid;
- how shared care and split care affect child support;
- what happens if someone denies they are a parent of a child;
- how the statutory child support services use personal information;
- what happens if the non-resident parent does not pay child support;

- information for a non-resident parent's employer;
- disputing decisions, making a complaint and appealing;
- changes that must be reported.

3. Other publications

Other CPAG handbooks
Welfare Benefits and Tax Credits Handbook (CPAG)
AskCPAG
The full text of the *Welfare Benefits and Tax Credits Handbook* online and updated throughout the year. See cpag.org.uk/subscriptions for details.
AskCPAG+
CPAG's full digital package which includes the full text of the *Welfare Benefits and Tax Credits Handbook* updated throughout the year, the *Welfare Rights Bulletin, Poverty* journal and decision-making tools and appeal letter generators. See cpag.org.uk/subscriptions for details.
Benefits for Migrants Handbook (subscription available on AskCPAG)
Council Tax Handbook
Debt Advice Handbook (available free on AskCPAG)
Fuel Rights Handbook (available free on AskCPAG)
Student Support and Benefits Handbook (available free on AskCPAG)
Benefits for Students in Scotland Handbook (available free on AskCPAG)
Children's Handbook Scotland (available free on AskCPAG)

Books from other publishers
Big Book of Mental Health, Tom Messere (subscription available on AskCPAG)
Disability Rights Handbook, Disability Rights UK (subscription available on AskCPAG)
Help with Housing Costs Vol 1: Guide to universal credit and council tax rebates, Shelter
Help with Housing Costs Vol 2: Guide to housing benefit, Shelter

CPAG guides
Universal Credit: what you need to know
Financial Help for Families: what you need to know
Personal Independence Payment: what you need to know
Winning Your Benefit Appeal: what you need to know

For CPAG publications and most of those in Sections 1 and 3:
shop online: cpag.org.uk/shop;
request an order form:
bookorders@cpag.org.uk.

Appendix 5

Abbreviations used in the notes

AAC	Administrative Appeals Chamber
AACR	Administrative Appeals Chamber Reports
AC	Appeal Cases
All ER	All England Reports
Art(s)	Article(s)
CA	Court of Appeal
CMLR	Common Market Law Reports
DMG	Child maintenance decision makers' guide, DWP, October 2020
col	column
EC	European Commission
EHRR	European Human Rights Reports
EWCA Civ	England and Wales Court of Appeal (Civil Division)
EWFC	England and Wales Family Court
EWHC	England and Wales High Court
FCR	Family Court Reports
FLR	Family Law Reports
HL	House of Lords
HMCTS	HM Courts and Tribunals Service
para(s)	paragraph(s)
r(r)	rule(s)
Reg(s)	Regulation(s)
s(s)	section(s)
SC	Supreme Court
Sch(s)	Schedule(s)
SCLR	Scottish Civil Law Reports
SEC	Social Entitlement Chamber
SLT	Scots Law Times
SP	Scottish Parliament
SSWP	Secretary of State for Work and Pensions
UKHL	United Kingdom House of Lords
UKSC	United Kingdom Supreme Court
UKUT	United Kingdom Upper Tribunal
WLR	Weekly Law Reports

Acts of Parliament

Legislative references are generally for '2012 rules' cases only, unless there is a particular reason also to refer to references for '1993 rules' or '2003' rules. Full sources for '1993 rules' cases can be found in the 2001/02 and 2002/03 editions, and for '2003 rules' cases in the 2013/14 edition, of this *Handbook*.

AA 1976	Adoption Act 1976
A(S)A 1978	Adoption (Scotland) Act 1978
A&CA 2002	Adoption and Children Act 2002
A&C(S)A 2007	Adoption and Children (Scotland) Act 2007
CA 1989	Children Act 1989
C(S)A 1995	Children (Scotland) Act 1995
CMOPA 2008	Child Maintenance and Other Payments Act 2008
CPA 2004	Civil Partnership Act 2004
CSA 1991	Child Support Act 1991
CSPSSA 2000	Child Support, Pensions and Social Security Act 2000
DPMCA 1978	Domestic Proceedings and Magistrates' Courts Act 1978
ERA 1996	Employment Rights Act 1996
FL(S)A 1985	Family Law (Scotland) Act 1985
FLRA 1969	Family Law Reform Act 1969
HF&EA 1990	Human Fertilisation and Embryology Act 1990
HF&EA 2008	Human Fertilisation and Embryology Act 2008
ICTA 1988	Income and Corporation Taxes Act 1988
ITA 2007	Income Tax Act 2007
IT(EP)A 2003	Income Tax (Earnings and Pensions) Act 2003
IT(TOI)A 2005	Income Tax (Trading and Other Income) Act 2005
LR(PC)(S)A 1986	Law Reform (Parent and Child) (Scotland) Act 1986
MCA 1973	Matrimonial Causes Act 1973
MO(RE)A 1992	Maintenance Orders (Reciprocal Enforcement) Act 1992
SSA 1998	Social Security Act 1998
SSAA 1992	Social Security Administration Act 1992
SSCBA 1992	Social Security Contributions and Benefits Act 1992
TCEA 2007	Tribunals, Courts and Enforcement Act 2007
WRA 2012	Welfare Reform Act 2012

Regulations and other statutory instruments

Legislative references are generally for '2012 rules' cases only, unless there is a particular reason also to refer to provisions in the equivalent regulations for '1993 rules' or '2003' rules. Full sources for '1993 rules' cases can be found in the 2001/02 and 2002/03 editions, and for '2003 rules' cases in the 2013/14 edition, of this *Handbook*.

AS(CSA)(AOCSCR)	Act of Sederunt (Child Support Act 1991) (Amendment of Ordinary Cause and Summary Cause Rules) 1993 No.919
AS(CSR)	Act of Sederunt (Child Support Rules) 1993 No.920
AUTCAO	The Appeals from the Upper Tribunal to the Court of Appeal Order 2008 No.2834
CB Regs	The Child Benefit (General) Regulations 2006 No.223
CS(AIAMA) Regs	The Child Support (Arrears, Interest and Adjustment of Maintenance Assessments) Regulations 1992 No.1816
CS(APD) Regs	The Child Support (Applications: Prescribed Date) Regulations 2003 No.194
CS(ARECI) Regs	The Child Support (Amendments Relating to Electronic Communications and Information) (England and Wales and Scotland) Regulations 2022 No.503
CS(C&E) Regs	The Child Support (Collection and Enforcement) Regulations 1992 No.1989
CS(CEMC) Regs	The Child Support (Collection and Enforcement and Maintenance Calculation) (Amendment No.2) Regulations 2021 No.763
CS(CEOFM) Regs	The Child Support (Collection and Enforcement of Other Forms of Maintenance) Regulations 1992 No.2643
CS(DEOAMMA) Regs	The Child Support (Deduction from Earnings Orders Amendment and Modification and Miscellaneous Amendments) Regulations 2016 No.982
CS(DOF) Regs	The Child Support (Deduction Orders and Fees) (Amendment and Modification) Regulations 2016 No.439
CS(MA) Regs 2018	The Child Support (Miscellaneous Amendments) Regulations 2018 No.1279
CS(MA) Regs 2019	The Child Support (Miscellaneous Amendments) Regulations 2019 No.1084
CS(MAJ) Regs	The Child Support (Maintenance Arrangements and Jurisdiction) Regulations 1992 No.2645
CS(MCSC) Regs	The Child Support (Maintenance Calculations and Special Cases) Regulations 2000 No.2001/155

CS(MOC&NCR) Regs	The Child Support (Meaning of Child and New Calculation Rules) (Consequential and Miscellaneous Amendment) Regulations 2012 No.2785
CS(MPA) Regs	The Child Support (Management of Payments and Arrears) Regulations 2009 No.3151
CS(NIRA) Regs	The Child Support (Northern Ireland Reciprocal Arrangements) Regulations 1993 No.584
CS(V) Regs	The Child Support (Variations) Regulations 2000 No.2001/156
CS(V)(MSP) Regs	The Child Support (Variations) (Modification of Statutory Provisions) Regulations 2000 No.3173
CS(VP) Regs	The Child Support (Voluntary Payments) Regulations 2000 No.3177
CSA(CA)O	The Child Support Act 1991 (Consequential Amendments) Order 1993 No.785
CSA(JC)O	The Child Support Appeals (Jurisdiction of Courts) Order 2002 No.1915
CSA(JC)(S)O	Child Support Appeals (Jurisdiction of Courts) (Scotland) Order 2003 No.96
CSF Regs	The Child Support Fees Regulations 1992 No.3094
CSF Regs 2014	The Child Support Fees Regulations 2014 No.612
CSI Regs	The Child Support Information Regulations 2008 No.2551
CSM(CBR) Regs	The Child Support Maintenance (Changes to Basic Rate Calculation and Minimum Amount of Liability) Regulations 2012 No.2678
CSMC Regs	The Child Support Maintenance Calculation Regulations 2012 No.2677
FT&UT(CT)O	The First-tier Tribunal and Upper Tribunal (Composition of Tribunal) Order 2008 No.2835
SS(C&P) Regs	The Social Security (Claims and Payments) Regulations 1987 No.1968
SS(DAWAP)(CA)O	The Social Security (Disability Assistance for Working Age People) (Consequential Amendments) Order 2022 No.177
TCG Regs	The Taking Control of Goods Regulations 2013 No.1894
TP(FT) Rules	The Tribunal Procedure (First-tier Tribunal) (Social Entitlement Chamber) Rules 2008 No.2685
TP(UT) Rules	The Tribunal Procedure (Upper Tribunal) Rules 2008 No.2698
UC,PIP,JSA&ESA(C&P) Regs	The Universal Credit, Personal Independence Payment, Jobseeker's Allowance and Employment and Support Allowance (Claims and Payments) Regulations 2013 No.380

Index

How to use this Index

Entries against the bold headings direct you to the general information on the subject, or where the subject is covered most fully. Sub-entries are listed alphabetically and direct you to specific aspects of the subject.

CMS Child Maintenance Service